PRAISE FOR JEFF MARGOLIS

"I'm happy to have gotten to know Jeff working together on the Oscars and so many other gigs over the years. Nobody has better stories or more to say."

–**Whoopi Goldberg**, EGOT winner and 4x Oscars Host

"Jeff Margolis and I have worked together for over twenty-five years on numerous TV specials including The Oscars. Over the decades, we've developed a deep professional respect for each other, a true fondness for one another, and an unshakeable and abiding friendship. Jeff is my brother from another mother. With *We're Live in 5*, the world will get a front row seat to Hollywood's biggest moments as they really happened."

–**Quincy Jones**, 7x Oscar–nominated, 28x Grammy–winning,
Emmy and Tony Award–winning entertainment legend

"The man who has called the shots, pulled the strings and been in the driver's seat of every major Hollywood TV spectacle has seen it all and now he's gonna show it to you. Break out the bejeweled sunglasses—you're in for a ride!"

–**Bruce Vilanch**, 2x Emmy Award–winner and 19x Oscars writer

"From my perspective, Jeff is an entertainer's director. He would be there in rehearsals with me figuring out camera shots to enhance my choreography. He would make sure the lighting and sound was immaculate and that the dialogue, staging and costumes were perfect. I knew that if Jeff was in the booth, it would be great."

–**Donny Osmond**

T0273359

MY EXTRAORDINARY LIFE
IN TELEVISION

WE'RE
LIVE
IN
5

JEFF MARGOLIS
WITH LOREN STEPHENS

Post Hill
PRESS

A POST HILL PRESS BOOK
ISBN: 979-8-88845-116-8
ISBN (eBook): 979-8-88845-117-5

We're Live in 5:
My Extraordinary Life in Television
© 2024 by Jeff Margolis
All Rights Reserved

Cover design by Conroy Accord

Post Hill Press
New York • Nashville
posthillpress.com

Published in the United States of America
1 2 3 4 5 6 7 8 9 10

"Three things in human life are important:
The first is to be kind;
the second is to be kind
and the third is to be kind."

—HENRY JAMES

TABLE OF CONTENTS

DEDICATION

I WANT TO DEDICATE THIS BOOK TO MY DAD, ROBERT MARGOLIS; MAY HE REST in peace. I thought a lot about him as I wrote this book. It was my dad who introduced me to television when I was five years old. And it was my dad who became tremendously supportive of my plan to be a television director and producer when he realized I did not want to become a doctor or a lawyer.

My dad was in the electronics business, and he always wanted to be the first person in our neighborhood to have the latest electronic gadget. One day he brought home a Philco eight-inch black-and-white television set—one of the early models—and I was hooked. He plugged it into the wall, and I pressed my face into the glass and searched for the tiny door that let the people in and out of that magical box. That was the beginning of my life-long obsession.

Television and I grew up together. By the time I was a student in the School of Theater, Film and Television at UCLA, and was working part-time holding cue cards for actors who needed assistance remembering their lines, I had a plan. I would become a director/producer and make a career for myself in Hollywood. Buh-bye to the doctor and lawyer career.

Years later—after sitting at the helm of the Oscars, and winning industry awards, my dad came up with the idea that I should write a book about my experiences in Hollywood. He wrote five pages of ideas that he thought would make for a good read. As I have been writing this book, I realize that he was right on the money! Many of his ideas are exactly what I'm writing about.

I used to get tickets for my parents to come to all my shows and sit in the audience. A lot of times, though, my dad preferred to sit in the control room with me.

In the mid-1990s, I took my parents to Washington, DC, where I directed *A Gala for the President at Ford's Theater*. My parents were guests at the event, and I introduced them to Bill and Hillary Clinton. My parents were thrilled to be embraced by the President and the First Lady, who gave them extra time in the receiving line because they were the producer/director Jeff Margolis's parents. Wow! I remember teasing them that day, saying, "And you wanted me to be a fucking doctor?"

My dad had a wonderful sense of humor. When I started directing live television shows, I told my parents, "I've got to figure out a way to go to the bathroom before the show goes on the air and hopefully not have to go until it's off the air. I can't leave my seat—not for anything."

That's when my dad started a tradition of sending me a present whenever I was directing a live show. He would secretly arrange for a production assistant to stop by his house and pick up a small jewelry box, which would be delivered to me in the control room.

The first time this happened I was surprised. The card on the box said, "To Jeff, From Dad." I opened the box, and inside was a solitary wine cork. And there was another little card next to the cork, and it said, "Shove this up your ass, and you'll never have to go to the bathroom during a live show." My father had a wry and clever sense of humor, and this joke was one of his best. (You'll hear more from my dad.)

From then on, every live show I directed until he passed away, he sent me a cork. I've saved them all. That tradition made me feel so loved and supported, and, wherever his soul might be, he'll always know how appreciative I was of his support.

When my dad passed away and the immediate family had an open-casket viewing for one final goodbye at the funeral home, the rabbi blessed my dad with a beautiful prayer, and when he finished the service, he asked if any of my dad's kids wanted to say something. We all did. I got up, and I told the cork story. Before the casket was closed, as I wiped the tears from my eyes, I took a cork out of my pocket, wrote my name and the date on it—May 29, 2019—and placed it next to my dad's hands. Rest in peace, Dad. Thank you. I love you.

Jeff Margolis

AUTHOR'S NOTE

OTHER THAN WHAT CAN BE FACT-CHECKED OR WHAT IS EXCERPTED FROM newspapers or radio transcripts, everything in this memoir reflects my memory of the events that I am sharing with you. It is sometimes difficult to mine the motherlode of memories, and how I remember may change over time. Had I written this book ten years ago or ten years from now the retelling might have been slightly or dramatically different.

It is impossible to fully know the truth, and if I have misremembered I apologize for any inaccuracy, but this is how I see it. What I can say is that I have enjoyed every minute of recollecting the events of my life and the emotions that encompassed them—even those that may not have been the most pleasant at the time. For those of you who were there with me, your recollection might be different from mine. But I couldn't have done it without you!

To be sure, I can lay claim to a jam-packed life and I wish the same for you. There is never enough time. But here we go in 5...4...3...2...1.

JEFF MARGOLIS

FOREWORD

THROUGHOUT MY CAREER I'VE WORKED WITH INCREDIBLY TALENTED PEOPLE, and some came at important moments in my life.

In 1990, legendary Oscars producer Gil Cates asked me to host the Academy Awards. The first time for both of us. Jeff Margolis was the director and, basically, after the disastrous 1989 telecast, we were all teamed up to help save the Oscars. Simply put, we did a very strong and well-received show, and there seemed to be an audible exhale throughout the industry. Jeff and I ended up working together on four of my nine hosting appearances. An event as huge as the Oscars is loaded with tension and anxiety. How to make it different and exciting was always my task. For anyone in that job you need a talented, creative, and instinctual director (and a good sense of humor helps). So when a billion people are watching and you hear the count-down to walk out there...5...4...3...2...1...you know that you are in safe hands.

What I liked best about those days was knowing the trust Jeff had in me. I would tell him what my entrance was and who in the audience I would mention in my monologue, so he'd be ready to cover them, but as far as the specific jokes, he was like the audience, seeing them for the first time on the air. Only a director with confidence in himself and his ability to react instantaneously could handle that. I also admired how Jeff knew how to capture my spontaneity, which he encouraged, always telling me, "Don't worry, I'll get it." I knew when I went off script—thank you Jack Palance and his one-armed push-ups, and one-hundred-year-old Hal Roach's speech without a microphone—that he would showcase the moment perfectly.

I could go on and on...but those stories are in my book, and this is Jeff's book, full of his fascinating stories about the people and the world of variety television in his now-tremendous career. So, when I count down from five, start reading...5...4...3...2...1.

BILLY CRYSTAL

CHAPTER 1

ON WITH THE SHOW

DURING MY SENIOR YEAR AT HAMILTON HIGH SCHOOL IN LOS ANGELES, I started to watch the Academy Awards broadcast on television. I told myself, "Boy, one day I'm going to direct the Oscars." That became my mantra. Looking back, it was unusual for a teenager who didn't come from a show business family to be so focused and driven toward a goal that to most people might have seemed a pipe dream, but to me it felt real. Life coaches say that intention is 90 percent of attainment and how you get there is 10 percent. I had the 90 percent in my pocket. I would just have to figure out the route to getting there. There's no one answer to "getting to the Oscars." It's alchemy: a mixture of drive and ambition, perseverance, talent, practice, luck, experience, education, and, last but not least, people who believe in you and go out of their way to help you.

Hollywood is filled with dreams, but so much of the time those dreams never come true. It's a highly competitive business. I started dreaming about directing the Oscars as soon as I knew I wanted to be a director.

Twenty-five years after I made that teenager's vow, I achieved my first Oscars directing gig in 1989. Not really such a long time to have climbed the highest peak in Hollywood! That same year, I received my first Primetime Emmy Award for directing the spectacular special *Sammy Davis, Jr. 60th Anniversary Celebration*. Six years later I won another Primetime Emmy Award, this time for directing the Oscars! Meanwhile, I also took home two Directors Guild of America Awards for directing the Oscars in 1991 and again in 1994.

I was so glad that I didn't trip on the way to the podium to receive the Emmy with my name on it. I told the audience in my acceptance speech:

> I knew I wanted to paint television pictures and have
> my signature on them, like every other famous artist.
> I never had a Plan B. This is all I ever wanted, and it
> is my dream come true. Thank you very much!

When I walked off the stage and the applause died down, I went right back to work, and I've been at it for more than fifty years. It's been an extraordinary ride, and I've loved every minute of it—even the tough times. This is my love letter to television. Whether you've chosen a career in the entertainment industry or some other field, there are lessons here that you might borrow, and it is my hope that you will be as fulfilled in your life's work as I have been in mine. And now on with the show.

I can barely remember my childhood without television: I was obsessed with the programs that the little Philco brought into our home. Television was more exciting to me than playing with my friends, doing homework, or practicing the piano. School was a sidebar to television as far as I was concerned, except for the time I spent with my shop teacher Mr. Marks learning stagecraft.

As television technology advanced with color television, sharper images, and an explosion of programs, I was hooked. Every spare moment when I wasn't in school, I was in front of the TV set. Yes, there was *Howdy Doody* and *Beany and Cecil*, but I also remember Arthur Godfrey and *My Three Sons*, *The Adventures of Ozzie and Harriet* (which was my favorite family sitcom), and, as I got older, I was a loyal follower of dramas like *Dragnet* and westerns like *Have Gun – Will Travel* and *Gunsmoke*. But it wasn't just what was on the programs that interested me but how they were made—who called the shots, who wrote the dialogue, who picked the actors, who made it all happen. It couldn't just have been the sponsors like Kraft Cheese, General Motors, or Lucky Strike. I thought there must be someone who put everything together, and I wanted to be that person.

There was a show in the early 1950s on Sunday morning starring the chubby-faced and friendly Bob Yeakel, a Los Angeles car dealer who had a home-grown variety show. Local talent came on, and he'd move cars out of the way in the showroom so he and his staff and friends could sing and dance. It was very folksy and lots of fun to watch. (Not-to-be-missed television for this kid.)

I was fascinated by musical talent. At six years old, I said to my parents, "I want to take piano lessons." I loved music, and my dad owned a fancy-dancy record player. He used to love to listen to Frank Sinatra, Tony Bennett, and Ella Fitzgerald. When high-fidelity sound was introduced and long-playing records (LPs) came on the market, my dad was first in line to buy them. I used to listen to music all the time. Then when I saw performers on television playing a musical instrument or singing on some of the specials, like Perry Como and Dinah Shore or Dean Martin or Nat King Cole, I wanted to do it too. I couldn't sing worth a crap, but I loved playing the piano. I heard all the tunes in my head, but I couldn't sing them. When I got older, I continued with piano lessons and added guitar and flute to my repertoire, but I never thought about becoming a professional musician. Music has been one of my life-long passions, and I brought this passion to my directing and producing career, as you will learn. And the stars that I've worked with know how much I admire their talent. We can't be good at everything, and I learned that lesson after years of practicing piano, flute, and guitar.

I was a young Jewish boy living in Cheviot Hills, California (almost right next door to Hollywood), in a very nice house that my mother's father, Sam Groper, built for us. I have two siblings: my sister, Jan, who is two years my junior, and my brother, Peter, who came along ten years after my sister. I was the happy, curious, fun-loving eldest child. From the time I started school my grandparents and my parents said to me, "You'll grow up and go to college and become a doctor or a lawyer." I'd smile and nod my head, but in my heart, I had other plans. I just didn't know how to articulate them or go against the family's wishes for their son, Jeff Margolis, who was such a good boy.

On the weekends, television was always a family event with my siblings and me sitting on the floor and my parents on the sofa in what became the "TV room."

Sunday night was *The Ed Sullivan Show*. It was one of the most popular shows on television, and Ed Sullivan had a knack for booking up-and-coming talent. He was known for his quirky expression, "a really big *shew*," his most famous, which he would say with a swing of his arm, like a baseball player winding up. (Johnny Carson adopted a similar gesture for all his years on his own show.) When he said that, we all perked up to hear who he would introduce.

Elvis Presley debuted on *The Ed Sullivan Show* nationally (although the cameras could only shoot him from the waist up, as I remember), and then Sullivan booked a new British rock 'n' roll group called The Beatles, on their first American tour. Pandemonium erupted at Studio 50 (later renamed the Ed Sullivan Theater). There were Sullivan copycats, of course, and eventually television programming became more diversified. I watched situation comedies, other variety shows, dramas, and talk shows. Each genre fascinated me, but I was especially fascinated with *The Jack Benny Program* and *The Red Skelton Hour*.

Television sets more than doubled in size, and the transmission of the picture greatly improved so that programs were no longer interrupted by some glitch where we'd all be sitting around watching "white snow" (referred to as static), and a message which came on for audiences to "please stand by." My dad brought home a thirty-two-inch TV. An antenna was installed on the roof of our house to receive many more stations for me to choose from. In Los Angeles there were the three major networks—CBS, NBC, and ABC, channels 2, 4, and 7—plus local stations KTLA, KTTV, and KCOP, channels 5, 11, and 13. Then public television, channel 28, was introduced and with it shows such as *Sesame Street*, *Evening at Pops*, *Great Performances*, and the science series *Nova*, none of which depended upon advertising revenue. Instead, they were supported by public donations widening the educational and cultural offerings. Public television was like a live encyclopedia with features that spanned the world and covered a range of topics not normally seen on the commercial networks.

My parents wanted me to become involved in extracurricular activities like tennis and swimming when I became a teenager. But I always made sure that there was time every day for me to sit in front of the television set to catch my favorite programs.

I wasn't the best student, and I owe it to my mother for helping me get good grades. My mother was a straight-A student herself. I struggled to get an A; most of my grades were Bs and Cs. I had an especially hard time with math (which wasn't a good thing for a boy whose family expected him to go on to medical school someday). In geometry I was in real trouble. Mom saw that and wanted to help me as best she could. She was very patient with me and explained geometry and whatever other subjects I was not doing well in. If I still didn't get it, I'd sit around and sulk. When it was bedtime and I hadn't completed my homework assignment, guess what? Mom would help me figure it out.

When it came time to take tests, I had to study hard on my own, but I had my own personal tutor to help me if I got stuck, and I always passed with flying colors.... Flying colors for me was getting a B on a test.

My parents were lenient about my bedtime. As long as I wasn't tired and I got at least eight hours of sleep, they were happy. By the time I was in eighth grade at Palms Junior High School, I had a lot of friends, and whenever I would go to their homes, we would study or play games or sports. But when they came to my house, it was television, television, and more television. But I still didn't know how it all came together—that is until Mr. Marks, my shop teacher, introduced a class called "Stage Crew" after school in the auditorium. Bingo! I couldn't wait to sign up and, of course, I was one of his most eager pupils, taking in every golden nugget he had to offer. Mr. Marks opened up a whole world to me, including receiving my first reprimand. Up to this point, I was what you'd call a "goody two-shoes," following orders from my parents and teachers.

Mr. Marks taught his eighth graders how to build scenery. The auditorium had stage curtains, and, in the back, there was a control room that controlled all of the sound—the microphones on the stage and the speakers in the auditorium. We also learned how to hang stage lights. I was so excited to learn about it all.

Sometimes I would walk to school early in the morning. I'd stop in to see Mr. Marks and ask him if I could have the key to the backstage of the auditorium so I could get a head start on whatever we were working on before classes began. That way I could start working on my piece of scenery, or the microphones that I was setting up on the stage for whatever the drama class was performing for the school play. He would give me the key, and I would give it back to him every day after I used it. I was over the moon that I'd be given a chance to fiddle around with all this equipment. I wanted to learn how everything worked—that was the "inventor" in me, something that I must have inherited from my father and from my grandfather (as you'll learn about soon)!

One Friday I had this plan in my head that I would surprise Mr. Marks and everyone else. I decided to keep the key on a Friday afternoon and return it the following Monday. I walked down to the school on the weekend. At this time there was no security. No nothing. There was no one around. I spent all day backstage in the auditorium, working on my set. I was putting my microphones in place and going into the sound room and testing things out, plus playing music and making sure the speakers were right. I did all that work on Saturday and Sunday, and I was so proud of myself. I thought everyone would be so pleased with what I did. Monday morning, I got to school, and standing at the front door with their arms crossed were the principal, the boys' vice principal, and Mr. Marks. I was found out. I had done something terrible—I kept this key, and I broke into the school. I got reprimanded for it, and I thought I was going to get suspended—or even worse, expelled. Luckily, I only got a good tongue-lashing.

Mr. Marks pulled me aside after I was reprimanded and said to me, under his breath, "Don't ever tell anybody that I told you this, but you really did good work. I'm very proud of you."

After the key incident, I kept out of trouble, finished up at Palms Junior High School, and went on to Hamilton High School, where I graduated in 1964. I was accepted into the University of Southern California, intending to follow a track that would lead me to become a doctor, fulfilling my parents' and grandparents' dream. But it wasn't my dream. I had other plans for myself, and by the time I was eighteen I knew that I had to be true to myself. Otherwise, I would never be happy.

CHAPTER 2

FROM ONE GENERATION TO THE NEXT

I WAS A TRULY LUCKY KID WITH A LARGE EXTENDED FAMILY FILLED WITH LOVING parents, siblings, grandparents, aunts and uncles, and cousins. I learned from a young age that keeping Jewish traditions was an important part of family life. It was what was expected of me, and I embraced Jewish values and holidays unconditionally. I couldn't have had a better childhood. I won the lottery in that department.

I was very respectful of my parents and grandparents. Every Jewish holiday was important to my family. My grandparents on my mom's side were Orthodox Jews. They kept a Kosher home and were very religious. My grandparents spoke Yiddish and Hebrew to each other. I heard both languages while growing up whenever I went to my grandparents' home.

My maternal grandfather, Sam Groper, escaped the pogroms against the Jews in Russia in the early twentieth century, emigrated to Canada, and from Canada to Los Angeles, bringing his tailoring skills with him. He left my grandmother Sarah and his first daughter in Winnipeg and settled in Boyle Heights, a predominantly Jewish neighborhood in Los Angeles shared with a mainly Latino population. That's where my mom (the middle child) and her younger sister were born. The center of Jewish life in Boyle Heights was the Breed Street Shul, which survived into the latter part of the twentieth century. It was ultimately converted into a community center serving the Latino population after most of the Jews moved away.

My grandpa was a tailor in Canada, and when he arrived in Los Angeles, he went to work as a tailor, but he really wanted to be a builder. Then he met somebody who owned a meat market, and he went to work for that guy, but he held on to his dream of becoming a builder. He just didn't know how he was going to get there.

At the meat market, when there were no customers, he would take a pencil and some of the meat-packing paper that he would wrap steaks and lamb chops in, and he'd draw on it. He would design buildings. As the story goes, he kept drawing and drawing. One day a man came in to buy some meat, and he saw my grandfather drawing.

My grandfather asked, "Can I help you, sir?"

The gentleman said, "What are you doing?"

"Oh, I want to be an architect and a builder one day. I'm just drawing."

"Son, let me see your drawing."

My grandfather put the drawing up on the counter, and the gentleman said, "I'm an architect, and I have my own company. Your drawing skills are phenomenal. I'd like you to come and work for me." How do such things happen? The universe must have been listening to what was in my grandfather's heart and led this gentleman into the butcher shop. As I like to say—you can't make this stuff up.

My grandfather became a very successful builder. Soon he had his own one-man company. I can drive through the streets of Los Angeles—from La Cienega to Vermont Avenues between Beverly Boulevard and Sunset Boulevard—and point out every apartment building still standing that my grandfather built. He became very successful and very wealthy. From tailor to butcher to builder, living his American dream!

On Friday nights, my mom and dad, my sister, Jan, my brother, Peter (who is thirteen years younger than me), and I, and my mom's two sisters and their families would all have Shabbat dinner at the Gropers' house to mark the beginning of the weekend, and of course to catch up on what was happening with each one of us. All of the cousins were together. It was always a wonderful, wonderful time. My grandparents lived in a big home with a swimming pool: the reward for my grandfather's hard work and passion for building. In the summer, the whole family lived at the pool during the day.

My grandmother and grandfather just loved their house which could accommodate big family gatherings. My grandfather worked from home. He had a big drafting studio in the house. He was such a good man. I loved him so dearly.

I don't want to admit that I was the favorite of all the grandchildren, but I was. Don't tell anybody. But everybody knew it. On Friday nights my grandfather said to me, "Do you want to go for a walk with me?" And we did.

On our Friday night walks we would talk about school. One night he got up the nerve to ask me, "So, Jeff, do you have a girlfriend yet?" Of course, I did—what, are you kidding? That was the end of that subject. What he really wanted to talk to me about came next. He finally said to me, "I've been watching you. I know you don't want to be a doctor or lawyer, but I'm not going to tell your grandma or your parents. I know how much you love television, and I know how much you love to watch me draw."

I used to try and draw with him, but I didn't have any of his talent. We continued our walks on Friday nights, and I shared with him my love for the entertainment industry—for music and drama. He knew that I wasn't going to fulfill my parents' dreams for me, and he was very supportive. It was always our secret.

One Friday night he said to me, "It's time for me to introduce you to your second cousin. His name is Monty Hall." Monty and his wife, Marilyn, and their kids had just moved to Los Angeles from New York; they were originally from Canada. Monty hosted a CBS TV show called *Video Village* and later created a show called *Let's Make a Deal* for NBC in 1963. He was a bona fide celebrity and a great entrepreneur in the burgeoning television industry. Just my good luck!

My grandpa said to me, "We don't call the slightly older generation cousins even though he's actually your second cousin. You'll call him Uncle Monty." And I did; Monty Hall was always my Uncle Monty. And what a great uncle he was to me.

My grandfather put us together at a family event, and Monty said, "Why don't you come over and let's talk." I stayed in touch with him, and he gave me an open invitation to come and watch *Let's Make a Deal*, the game show he hosted and produced. I walked into the television studio, and Monty laid out the red carpet for me. Everybody was extra kind. They took very good care of me.

I went into the control room and saw the director work. At that time there was live music on the show, and I watched the bandleader with the four-piece band. They used to play all the jingle music. I got to go backstage and see them set up the prize packages for the contestants to bid on when the curtain opened. Oh God, I loved it. I just absolutely loved it. This was my first exposure to a real television studio. I felt like this was where I belonged.

At the time I was already in high school. My parents and my grandma still thought I was going to be a doctor. My grandpa knew that Grandma was really, really set in her ways, and all she could imagine for me was the doctor thing. My grandpa wasn't henpecked, but he knew what to do and not to do with my grandma. He never told her about my plans, and he always agreed with her. "Oh, yes, Jeff's going to be a doctor."

Meanwhile my older cousin Dick was already in college and preparing to go to medical school, so it took a little bit of the pressure off of me. At least one of my grandma's grandkids was headed "in the right direction" as far as she was concerned. He is today a very successful psychiatrist.

What can I tell you about my father's parents, the Margolises? Every other Sunday night, we'd have dinner with them. My dad's dad was a hard guy to get to know, but my grandmother was a sweet, sweet lady. Grandpa had a jewelry store in Compton which is south of Los Angeles. He went to work every morning by trolley car to his store, worked there until dark, came home, and my grandmother would have dinner waiting for him. He watched television to unwind and then went to bed. That was his life. Sometimes on the weekends, I would get on the trolley car with my grandma and ride it all the way from Third Street and Fairfax to Compton and spend the day with them. It's hard to imagine today taking public transportation all that distance, but I didn't have a license or a car until sometime later, and neither of my grandparents drove.

My grandfather worked very hard and finally became somewhat successful. My dad said to him, "You're such a good jeweler and such a good watch repairman and such a good salesman—you should move to Beverly Hills!"

Of course, my grandfather replied with, "Ah, I don't know. I'm comfortable in Compton; my customers know me, and Beverly Hills is too fancy." My dad made the decision for him and rented him a little space right next to the Music Hall Theater on Wilshire Boulevard. My dad knew he didn't need a big space. He had no employees. His store—wait for it—was called Margolis Jewelers. It was the first time my grandfather had his name on a storefront and the first time I saw him smile from ear to ear. His income probably tripled in the first five years he was there with all the foot traffic on Wilshire Boulevard and his reputation for doing good work. He and my grandmother got a fancy-dancy apartment on Doheny Drive in Beverly Hills near the store. They used to walk to work and walk home from work every day. They worked six days a week and only took Sundays off. I think my grandma's greatest joy was to spend time with our family.

Going to Compton and spending time with them, I appreciated the Margolis work ethic and realized how important it is to work hard and persevere. They were an important example to me of how to be successful.

Both the Margolis and Groper grandparents were survivors of anti-Semitic violence in Russia. My grandma Sarah Groper spent days with one of her cousins in a storage chest at the bottom of a boat without food or water; she almost didn't make it. She used to tell that story all the time, and every time she told it she'd cry. I wasn't fully aware of just how horrific this experience was or how they feared the Nazis later on, but I do know that their personal histories made my grandparents even more grateful for the blessing of family and the success they attained in America.

When I turned sixteen—I was in the eleventh grade at Hamilton High School—my parents and my mother's parents gave me a very generous early graduation gift and told me I could go out and buy whatever I wanted. And, of course, as any teenager is wont to do, I went out and bought myself a car. What I could afford was a 1961 German Volkswagen bug. I put some money down and my dad cosigned the loan on the car. I waxed it, I shined the tires, I cleaned the inside. I was incredibly proud of this car.

When I got my driver's license and before I bought my car, I used to take my mom's car and I would pick up my grandma Sarah Groper and take her to the hairdresser every Friday afternoon before Shabbat dinner. After her appointment, I'd drive her home, and she'd make me a cup of tea and we would sit, talk, and wait for the rest of the family to arrive for dinner. Sometimes she'd give me a delicious piece of fruit cake. I loved those visits—they were my Friday afternoon ritual, just as my walk with Grandpa Sam was also a ritual for me. All was good until I went to pick Grandma up in my VW. I was so excited to show off my car. I pulled up to my grandparents' house, honked the horn, and waited for my grandmother. She came outside. I rolled the window down and said, "Hi, Grandma. I'm here."

She refused to get into the car. She said something like, "I'll call a taxi," or "I'll walk. I'm not getting into that German car. Not on your life."

I was, of course, crushed, but I eventually understood her repugnance for my VW. At the time, I did not realize that VW was made by a company that had close ties with the Nazis during World War II. It brought up terrible associations for my grandmother. I'm not sure why I didn't put two and two together sooner, but like so many Jewish kids of my generation, the Holocaust and the anti-Semitic pogroms of Russia were just stories we were told. And in our defense, many survivors didn't want to talk about what they went through in great detail—to spare us from reliving their pain.

I discovered wrestling in high school. I was really good at it, and I became captain of the wrestling team. I tried football, and I was a disaster. I tried baseball, and when I was up at bat, I was really good. But when I was out in the field, I was terrible. I loved basketball, but my high school had giant sixteen- and seventeen-year-old boys, who just towered over me. I loved wrestling and excelled in that, and I played a lot of tennis in high school, but I wasn't good enough to earn a college scholarship.

My interests were in show business—music, dance, scenery, lighting, and staging—not sports.

I did take some drama classes in high school but was never in a school play. Every time there was a talent show, I would try out. I always wanted to do something musical. When I was in the eleventh grade in 1963, The Beatles were performing at huge arenas and theaters to the screams of adoring fans. (And, of course, they had appeared on Ed Sullivan's really big *shew.*)

I got some friends together and said to them, "Let's be The Beatles in the talent show. I want to be Ringo. I'll play the drums. And why don't you be John and you be George and you be Paul?" I put together this group, and we lip-synched to The Beatles song "I Want to Hold Your Hand." We entered the talent show, which we won because everyone loved The Beatles at the time, and nobody else thought of it, I guess. Or they heard that we were doing it and didn't want to compete with us.

It was great. We all had The Beatles wigs and facial expressions. I mimicked playing the drums just like Ringo Starr. It was a whole lot of fun. I wanted to do anything that I could to get me as close as I could to where I wanted to go. (Spoiler alert: years later I directed a TV special with Ringo, and of course I had to tell him this story!)

I was a very lucky kid in every way. My parents gave me so many opportunities and introduced me to cultural events—music, plays, museums, and so much more. We used to go to the Music Center in downtown Los Angeles. My dad loved to travel, and we were always going somewhere. I remember my dad saying to me, "Jeff, this summer we're going here, here, and here for three weeks." I told him, "Dad, you know what, I think I'm going to pass." I was in junior high school at the time. My dad looked at me with a quizzical expression, "Why?"

"'Cause I don't want to leave Paula." Paula was my girlfriend at the time.

"Is she going anywhere?"

"No."

"Well then, she'll be here when you get back."

I went on the trip with my family, but I did spend time in the hotel room on the telephone with Paula. I loved what my dad had said to me, and I loved his logic—he was practical and witty at the same time. What I saw on our trips enriched my appreciation of the world beyond Hamilton High School and Beverly Hills. I was bitten by the travel bug, which has served me well in my television career. If you're not willing to pack your bags at a moment's notice, don't think about being a director/producer.

CHAPTER 3

FROM A TROJAN TO A BRUIN

AFTER GRADUATING FROM HAMILTON HIGH IN JUNE 1964, I WENT TO SUM-mer school at Los Angeles City College to take extra classes so I could qualify to major in pre-med at USC. Yes, I initially responded to family pressure, and I was going to fulfill their dream of becoming a doctor (that is, with the exception of Grandpa Sam, who knew what I really wanted to do). I got into USC in the fall semester as a pre-med student. I had to take Logic and Biology 101. We had to dissect a frog, learn about all the body parts that helped the frog go, "Ribbit," and see the little heart dead as a doornail. I hated it. That poor frog.

I said to myself, "Oh, God. I don't want to do this." I made it about halfway through the first semester at USC, and I thought, "What the fuck am I doing? I've got to do what I want to do. I can't live my life for what my parents and my grandparents expect me to be. I can't do it." I thought to myself, "I'm not happy; I'm never going to be happy. I've got to make a change."

One day, early on in the first semester, I drove to USC in my VW, and I didn't go to my first class. I went directly to the counselor's office and said to the receptionist, "I've got to see the counselor."

"She's very busy in meetings this morning. You'll have to wait."

"I'll sit here all day if I have to."

Before lunch I saw a counselor. I went in and said, "I can't do this anymore. I've got to change my major. I can't be a pre-med student. I want to be in television."

"You know we don't have a television school here at USC. We have a film school."

"Yes, I'm aware of that. I'll go to the film school." Which I did. She allowed me to make the change, as it was early enough in the semester to do so. We worked out all the classes that I would need to take. I knew that I had to stay at USC because my parents had already paid a fortune for the full semester tuition, and I wasn't about to waste their money. That would have put salt on a wound. Bad enough that I'd never have an MD after my name. No more bragging rights for my parents, but I'd eventually give them reason enough to be proud of their son—just not in the way they envisioned.

I enrolled in the beginning classes in film school, and I loved it, but it wasn't television. I wanted to be in television. I learned that when you make a film you may spend years preparing. Sometimes it may take as much as a year or more to shoot it. And then you have to edit it. I think that I was too impatient to be a film director or producer. Television was fast-paced and suited my personality better. I didn't want to have to wait years to see the fruits of my labor—or maybe never see them because getting a film financed and distributed can be a road of endless frustration.

There I was in USC film school, still unhappy. It was the second half of the semester. I had an idea. I drove to UCLA in Westwood. I knew that UCLA had one of the only television schools in the country, and it was ranked number one. I walked into the dean's office and asked the receptionist, "Is there any way I can speak to the dean?"

She said, "Who are you?"

I said, "My name is Jeff Margolis, and I'm in the film school at USC. I'm very interested in transferring to UCLA and getting into the television school."

"Well, I don't think that's going to happen. That's virtually impossible."

"Could I just speak to the dean?" I wanted to say, "Who the hell are you to make that decision?" but I knew that wouldn't get me anywhere and would just piss her off royally. Then I said, "I would really like to see the dean. May I just wait, please?"

"Okay, I'll see what I can do, but I don't think he's going to see you. I don't think it's going to happen." I thought, "*Shut the fuck up with your opinions and just let me talk to the dean.*"

I waited and waited, and finally she took me into the dean's office and I introduced myself. I talked about my childhood obsession with television—that it was in my blood. I explained that I started as a pre-med student and then I changed to film and I was at the USC film school. At the end of the conversation he said, "You know what, kid? I like your spunk. When are you ready to make the move?" He sounded just like Ed Asner from *The Mary Tyler Moore Show*.

"Yesterday," I quickly responded.

"Do you have to finish up the semester at USC?"

"No. I don't think so." (Oy, how was I going to tell my parents?)

"I can't get you into a program formally until next semester because it's too late for this semester. But you are welcome to come here and audit any class that you want."

I went back to USC to the counselor and thanked her very much for allowing me to make the change to the film school. Then I told her about meeting with the dean at UCLA who arranged for me to matriculate starting the next semester. I politely said, "Thank you so very much for all you did for me, but I am going to transfer to UCLA."

"Good luck. I hope I see your name in lights someday."

"Oh, you will," I told her. "Oh, you will." I was brimming with self-confidence because I knew I was being true to myself.

CHAPTER 4

TAKING A CUE

I WAS EXCITED ABOUT CLASSES AT UCLA, BUT I FELT INSTINCTIVELY THAT I also needed practical hands-on experience. I reached out to Uncle Monty who was the executive producer and the host of *Let's Make a Deal*, which was one of the most successful game shows on television at the time. I told him, "I'm taking classes in directing—a little bit of producing, but mostly directing at UCLA. And very soon, maybe not this semester but the following semester, I'll be able to get into a control room at school and actually start doing things on camera as a director. I need to get my foot in the door at a real television studio."

"Jeff, I've been waiting to hear from you. I know exactly what I can do to help you get that foot in the door.

"Sit right here. I'm going to make a phone call."

I was at Uncle Monty's house at the time. I didn't feel any pressure, but this call was about to change my life. Had I known, I probably would have had a bad case of sweaty palms, but I didn't realize what was at stake and how rare this opportunity was. To me I was just talking with my Uncle Monty.

He called the associate producer of his show and said, "I want you to set up a meeting for my nephew Jeff Margolis with Barney McNulty."

Barney McNulty owned the only cue card company in the television industry. He had a monopoly. He happened to be at the right place at the right time. He was working with Bob Hope. When Hope was getting ready to go on camera for a television show, and McNulty was on the stage doing something, I don't know what, he said to McNulty, "I can't remember all this dialogue! I need somebody to hold up the script to help me remember my lines."

McNulty heard that and said, "Mister Hope, I'll be right back." He tore up some cardboard boxes, got a pen, wrote Mr. Hope's dialogue on the cardboard, and held it up next to the camera lens. That was the beginning of the cue card industry. Just like that. It was amazing that no one had thought of it before.

McNulty had a monopoly in Hollywood. In New York they were still using teleprompters. I heard a rumor once that one of the many reasons Johnny Carson moved his show to Los Angeles was because he didn't want to use a teleprompter anymore. He wanted to use cue cards, and there were no cue card companies in New York. It was only a rumor, however.

McNulty was doing almost every show on live and taped television because producers/directors were turning to cue cards. It made life much easier for the on-camera talent. They didn't have to worry about forgetting their lines, and cue cards were more flexible than teleprompters for lots of reasons.

Monty set up a meeting for me with Barney. We met, and Barney asked me, "What do you want to do?"

"I'm going to be a producer and a director one day."

"Oh, you are, are you?" Barney had probably heard that a million times, but to his credit he didn't laugh in my face.

"Yes, but I'm willing to learn, pay my dues and do what I have to do. And I'd love to do cue cards."

"Okay, you're hired." I couldn't believe my chutzpah, but Uncle Monty had my back, and his endorsement meant everything. He was the "eight-hundred-pound gorilla," with a huge fan base and the respect of the network behind him. That's one of the lessons I've learned over the years. Try and find someone with connections and a stellar reputation to help you achieve your goals. And if they are your uncle or aunt, all the better.

What are cue cards, anyway? Cue cards are white cardboard cards about the size of a thirty-two-inch desktop computer. What you do with them is write, with a black marking pen, the dialogue in the script for a host to introduce a guest, the words to a singer's song, dialogue for a sketch, or anything else someone might need to say. Those

WE'RE LIVE IN 5

words are printed on consecutive cards. The job is difficult in the sense that when you "pulled" the cards for the talent who was saying their lines, you'd have to make sure that the home audience was not aware that the talent was actually reading their lines. The trick was to make sure that you followed the talent's eyes and positioned the cards where the talent was looking—so that it looked like they were looking straight into the camera. You also had to make sure that you broke up the dialogue on the cards in the same way that the talent takes a pause—for example, you'd only put five lines on a card, flip that card, and the next card of dialogue would be behind it. And of course, you'd have to make sure that you used the most current script. Often directors and talent revise dialogue almost until the minute the show is taped or goes live on the air. If it sounds like a three-ring circus, it sometimes was, but it was exhilarating and exciting. Especially for a kid like me who was still a college student. (I don't think anyone in my program was actually working in television at the time.) Cue cards are used on game shows for the host to read (such as Uncle Monty, of course); on soap operas for the stars to read so they don't have to commit all that dialogue to memory every day; on variety shows for all the guests; and as I mentioned earlier, for singers who need an assist with their lyrics. Cue cards are still used today on many shows, although for big arena venue shows, such as award shows and concerts, it's always necessary to use big screen monitors.

It was exhausting printing up cue cards. We always came in before the first day of rehearsal, and we'd look at the schedule to learn what sketches were being rehearsed on the first day. Then we'd print those cards to be ready for the full day's rehearsal, and while a couple of us were holding cue cards, there were sometimes three or four more guys backstage printing the next day's dialogue.

Back in the days of weekly variety shows, there were three days of rehearsal in a rehearsal hall, and then you'd go into the studio, and you'd shoot for two days. You'd block and tape, and then, at the end of the second day, you'd let an audience in and do certain parts of the show so that the performers could hear real laughter and live applause.

Let me take a moment here to explain what "block and tape" means on a variety show or entertainment special. Blocking is rehearsing "on camera." The director gets to see if the shots he or she has planned for a comedy sketch, musical number, or interview work the way he or she planned it in his or her head. The performers get to "practice" to see if they are comfortable with what they have to do, whether it is singing a song, dancing, doing comedy, acting in a sketch, and so on. You get it. The lighting designer, the set designer, the audio engineers, the prop department, and all the other departments involved get to practice making sure that their part is working properly.

The cue cards used in rehearsal were pretty much the finished product. Sometimes the director, writer, or talent would change lines, and you'd go back and print a new card. Or if it was just a word, you were able to put a piece of white tape over the word and then just print over the tape. But that's what rehearsals were for: to make sure that everything worked seamlessly and that there would be no glitches.

There are usually five people dealing with cue cards on a one-hour variety show—two backstage prepping cards and two or three on stage holding cards. It's extremely labor intensive. Without cue cards there would be a lot more bloopers and outtakes.

I went to work doing cue cards on guess what show? *Let's Make a Deal*. It was the number one game show on television and aired on NBC. That was my first show, and man, I loved it. I was on stage. I would stand next to a camera holding cue cards for Monty. The only one happier about it than Monty was me.

The show was live on air at the start, but eventually it went live-to-tape because Monty and everyone else on the staff and crew couldn't keep up with that five-day-a-week schedule. So, they began taping two shows each day for three days in a row, six shows a week. After five weeks, when they'd taped an extra week's worth of shows, Monty and everyone else who worked on the show took a week off.

I learned from Monty that you could adapt your schedule to accommodate a personal life (that is, if you are the boss).

I went back to UCLA after days of working on the show, and everybody knew what I was up to because I'd figured out a special schedule. I had to take a certain number of units every semester, but I didn't want to go to school eight hours a day, five days a week. I found a way to get all the units that I needed per semester and still make time for my job. I registered for early morning classes and was done in time to get to NBC and write up the cue cards and be ready for the taping.

When I wasn't in the studio or in class, I was watching television. I studied all the shows I loved. Two television directors in particular were my idols. Dwight Hemion was the king of the musical variety specials. His career is legendary. Among the hundreds of shows he directed were the Kraft Music Hall specials, "which defined the fast-paced look and glamorous style of the American comedy variety."[1] His credits include *My Name Is Barbra,* for Barbra Streisand (1965); *Frank Sinatra: A Man and His Music* (1965); and *Baryshnikov on Broadway* (1980). Director/producer Marty Pasetta was best known for his work on the telecasts for multiple awards shows including the Oscars (I succeeded him in 1989), the Grammys, and the AFI Life Achievement Award. He also directed *The Smothers Brothers Comedy Hour* along with the game shows *Wheel of Fortune* and *Love Connection.* Marty was great at discovering new gizmos for television and figuring out a way to adapt them. From news and weather people he took the idea of using a green screen. It was called "chroma-key" in television back then. A green screen is a visual effect and postproduction technique that allows the director/editor to drop in whatever background images they want behind an actor. For example, an actor can be in an empty studio with only a green screen and when the program is locked down that actor is on a beach in Hawaii one minute, and on the Champs-Élysées in Paris the next. Both of these television

---

1   Larry Melton, "Harrigan's Orpheum," *The Syncopated Times*, June 30, 2021. https://syncopatedtimes.com/harrigans-orpheum/.

pioneers taught me so much and enhanced what I learned from my professors and from hands-on experience.

I worked for Barney McNulty for about six months, and during those six months I was constantly reminded that he had a monopoly in the cue card business. The only other monopoly that I was aware of at the time was the phone company. It was Ma Bell. Everybody had a Bell System phone. And Barney McNulty had a monopoly in cue cards. I heard rumors that the producers on many shows were unhappy with Barney because he was always making mistakes with scheduling people, and his billing system was a nightmare.

I thought, if there are so many people who are unhappy with this guy and he has a monopoly, why don't I start my own cue card company? I thought about it for a long time. A long time for me back then was a couple of days. I was an impatient nineteen-year-old, particularly when I came up with what I thought was a really good idea.

CHAPTER 5

A NEW SHERIFF
IN TOWN

I PICKED UP A SECOND SHOW TO DO CUE CARDS FOR—*THE ANDY WILLIAMS Show*, which was one of the most popular variety shows on television at the time. The show attracted a lot of first-rate talent, helmed by the singer Andy Williams. He had a string of great hits and recorded over forty-three record albums during his eighty-year career. (Among the biggest singles were "Can't Get Used to Losing You" (1963), "Can't Help Falling in Love" (1970), and "Where Do I Begin" (1971), the theme from the 1970 film *Love Story.*

I couldn't manage *Let's Make a Deal* and *The Andy Williams Show* at the same time and keep up with my classes at UCLA. I spoke to Monty and asked him if I could drop his show, as much as I loved working with him.

"Hey, kiddo. I've got your back. I know what you want to do. I've always known what you want to do. I just opened the door for you." He gave me a big hug and a kiss and said, "I'll see you in the hallway."

And then I was offered a gig with *The Smothers Brothers Comedy Hour,* in addition to my assignment with Andy Williams. I was on a roll. I became friendly with Tommy Smothers very quickly. Every Friday night after the taping of the show Tommy would invite people up to his dressing room. (By this time, I had to give up going to Shabbat dinner on Friday nights, as did many of my cousins. It was a beautiful thing all those years. I'll never forget my Friday night family dinners at Grandma and Grandpa Groper's house, but all the grandkids were so busy following our careers and our dreams.)

One Friday night after the taping of the show, I asked Tommy if I could talk to him. He said, "Sure." We went into his dressing room and closed the door.

"What's up?" he asked.

"I don't want you to say anything, but I'm thinking about starting my own cue card company."

"That's the best idea I've heard. How are you going to finance it?"

"Well, I have money I've saved up."

"Okay, but if you ever need any help, I'm here. I will bet that within the next six months, you'll have twenty-five percent of the cue card business."

"You're on." We hugged, and I left.

I went to four other guys I worked with. They were disgruntled employees who also worked for Barney McNulty. I said to them, "Hey, guys, I've got an idea. Let's start a cue card company. I'll get the business license."

"That's so expensive. Do you expect us to contribute?"

"No. I know that only one of you is Jewish, but do the rest of you know what a bar mitzvah is?"

They said, "We've heard of it but we really don't know...."

I said, "Well, a young Jewish boy becomes a man on his thirteenth birthday and you have your bar mitzvah and you usually get money from your family and the guests. I've got enough money to cover us. I'm going to use my bar mitzvah money to start this business."

At my bar mitzvah—when I was in seventh grade—my family and friends handed me envelopes as I stood in the receiving line after the ceremony. A lot of the older people who were there said, "Take this and stick it in your pocket. Look at it when you get home."

I got a lot of money and Israeli bonds (a traditional bar mitzvah gift), and I saved most of it. I wasn't sure what I was going to do with it, but it was growing in value over time, and when I was ready to go into business, I cashed in all the bonds. What a great nest egg! I was one lucky kid.

We called the company Cue Cards Incorporated. I told the guys that Tommy Smothers was going to hire us for our first show. What a way to start a business!

We got a business license and went to Tommy and told him we were all set.

He said, "Pick up the script from the production office. You're doing your first show this week." He was just as impatient as we were.

I have the ability to be a good leader; maybe it comes from being the second eldest son in my big, beautiful extended family—and I am lucky enough to have other people who want to jump on board. This quality has carried me a long way. Cue cards were just the beginning of pulling a team of people together to make something happen in television. Someday in the not-too-distant future I'd have my own production company. Even as a nineteen-year-old I could actually visualize it. I was just that ambitious, but I was smart enough to know that I had a lot to learn.

At first, I printed and held up the cards with my partners, but when we started hiring employees, they'd print and hold up the cards with us, which gave me the time to do other things. I was interested in moving ahead in the television business. I knew that Cue Cards Incorporated was just the beginning for me and that there was so much more to do. But holding cue cards for actors helped to build important relationships, not only with the talent, but also with the crews on set who could make you very happy (and successful) or make your life miserable.

I'd sit in control rooms and watch directors at work. I would listen to producers talking about what worked and what didn't work and why, and if they wanted to do a pick-up for someone. (A "pick-up" means that you might only have to do a certain line in a sketch over again, or four bars of a song that sounded wrong.) I kept my eyes and my ears open and spent as much time as I could in control rooms, scoping out other opportunities.

After a few years I left Cue Cards Incorporated because my career in television had taken an amazing turn. I became an assistant director and could no longer do both jobs. I don't know very much about the company anymore, but I do know it's still around today.

CHAPTER 6

MURRAY ROMAN'S TV SHOW

SENIOR YEAR IN THE TELEVISION PROGRAM AT UCLA, I HAD TO COME UP WITH a final project. All the students were talking about doing newscasts and using chroma-key. We were all excited about the new color cameras at the school. The cameras were made by RCA and had turret lenses—four lenses that you could use to get a closeup or long shot but you couldn't zoom in or out. You had to switch from one lens to another to get a distance shot or a closeup. (If you want to see what an old turret camera looks like, there is a great scene in *The Aviator* where Leonardo DiCaprio, playing billionaire tycoon Howard Hughes, testifies before a US Congressional Committee chaired by Alan Alda. The cameras are on them, and you can hear the sound of the lens turning. It's an incredible scene, made more dramatic by including shots of the cameras.)

I thought about what kind of project I wanted to submit: "I'm actually working in television. I'm on these variety shows doing cue cards for Andy Williams and the Smothers Brothers. I have learned how a lot of television production is actually done. I want to do something bigger than a newscast or a short scene from a play—something that will set me apart from the other students and will demonstrate my hands-on experience."

I went to the dean and said, "Listen, I know I'm asking a lot, but I don't want to do a five-minute news broadcast. I want to do a one-hour variety show."

He laughed at me. "I appreciate your ambition, Jeff, but we don't have the money or the time."

"I'll tell you what. I'll pay for everything."

"I don't know if I can let you do that."

"Well, don't tell anybody. I'll cover everything. Look, you've got the cameras and, over the years, all the networks have donated scenery to the school. I'll go into the scene shop, and I'll find everything that I want to use so we don't have to build anything. I'll just make it work!" (Thank you to Mr. Marks, my junior high school shop teacher, for showing me how to build scenery.)

"How are you going to do it? Lay out your schedule for me."

"Give me a day to think about it."

I came back the next day and told him my plan, and the dean agreed. I didn't tell him how I was going to recruit talent for the show. After all, it was a variety show, and there is no variety without a lineup of singers, comedians, a host, and so on.

I went to Tommy Smothers and said, "For my final project at UCLA, I'm doing an hour variety show. Can you help me?"

"What do you need?"

"Well, I'd like to have you and Dick do something for me, and maybe you could help me get some other talent…." It was chutzpah, but Tommy and I had a close enough relationship, so I just forged ahead, and he was totally game to help out this nervy twenty-year-old.

"I think I might be able to help," he said. And he did.

When I was doing cue cards for the *Smothers Brothers*, I also became very friendly with one of the writers on the show, Murray Roman. Murray was a comedian. He used to perform all over Los Angeles in clubs, and man, he wanted to be a television star in the worst way.

I thought, "Oh, this'll be great." I said to Tommy, "Murray wants to have his own show. Should I ask him to host? He'd be great."

Tommy encouraged me, so I went to Murray and told him I was doing my final project for UCLA.

"Thank you, next!" was his response.

"Wait, hear me out! They're allowing me to do a one-hour variety show. I'm going to do it right, and I want you to host."

After he got up off the floor, there were kisses and hugs. This was the greatest thing that ever happened to him. I called it—what else—"Murray Roman's TV Show." The UCLA television department gave me six hours on each of two Fridays in their studio. I did the whole show in twelve hours, and Murray was the host. Glen Campbell, Tom and Dick Smothers, Pat Morita, and Hamilton Camp were all guests.

I recruited student camera operators, and all these stars came to UCLA for the show. I put out coffee and donuts for them in the morning, and cheese and crackers in the afternoon—craft services are often the key to a good day on a set. I really did it up to show the students that this is how it's done in the real world. When we were shooting on the two Fridays, word got out around campus that one or another of the stars would be showing up. Students gathered outside the glass-paneled studio to watch what was going on. It was unbelievable!

I edited the show on donated equipment, which included the old Ampex two-inch tape machines, which were as big as a house. My student editor years later became the head of the editing department at CBS Television City in Hollywood.

Of course, I showed my final project to the dean and my professors, and I got an A plus, plus, plus.

~ ~

I heard that KTTV—an affiliate on Metromedia—was airing mostly sports, cartoon shows for kids, the roller derby, long news broadcasts, and old movies. KTTV also used to have a variety show on Sunday mornings from the Bob Yeakel Oldsmobile parking lot, which had been one of my favorite shows in my early television-watching days. I heard on the street that KTTV was looking for more professional programming to compete with the major networks and appeal to a younger audience—the owners believed that a variety show was the way to go.

I thought, "I'm going to go for it." I did my research and found out the name of the executive vice president of programming for KTTV in Los Angeles: Jim Gates. I called his office, and I couldn't get past his assistant. She said, "Forget about it." As you have learned, you don't say that to Jeff Margolis. It's an invitation for me to go into action. Remember every No is one step closer to a Yes. I just needed to get my foot in the door.

I put the two-inch tape of my edited show under my arm, and I went to KTTV. At that time there were no security guards. I looked at the directory, saw where Jim Gates's office was, and walked in.

The assistant said, "Uh, excuse me. Can I help you?"

"Yeah, I'm that guy Jeff Margolis, who called you on the phone, who you hung up on."

"Oh, I'm so embarrassed! Hi! It's nice to meet you."

"Nice to meet you, too. You wouldn't answer my phone calls so now I'm here in front of you, and you don't have a choice. I want to see Jim."

"Well, it's probably not going to happen today because all the affiliates from around the country are here. They're talking about new programming ideas, and they're reviewing different shows to choose from."

"I'll wait." And I sat outside his office.

When there was a lunch break, Jim came up to the office. I stood up and said, "Excuse me, Mister Gates. My name's Jeff Margolis."

"You were the kid bothering my assistant, right?"

"Yeah, that was me. Here I am." (I said this with a huge smile on my face, feeling a little bit guilty.)

"Well, come on in. Why are you carrying a two-inch tape with you?"

"This is a one-hour variety show I produced and directed at UCLA. It was my final project. I know that you're looking for variety shows that appeal to a younger audience. I want you to look at this, and maybe there's some way we can reproduce this for you at KTTV."

"Jeff, I really appreciate you bringing the show idea here, but we're not ready."

I wasn't giving up. "I'll leave the tape with you. If you could just look at the first ten minutes and tell me what you think and if you're interested at all."

"Okay. I'll do it when I have time."

The pushy little prick that I am, I said, "Why don't you take it down to the videotape room, and look at the first ten minutes yourself? It might be something you want to show your affiliates."

"Boy you're a pushy little prick, aren't you?" (See, I told you.)

"I am. I hope I don't offend you in any way, but I'm really excited about this. I think it's something that you might be interested in. I'll tell you what a pushy little prick I am. I'm not going to leave until you look at it. If I have to sit here for three days, I will." (I don't know how I got away with this, but whatever. It must have been my big smile.)

He laughed and took the tape from me, went down to the tape room, looked at ten minutes, and then he came back up to the office and said, "Today's your lucky day, Margolis. I love it. I'm going to go back into the affiliates meeting, and you go down to the videotape room with the operator. At some point I'm going to call down and ask him to roll it," which he did.

After about thirty minutes into the show, he called down to the tape guy and said, "Okay, you can stop it." Then he said, "Send Jeff up to my office."

"I've got to finish all these affiliate meetings, but everybody really liked your show. I want to talk about it some more. I'll call you in about a week."

On the call he asked me, "Can you really reproduce this show and make an hour special for KTTV? Some of my other affiliates will probably pick it up."

"You bet."

I went to Murray Roman and said, "Murray, your dream is coming true. *Murray Roman's TV Show* is going to be on KTTV and some of the other Metromedia affiliates around the country."

"You're shittin' me!"

"No, we're going to do it, although I don't know when. I want to start thinking about it and booking it right now. I'm going to sit down with Tommy [Smothers] and see what he can do to help us."

Tommy helped me book the show, just as he had promised. "I think I will be able to get you a new singer named Linda Ronstadt, and maybe even Donovan. I also got Pat Morita, Glen Campbell, and Hamilton Camp to return." Can you imagine having access to this talent as a senior in college? It was unbelievable but that was my reality. God bless you, Tom Smothers; I will be forever grateful.

I had made some connections myself by that time from holding cue cards for talent. We ended up at KTTV. It was a big, big deal. At the time, the station was required to hire only union tradespeople to run the equipment. I asked Jim Gates, "Can I bring a couple of my fellow students in from UCLA to work on the show? Maybe one of them can assist on camera and one of them can be an assistant audio person. It would give them a chance to be in the real world."

"Sure, I'll make it work somehow. No problem." And he did.

We shot the show with a live audience. We taped it twice and pre-taped some stuff. I had Tom and Dick Smothers (on tape), Glen Campbell, Donovan, Frank Zappa—not the Mothers of Invention, just Frank Zappa—Nancy Sinatra, Linda Ronstadt, Pat Morita, and Hamilton Camp.

I hired a couple of writers from *The Smothers Brothers Comedy Hour*. I had also met writers on some other shows, and I asked them if they wanted to help me out. KTTV gave me a certain amount of money to do the show, and it was not quite enough for me to do what I wanted to do. There went the rest of my bar mitzvah money!

We did this hour show, and I edited it and put in all the spots for the commercial breaks. Linda Ronstadt sang. Donovan sang. Frank Zappa did a one-on-one interview with Murray. And Murray was pretty good at asking Zappa questions, and Zappa's responses were phenomenal. Nancy Sinatra recited the lyrics to a Paul McCartney song as Donovan accompanied her on guitar. All I remember is that it was great, and from that point on, I felt like I was on my way.

KTTV Los Angeles put it on a Sunday night right after *The Donald O'Connor Show*, which had garnered good ratings. Our show did very well. Then some of the other affiliates around the country decided to carry it, and KTTV decided to rerun the show a week later. They spent some money on promotion and built a viewership for the show and the ratings were really good.

At the Los Angeles Emmy awards for 1970—not the big Emmy awards but the Los Angeles local Emmy awards, which were still a pretty big deal—*Murray Roman's TV Show* won Best Variety Show of the Year, and I won Best Director. I was only in my early twenties. Right out of the box, I had my first award. I really couldn't believe what was happening. A lot of good luck and some talent, too. (Remember, if you get a lucky break, you better have the talent to back it up.)

I'll tell you something interesting. Jim Gates came back to me and asked, "Do you think you could do a weekly variety series for us?"

I thought, "My God, the *Murray Roman TV Show* as a weekly series?" I said to Jim, "I've got to think about that. I want to make sure I can deliver to you on a weekly basis, and that I'm not going to let you down."

Meanwhile Chris Bearde and Allan Blye, who were producing *The Andy Williams Show*, soon to be producing the new *Sonny and Cher Comedy Hour*, asked me if I wanted to get into the Directors Guild.

"Of course, I do!"

Allan said, "I want you to be the associate director on the new *Sonny and Cher Comedy Hour* which Chris and I will be producing."

"Okay. Get into the Directors Guild. Be with Chris Bearde and Allan Blye on a new CBS Primetime Network series, or do I want to do a weekly local show on KTTV?" I weighed both options. It was truly incredible. What a difficult decision. I thought and thought about it and finally decided, "Hey, this is my opportunity to be working on a weekly network variety show and get into the Directors Guild. I gotta do it."

I invited Jim Gates out for lunch and told him how honored I was that he took a chance on me. "You gave me an opportunity, and

I'll forever be grateful to you. Your kind and generous offer to do a weekly variety show—it's a dream come true! But let me tell you what else I was offered at the same time. It's been a really hard decision for me." I filled him in. This speech may sound a bit corny, but I was being entirely sincere—I meant every word of it.

"You don't even have to explain yourself. If I were in your shoes, I'd do exactly what I know you're going to tell me you're doing. You're making the right choice. Maybe one day when you're a hotshot producer/director, you'll come back and produce a show for me." That sounded great to me, and then I remembered that I had to tell Murray what I decided to do.

I stayed in touch with Jim Gates over the years. (When someone helps launch your career, don't forget them. That's something you should always remember and be sure to express your gratitude.) Jim followed my career, and a couple of times he called me and asked if he could come to see something I was doing. I always accommodated him. Never ever turn your back on friends. (It's been done to me, and it doesn't feel good.)

Anyway, back to the DGA; on my application for the Directors Guild, the first signature I got was Tom Smothers.

There is a sad postscript to this story. A week after I made my decision to turn down Jim Gates's offer to produce *Murray Roman's TV Show* for KTTV, Murray died in a horrific car crash. Murray used to perform in comedy clubs all over the city. He had been on stage at a small club in the San Fernando Valley—Studio City, I believe—and after he finished his set, he got into his car to go home. He made it about halfway through Malibu Canyon and went over a cliff on a winding and dark road. He did not survive the crash. It was a tragic ending to a friend's career. I was devastated.

During the time I was at UCLA and I was one of the owners of the cue card company, I also started associate directing. In television, an assistant director is called an associate director, and the associate director does a different job than an assistant director does in film. An associate director sits in a control room next to the director and readies the camera shots for the director to take, readies the music cues, and readies the light cues. A good associate director paves the way for a director. By the time you are taping the show or doing the show live, a director shouldn't have to do much more than call camera shots, and say, "Take it, or dissolve...." Same thing with lighting cues, music cues, scenery cues, you get the drill. It's like being the advance person. Associate directors do so much more before they finally get into the control room. There is so much prep to do on all these shows, and the director relies quite a bit on the associate director. ADs, as they are referred to, really work for their money.

I learned a lot by holding cue cards on *Let's Make a Deal*, *The Andy Williams Show*, *The Smothers Brothers Comedy Hour*, and all the other shows I had the good fortune to experience—*but* when I became the associate director on *The Sonny and Cher Comedy Hour*, that's when I felt I was in television graduate school. And working with the legendary director Art Fisher, oh my God! What a piece of work he was. I learned as much from him about what not to do as what to do.

CHAPTER 7

NOT THAT CHAIR!

I EXITED UCLA IN 1968 AFTER TURNING IN MY ONE-HOUR VARIETY SHOW. Armed with Murray Roman tapes, and my experience on set holding up cue cards for talent, I had enough ammunition at twenty to earn my way into the Directors Guild of America (DGA) and land associate directing gigs that would draw attention to this kid who was a hard worker and pleasant enough to be around. And then along came Art Fisher. He really tested me with his gruff manner and take-no-prison-ers attitude. He thought he'd put me in my place.

I learned a lot about directing from Art Fisher. I worked with Art for five years. A lot of people who worked with him didn't like the way he treated them, and for good reason. Art was extremely orga-nized (as well as sporadically temperamental). A lot of directors at the time flew by the seat of their pants—that never cut it with Art. Art was thoroughly prepared for every day in the rehearsal hall and the studio. Everything was marked in the script book from day one. I still do that today, too.

Nobody ever said to me, "This is what you should do as a direc-tor. When you're doing a musical number, you should do this. When you're shooting comedy, you should do that." I learned by watching carefully, and sometimes I'd come up with a better way of doing something. I eventually got the chance to "do it my way," but that would take a while. I had to earn my stripes and gain the confidence of the producers and directors whom I looked up to.

Let me tell you more about Art. We met in 1971, when I was working on *The Andy Williams Show*. Chris Bearde and Allan Blye, who were producing the show, asked me if I wanted to take on the role of associate director on a new series they were going to produce called *The Sonny and Cher Comedy Hour,* with Sonny Bono and Cher. Ever heard of them? That's of course a rhetorical question. At the time, they were known for their hit song "I Got You Babe" and a few others. Fred Silverman, who was running CBS, got the brilliant idea that Sonny and Cher would be great on their own show, and there you have *The Sonny and Cher Comedy Hour.*

Allan and Chris hired Art Fisher to direct the show, and I thought, "Well, this'll be a challenge." Art's reputation preceded him.

I said to Allan, "Are you sure we can do this? Art's known for picking his own people, and to tell him that he's got to use me as his associate director, he's not going to be happy." (He wasn't happy about much. That was just his personality!)

Allan said, "I want you to be the AD. I have a reason for wanting you to be the AD, and I can't tell you now but don't worry about Art. I'll take care of him. Okay?"

Art would not go into an editing room. He just wouldn't. And anybody who hired him knew that ahead of time. It was one of his quirks. Who ever heard of a director staying out of the editing room? That's where the magic sometimes happens, and the finishing touches are put on a show to make it sparkle and shine.

I went to Art Fisher's office about a week before I started working on *The Sonny and Cher Comedy Hour.*

"Hi, Art. I'm here for our meeting."

He barely looked up at me. "Close the door."

There were only two chairs in his office, both of them directly across from where he sat behind his desk. I sat down in one of those chairs, and he looked directly at me and said, *"Not that chair."* I moved to the other chair. He folded his arms, and he put his head as close as he could get to mine, and said, "I don't like you. I don't want you here, and I'm going to make your life fucking miserable."

"It's nice to meet you, Art."

"Now get the fuck out of my office."

Someone else might have been quaking in their boots, but I figured I'd find a way to work with Art, come hell or high water. I was not going to let him get the better of me. And I certainly was not going to disappoint Allan Blye and Chris Bearde. I'm not sure where I found the confidence, but there it was. I said to myself, "No, he's not going to make me miserable. He doesn't know who he's dealing with."

First day of rehearsals for *The Sonny and Cher Comedy Hour*, Art's holding a script reading in the rehearsal hall. Normally the AD sits next to the director to see the notes the director is making regarding camera blocking. (Remember, blocking is where the director decides which camera he wants to shoot a certain line of dialogue in a sketch or a certain line of music in a song.) Art sat at the head of the table, and I went to sit next to him, and he said, "What are you doing?"

"I'm sitting next to you so I can look at your script book and see your camera-blocking notes."

"I'll give you my script book when I'm ready if I want to. Don't sit next to me; go sit over there." He pointed to his far left.

"You know what, Art?" I said. "If you're going to treat me that way, this is not going to work. I'm here to help you. Take advantage of it. Don't treat me like a piece of shit. I'm supposed to be your shadow. I'm supposed to take a load off your shoulders. I'm supposed to make your life easier. If you keep pushing me away, you're not going to take advantage of what I have to offer. It'll be your loss."

He looked at me, and then he looked down. He always used to rub his eyes. He rubbed his eyes, and then he rubbed his eyes again with one hand, and then he looked back up at me and said, "Fuck you! Sit down." So, I sat next to him. There was no big reaction in the room. He had talked quietly so as not to make a spectacle. Some people smiled while others at the table turned away. I'm sure they'd seen this kind of behavior from him before. But perhaps they hadn't seen someone as young as I was or as new to the business hold their ground.

That was the first time in my adult life I really had to stand up for myself, and I did it.

Surprisingly, after that rocky start, Art and I became really good friends, only Art didn't want anybody to know it. He really respected me and understood that I understood him. I always delivered for him, and he realized that I had certain skills that he lacked like being able to deal with complicated situations involving a difficult person, or for that matter, communicating with just about anybody. I was patient, willing to listen, and wanted to be able to "fix" the problem. I have always been a problem-solver, never a problem-maker. It must have been a bitter pill for him to swallow in a sense, but he was thankful that I was there to always clean up his "mess" or prevent a "mess" from happening.

Let me pause here briefly to tell you a story about Sonny and Cher and how I came to be the owner of an unwanted birthday present for Cher.

I was working on their show; it was a Monday morning, and we were in the rehearsal hall, ready to do the script read, which we did every Monday morning. Cher didn't show up. That was very unlike her. Sonny was already there, and he looked white in the face and preoccupied about something—he didn't have his A-game face on, that's for sure.

Cher arrived about fifteen minutes late, crying her eyes out. She heard on a rock 'n' roll radio station, KFWB, on the way to the studio, driving to rehearsal, that Sonny had filed for divorce. That's how she found out about it. So, it was a tense script read that Monday morning, to say the least.

A few shows after this "shot across the bow," the couple was trying to work out their differences and salvage their marriage. It was Cher's birthday. She had told Sonny she wanted a Mercedes 280 SL. That was the small two-door Mercedes sports car. It was a great little car, and Sonny apparently hadn't bought her a birthday present as far as she knew.

On the lunch break Cher said to me, "I might be a little late getting back from lunch. I'm going to buy myself a birthday present."

Sonny had already left the lot. He had ordered a 280 SL Mercedes for her, and it was a day late coming. He went to pick up the car, and he drove back to the artists' parking lot at CBS and parked it in Cher's spot.

Cher, on the lunch break, went to Hollywood Mercedes and bought herself a 280 SL. She drove the car back and there in her parking space was a brand new 280 SL.

Now there were two Mercedes 280 SLs.

Later that afternoon, I was talking to Denis Pregnolato, Sonny and Cher's manager, who said to me, "Sonny is going crazy. He doesn't know what to do. He bought this car for Cher, and Cher bought herself the same car. He called the Mercedes dealership as soon as he realized what had happened, and they said if he tries to give the car back to them, it'll now be a used car because he drove it off the lot!" I said, "Oh my God, Denis. I've always dreamed about owning a 280 SL. I wish I could buy it from him but I don't think I could afford it right now."

Denis said to me, "Let me talk to Son. See what I can do."

"Really?"

"Yeah."

An hour or so later, Denis called me, "Can you come on up to Sonny's office?" I told him I'd be right there. Visions of a 280 SL danced in my head.

Sonny said to me, "I hear you've always wanted a 280 SL."

"It's my dream car, but I really can't afford that car." (I had, of course, long since graduated from my cherished VW.)

"Well, how much do you want to pay? How much money you got?"

I thought about it for a minute. I knew how expensive the model was, and I knew I couldn't afford a new one.

Sonny persisted. "How much money do you have to spend?"

"Well, I've got about this much money. I can probably put about this much down and maybe I can make payments to you."

"How much did you say you had to put down?"

"This much."

"Good enough. Write me a check. The car's yours."

What just happened? I couldn't believe it.

I had myself a 280 SL. Thank you, Sonny Bono. I'll be forever grateful.

I learned a lot working with Sonny and Cher—because we were all novices in television. We were learning together, experimenting, determining what played well to an audience, and how to make them laugh and entertain them. The show was a huge success.

Before they appeared on their own show, one of their appearances on CBS was on *The Merv Griffin Show*. They had, of course, appeared on Dick Clark's *American Bandstand* singing "I Got You Babe." Both of them looked so tentative and uncomfortable in front of the camera, but the kids dancing to that tune loved them. Merv asked them to substitute host for him on his talk show for a week, so they hosted while he was away. Maybe that appearance gave Fred Silverman the brilliant idea that they could carry their own show and not be simply a variety act in Las Vegas, which is where they made their name like so many other great performers.

Donny and Marie Osmond, Sonny and Cher, Tony Orlando and Dawn—it was television school for all of us alone and together. I also learned a lot by watching television producers Allan Blye and Chris Bearde work with Sonny and Cher, teaching them how to deliver a primetime television show on CBS. Allan was especially important to my career, and I looked up to him as I honed my directing and producing skills.

Cher and I became buddies. She used to call me into her dressing room to talk. She wanted me to tell Art Fisher that she planned to ad-lib something and didn't want him to be surprised or have a "shit fit." That became one of her hallmarks—ad-libbing off something Sonny said. He became her "straight" man, and she had fabulous comedic timing! Something you don't know about Cher. She is dyslexic, so it was probably difficult for her to read her cue cards and she'd often memorize her lines, but ad-libbing was her specialty. What a talent!

I spent four years with Art Fisher on *The Sonny and Cher Comedy Hour* (1971–74) and another year with him doing specials—at which point I had already set my sights on directing specials without Art. I had been through the "School of Art Fisher" and was ready to graduate.

Art went through associate directors, one after the other, like Kleenex, but I managed to last with him. We developed such a good relationship. I understood him and his quirky personality. I knew how to deal with him. I was no work for him. I gave him everything he needed, and he didn't have to think about it.

Believe it or not, he gave me a lot of freedom. While in the rehearsal hall, he would say to me, "Why don't you do the camera blocking for this sketch?" Sometimes he looked at my shots and said, "Good job." He used my shots and my blocking because I was good. I loved what I did so much, and I was so passionate about it.

I consider Art to be one of my greatest teachers—both in terms of what to do and what not to do. Both lessons are valuable. While I was working on *The Sonny and Cher Comedy Hour*, one day Art Fisher didn't show up in the studio for camera blocking. Very unlike Art. I was sitting in my AD chair, right next to the director's chair. When it was time to start blocking, Art still hadn't arrived. Allan Blye tapped me on the shoulder and said, "Move over, Jeff." I said, "What do you mean, Allan?" He wanted me to take over as the director because Art had not shown up, and Allan wanted to get going. He had lost his patience. That was one of the luckiest days of my life. I have a saying, "When luck comes your way, you better have the talent." Up to that point I had been the AD, and I knew what I was doing, and the crew was very supportive of my move into the big chair. Transitioning from AD to director was easy for me because I was totally prepared. I was ready. Art never showed up for that show. What happened to him that week is such a complicated story; I really can't get into it now. Sorry.

Art was unpredictable. One day, he decided that he wanted to learn how to fly a helicopter, which he did. Unfortunately, he was killed in a crash in 1984. It was a cloudy, rainy night in Los Angeles, and he wasn't supposed to be flying, but that was Art. On his way home from Malibu, he was flying too low, and the control tower kept telling him, "You've got to increase your altitude."

"But I won't be able to see anything through the clouds."

"We'll talk you through getting back to Burbank."

He didn't listen to them—I think he thought he was invincible, and he certainly wasn't about to take direction from anyone else, on or off the set. Sadly, the rotor got caught on an electrical cable, and his helicopter went down and exploded. (A dentist from Beverly Hills who Art was teaching how to fly was also killed in the crash.)

I have so much to thank Art Fisher for. He was a legend. He helped launch my directing career and also enhanced the careers of many stars—not only Sonny and Cher, but Andy Williams, the Osmonds, and so many more. Art Fisher, rest in peace.

Cher and Me, friends forever.

CHAPTER 8

TIE A YELLOW RIBBON

FRED SILVERMAN, WHO WAS A TOP EXECUTIVE AT NBC, CBS, AND ABC during his legendary career, gave me so many opportunities over the course of my career and was one of my champions. I met Fred because he put *The Sonny and Cher Comedy Hour* on the air. He used to come down from his office at CBS and sit in the control room every time we taped the show. I was the associate director, until I was asked to direct the last couple of episodes when I took over from Art Fisher. Fred saw how I worked and became a big fan, which was lucky for me because Fred was the most powerful executive in television and could move mountains when he needed to.

Fred was always on the lookout for new material and new talent for CBS. So when his wife told him about this hot group she and some of her girlfriends had seen in a New York club, he was intrigued. "Fred, you won't believe these kids," she told him. "There's this Puerto Rican guy and two black girls, and they are incredible! You've got to see them; they call themselves Tony Orlando and Dawn." (They had released two big hits, "Knock Three Times" and "Tie a Yellow Ribbon Round the Ole Oak Tree.")

Fred told her, "Well, I'm coming home this weekend. Let's go." Fred and his wife lived in Manhattan, and he shuttled back and forth to Los Angeles—which was not unusual for executives of his rank and stature. It's also par for the course since LA and New York are the two anchors of everything that is happening in television.

Fred went to one of their shows, and afterward he asked Tony if his group had representation. The answer was no.

"Well, I want to put you on television."

Fred recognized talent when he saw it, and he wasn't afraid to take risks. He liked Tony's energy but sensed that Tony would need lots of guidance because he really wasn't a performer; he was a record label executive who wanted to change his career. That's when Fred hired Saul Ilson and Ernie Chambers, who were among the best go-to TV producers of television specials and series at the time. Fred Silverman thought—with all their credits and their stellar reputations—they would be perfect for Tony Orlando.

Fred told Saul and Ernie that he wanted them to meet with me. "Jeff was associate director for Sonny and Cher, and he's directed a couple of specials for Allan Blye and Chris Bearde."

I met with Saul and Ernie. I was in my late twenties. It was really unheard of for someone my age to be directing a primetime network show, but when you have Fred Silverman in your corner, and Saul and Ernie behind you, magic happens. Never, ever underestimate the power of connections.

Saul and Ernie hired me on the spot to direct four episodes of *Tony Orlando and Dawn* during the summer of 1974. It was a summer replacement for the regular network programming and putting it on air during the summer gave the executives time to assess if it had legs to make it into the regular fall lineup. And it did. The show was picked up for the 1974 fall season. Instead of it being a mid-season replacement the following January, Fred wanted it to go on the air right away. We shot the summer shows, took a week off, and were back rehearsing for the September 1974 premiere of the show. The significant takeaway here is that Saul and Ernie (along with Fred Silverman) gave me my first job as a director of a major network primetime variety series—I was now in the big leagues. I will forever be grateful to them. And to this day, they are two of my very dearest friends.

Tony Orlando could barely believe his luck. He said, "You know what? I like this show-business stuff. I'm going to leave the record label, and I'm going to be a star!"

I think Tony was twenty-nine or thirty, and he was kind of insecure because this was all so new to him. We were about the same age, and he knew it was my first big directing gig and it was his first big break in television. He hung on to me for dear life. With fear in his eyes, he said, "Jeff, you've got to get me through this, man. I don't know what the fuck I'm doing, but you know what you're doing. Tell me what to do and where I should go and where I should look. But I don't want anybody to know that I don't know what I'm doing. Make me look good!" What pressure? This was his first shot at real stardom, and I was right there with him. It's almost laughable that such a big talent as Tony Orlando was leaning on me to keep him upright and looking good. I didn't want to let him down, disappoint Saul and Ernie, or make a mistake that could torpedo my career. We were in the same canoe paddling as hard as we could.

I never wanted to hang out with performers when we weren't working. Sometimes they wanted to, though. I always told them, "We need to keep this relationship like it is. We can be good friends here at work, but you're the star, and I'm the director. I really would rather not hang out socially. I just don't feel comfortable doing that." I have always maintained that policy throughout my career—I always want to keep the relationship professional with the talent and stay away from the "after-hours" scene. I made sure to follow that rule with Tony, and I did it in a way that would not be taken as an insult or a "brush off." I rarely break this rule.

I have another secret to share. No matter how important the star is that I'm working with—whether it's Cher, Barbra Streisand, Whitney Houston, Paul Newman, Kirk Douglas, Clint Eastwood, Garth Brooks, Michael Jackson, Meryl Streep, Bette Midler, and on and on, I always try and remember, "They get up in the morning just like I do, brush their teeth like I do, take a pee, and whatever else." It's kind of like the saying, they put their pants on just like everyone else—one leg at a time. With those thoughts in my head, I am able to stay calm when I first meet a star; it's a version of what actors are often told when standing in front of a theater or studio audience, "Just imagine the audience is buck naked, or that you're in your own living room performing for friends. It will calm your nerves!" Most stars and celebrities appreciate that they are being taken care of by someone who stays calm and gives them an honest opinion—not someone who is intimidated by their celebrity.

Tony Orlando's weekly variety show was the first network prime-time series that I did all on my own. It became CBS's number one hit on Wednesday nights at eight o'clock. Kismet. The chemistry between Tony and me was magical, and it worked for both of us.

I remember the first day on the set. Tony was so nervous; Saul and Ernie were right there by his side, and I also really helped him through, but at the same time I had to prove myself!

Fortunately, I had a CBS staff crew; the guys that were assigned to do *Tony Orlando and Dawn* knew me from other shows and my cue card days. In those days, directors or producers didn't get to pick their own crew. You were doing a network show at a network, you had staff guys, and they were assigned to you. It was a way to keep a lot of people working consistently. The crew on *Tony Orlando and Dawn* were seasoned professionals, and they thought it was great that I had this opportunity. In the first camera meeting for the first show, they all said, "We got your back, buddy." It was so comforting. There was no cameraman that said, "I can't get you that shot," or "You don't know what you're doing; I'll show you what the shot should be." I never heard that ever.

When we debuted *Tony Orlando and Dawn*, we were still recording on two-inch tape. It was pre-tape all day Thursday. You'd tape some of the comedy sketches. Sometimes, depending on who the musical guest was, you would pre-tape a song even though you might do it again in front of the audience on Friday. And then Friday morning, you would come in, and you would rehearse on camera everything that you were going to do in front of an audience. Then you would let an afternoon audience in to watch the dress rehearsal, which you would tape. Sometimes sketches or musical numbers worked better in the dress rehearsal than the air show (that's what we called the second taping), so those spots would be edited into the aired show. We would splice and dice between one taping and the other to use whichever segments were better.

On *Tony Orlando and Dawn*, we always did their opening number in front of an audience. "Ladies and gentlemen, Tony Orlando and Dawn!" and they would enter the stage, singing "Tie a Yellow Ribbon," which was their theme song. And then they would perform a monologue where Tony talked to Dawn, his two backup singers, Telma Hopkins and Joyce Vincent Wilson, and they would sass him, and he would have comebacks.

Then they'd sing a reprise of "Tie a Yellow Ribbon," and the audience would go crazy and clap and scream. And then Tony would say, "We're going to go change our clothes for the next thing we've got to do. But you should have been here yesterday to see what was going on." And we'd play back a sketch that we recorded the day before to get the audience's reaction.

I recorded the audience reaction which I would later put in when I went into the editing room to sweeten the show so that I didn't have to use that fake crap (canned laugh tracks and canned applause). I had a real audience applause and laughter.

I think the great comedian Carol Burnett probably set this style on her own weekly variety show. It's called "block and tape on Thursday"— all the things that you might have to do twice because somebody somewhere might have screwed up. There were things that the producers didn't want to take a chance on doing in front of an audience and possibly embarrassing the stars, so we always had a backup tape.

For me, once I camera-blocked and rolled tape, it was always like shooting something live because I wouldn't stop. I did not want to have to go to the studio audience and say, "Sorry guys, we have to cut!" because one of my camera operators was out of focus or made a mistake. That was my problem, and I had to fix it in the editing room. I never stopped for any problem that was mine. Occasionally a star would stop and say, "Cut, I just really messed up. We've got to do it again." Of course, I'd accommodate them. Always make the talent look good. That is one of my hard-and-fast rules. Especially if you want to work with them again.

The first day on the set, Tony was a bundle of nerves, as I mentioned earlier, and Telma and Joyce were really nervous as well. I couldn't be nervous because I wasn't allowed to be nervous. And I never got nervous anyway. I never ever, ever got nervous in my entire career. I only got excited.

One of my greatest thrills working on *Tony Orlando and Dawn* was Jerry Lewis's appearance on the show. (Because of the show's popularity, we were able to book a lot of top-notch stars.) When I started watching television as a kid, there were two people I wanted to meet one day: Jerry Lewis and Jackie Gleason. For some reason Jerry Lewis made me laugh. I loved all of his "hey, lady" stuff, and Jackie Gleason—with his gruff manner and brilliant physical comedy on *The Honeymooners*—was priceless.

First, a couple of stories about Jerry Lewis. Tony Orlando loved Jerry Lewis and really wanted to get him to guest on the show. When Jerry said yes, Tony almost peed himself. Jerry did a ten-minute comedy sketch called "We're in Politics" with Tony. The set was dressed like a stop on a campaign trail with a sign, "Lewis and Orlando." It was really the only time I saw Tony as nervous as he was on all the shows we did. Nervous, but so flattered and excited, because he was in the presence of the master of comedy, Jerry Lewis.

It was hard to direct Jerry Lewis doing comedy. I was kind of intimidated, so I said to him, "Hey, Jerry, why don't you just do what you would do? Let me see it! Tony, is that okay with you?" Tony said, "Psh, are you kidding!" They went through it a number of times in the rehearsal hall. Jerry would say things to Tony like, "Hey Tony, what if—when we get to these lines—what if we do this?" Tony would say okay, then Jerry looked at me and said, "Is that okay with you, Jeff?" And I said, "It's perfect," because it was.

The sketch was genius. Jerry is running for president, and he asks Tony to be his vice president: "Strike up the band for Lewis and Orlando." And they were off and running. At one point Jerry's image consultant from the firm of Button Comma, Button Comma tells Jerry: "You've got to have the enthusiasm of Monty Hall; the sex appeal of Robert Redford; but above all, be yourself." They remind the audience that this is the year of the woman, and Jerry puts on a wig and says, "We want equal pay." And then he looks at Tony and asks—in a voice that sounds like Bella Abzug—"What do you think of that, *bubbe?*" To Tony's great credit, he kept right up with Jerry, and, when the sketch wrapped with a song, "We're in Politics," the audience went wild.

That was my first time working with Jerry, and it was such a good experience. I had heard horror stories about him, but he was really lovely, and I learned a lot about comedy directing, from the master no less. He knew how badly Tony wanted him to be on the show and that he was Tony's comedy idol, so he couldn't have been more pleasant.

One more quick story from *Tony Orlando and Dawn* before I tell you another Jerry Lewis story. It was the February 18, 1976, episode and Tony's guests were Milton Berle, Joey Bishop, and Sid Caesar... oh my God...! I don't know what Tony was thinking when he booked those three comedy geniuses with giant egos on the same show. Well, it started on Monday morning at the script reading when Milton Berle and Joey Bishop got into it; they started rewriting. Tony asked the writers to accommodate Berle and Bishop's changes. At Tuesday's rehearsal, Caesar was not scheduled to come in, Berle and Bishop were directing each other, and I sat back and watched because I knew that there was nothing I could say or do. Soon Tony and I both had to become Henry Kissinger as Berle got pissed off at Bishop and vice versa. We tried to keep the peace, but that didn't happen. I was not looking forward to Wednesday morning, but before I knew it, there we were, Berle, Bishop, and Caesar doing a song-and-dance number with Tony. That did not go well at all, as Berle and Bishop continued their spat. That night, I got a call from Saul Ilson, the producer, who told me that he had just received a call from Sid Caesar, who said, "Please, take me out of the fucking number. I can't work with those two maniacs; they're nuts." Well, I couldn't wait for Thursday's camera rehearsal to see what was in store for all of us. Skipping now to the end of this story, at the taping of the show, everybody put on their professional hats, and it was all fine. But *oy*, getting there, man was I happy when that week was over.

And now back to Jerry Lewis.

The next time I worked with Jerry was on the Muscular Dystrophy Telethon. George Schlatter produced it, and I directed it, and that was twenty-one hours on the air, live. Oy vey. That show meant so much to Jerry; it was his baby, and he was very uptight. Thank goodness for Debbie Williams, the stage manager. Jerry loved her, and she knew how to keep him calm. I stayed as far away from him as I could on that show, and I let George and Debbie deal with him.

If George needed help, he called me. But George very rarely needed help, so I never heard from him. George knew how to deal with anybody.

Then I had a really interesting experience. I was directing a country music special at a hotel in Las Vegas, and Jerry was in Las Vegas at the same time performing at the same hotel. One of my stage managers said to me when we were in the middle of rehearsal, "Jeff, fasten your seatbelt. You've got a guest coming to visit you in the truck."

I said, "Can you tell me who?"

He said, "Nope!"

I was directing a musical number, and I heard the door of the remote truck open. I was so busy I didn't have the chance to turn around. And finally, when I had a moment, I turned around to see who my guest was, and there was Jerry Lewis sitting right behind me. I thought, "Holy shit! Jerry Lewis is sitting in my truck watching me direct! Jerry Fucking Lewis!" I went over to say hello, and he hugged me. It was like another dream come true for me!

After the hug, he said, "Carry on. I don't want to bother you."

I said, "I can give everyone a five-minute break, and we can talk."

He said, "No, no, no. I'm here to watch. I want to see the master at work."

Eventually we took a break, and I said, "What are you doing here?"

He said, "Well, I'm in the same hotel you are. You're in one showroom, and I'm in the other. I heard that you were here, and I wanted to come and say hello." From *Tony Orlando and Dawn* and everything else we did together, he remembered me. What a mensch he was. I will never forget that.

By the time I finished the first full season of *Tony Orlando and Dawn* as their director, my life started to get nuts. By the second season a lot of producers were calling wanting me to work on their shows once they saw how I handled comedy, music, and live interviews. I was booking shows that started as soon as the second season wrapped. I barely had time to change my clothes before I was on to the next project. It was one show after another until the next season of *Tony Orlando and Dawn* started up.

I was hot. To me, hot meant the phone rang constantly. Television producers wondered what was different about Jeff Margolis and if they could have some of it.

CHAPTER 9

THE PHONE DOESN'T STOP RINGING

As the new kid on the block, I was in demand as a director. I had proven myself with my work on *The Sonny and Cher Comedy Hour* and on *Tony Orlando and Dawn*. I was on a roll, and television producers looking for a director thought that my talent would bring a new perspective to variety shows. My agents at William Morris, one of the most venerable talent agencies in Hollywood at the time, fielded inquiries about my availability. Often a producer or network executive wanted to meet with me, or they'd call me directly so they could hear my voice and get to know me on the phone to ascertain if I was the right person for the job. Hearing my voice was apparently an important clue, and if they liked the sound of my voice and what I had to say, that initial conversation might seal the deal. Then my agent would step in and negotiate the terms of engagement. They were curious about this kid who didn't come from Hollywood royalty. Sure, Uncle Monty had given me my first big break, but I wasn't the son of a television or film executive. My dad, as you remember, was in the electronics business. They thought I brought a fresh perspective to the medium and knew that I delivered without a lot of psychic drama, pencil throwing, or screaming and yelling.

By the mid-1970s I realized I was doing a lot more than directing a show—I was actually producing some of the shows for the producers who hired me. A lot of the creative ideas on the show were mine. I would be hired to do a show, and I would be called in weeks before directors were usually called in at the development and concept stage.

I worked with a lot of producers who would say to me, "Hey, man, we're so glad you're here; this is your show. Tell us what you want to do." But there were other producers who had very specific ideas about what they wanted and knew I could execute their plans.

I thought, why not start my own production company? If I'm producing and directing, I might as well get the credit for it and get paid accordingly.

And just like that, Jeff Margolis Productions was born in 1976.

My agents at William Morris made it known that I had established my own production company. Just to keep my options open, I told them, "Look, if I intimidate a producer by taking on that role and they think I might have too much power or take something away from them, then I'm happy to just be the director. When an opportunity comes along to do both jobs, great."

I remained flexible and kept my ego in check. I was always looking for ways to make the set a great place to work, where everyone got along, worked hard but had fun doing it, and the talent felt supported.

As a producer, there's no liability. There's a responsibility. You are given money from a studio or a network, and you have a budget. Red alert: you better come in on budget because if you don't, you are going to piss a lot of people off. I wanted Jeff Margolis Productions to reflect the collaborative style I had established as a director—to create a team of people who enjoyed what they were doing and did their job to the highest standard possible. (Remember, I was a Margolis/Groper, and I saw my parents and grandparents work hard, never cutting corners— there were no slackers in my family, as I've said before—and I carried their examples throughout my career in television.)

When I hired people to work with me—notice I said work *with* me, not *for* me—and they had worked on other shows, they would say, "Jeez, Jeff, this is so different. It's so good. It's so much more fun. It's so much more creative! In the long run it makes everybody's job so much easier!" It's a pleasure when people like working with you and you've created a collegial atmosphere instead of a work environment where people are constantly butting heads and wishing they were somewhere else—say, a beach in Hawaii, for example. For me, work was a pleasure and a passion, and I hoped to convey that message to everyone who elected to sign onto my team.

I built a great team around me, some of whom have been with me since the beginning. Gloria Fujita O'Brien, Benn Fleishman, and Mick McCullough all served as co-producers. Within a few years we could finish one another's sentences, and together we created a well-oiled machine that delivered great programming, whether it was a special or a series or a one-off. (You'll find out what all of that means later on.) I could pick and choose what I wanted to do at this point, and I loved every minute of it. I could also select the people I wanted to work with—there is never a reason to work with difficult people who make your life miserable—there is so much great talent out there, why not find people who are gifted and pleasant to be around, who are problem-solvers not problem-makers?

Some of my other family members are the writers Stephen Pouliot, Bruce Vilanch, Jon Macks, and Dave Boone; production designers Joe Stewart, John Shaffner, and Ray Klausen; lighting designer Jeff Engel; music director Diane Louie; production manager Chris Carr; associate directors Peter Margolis, Allan Kartun, Debbie Palacio, Wendy Charles Acey (may she rest in peace); and really, the list does go on, but these people were there for almost every production I worked on. That's longevity, and it's as rare as a fifty-year marriage in Hollywood.

Speaking of marriage, I was busy dating from a relatively early age—remember Paula? We dated for four years, but when we went on to college, the flame went out. I had a lot of fun at UCLA. I moved out of my parents' home and into my own apartment when I enrolled in the television school. At twenty-two I met my future wife, Leslie, who was just eighteen. In those days that might have seemed like a dramatic age difference but we really got along, and she was incredibly supportive of my ambition to become a television director. I probably told her of my secret wish to direct the Oscars someday. Instead of laughing, she encouraged me and totally believed in me. And that's what you want in a partner.

We just clicked. I think you could say it was love at first sight, and we got married in 1971, a year after we met. It sounds a bit premature, but back in the day getting married at the age of twenty-three and nineteen wasn't all that unusual. My parents loved Leslie. Her mom loved me. I was never quite sure how her dad felt about me though. Anyway, it was all good. Leslie would visit me in the editing room when I was pulling all-nighters, bringing me snacks or entire meals just to make sure that I was taking care of myself. At some point she quit her job as a dental assistant and taught cooking classes at UCLA. I was the appreciative beneficiary of her culinary talent.

Being the partner of a busy director/producer is challenging, but Leslie adapted to all the managed chaos. Five years into our marriage, life was one assignment after another—each one bigger than the previous one—but I was ready for it all, and with my wife by my side, everything seemed possible, which included a six-month stint in Hawaii directing *The Don Ho Show*. Could it get any better?

CHAPTER 10

FAMILY FIRST

I HAD JUST RECOVERED FROM DIRECTING A HELLACIOUS SHOW WITH BILL Cosby, *Cos,* which was a short-lived series on ABC Sunday nights opposite *60 Minutes,* and so an invitation to head off to Hawaii to direct Don Ho was a blessing. Apparently, Don had a disagreement with the director on his daytime variety series, *The Don Ho Show.* His producer, Bob Banner, asked me to step in. I hadn't worked with Bob before but, of course, I knew who he was—one of the pre-eminent movers and shakers of the Golden Age of Television. He was the director of *Omnibus,* which was the forerunner of PBS. When he formed his own production company in the 1950s, he produced *The Dinah Shore Chevy Show,* an early example of variety programming, for which he won Emmys and Peabodys; he was also credited with producing over two hundred episodes of *The Garry Moore Show.* In the sixties, he put together *Carnegie Hall Salutes Jack Benny* and then went on to produce a special, *Julie and Carol at Carnegie Hall,* starring Julie Andrews and Carol Burnett, which won three Emmys. He and Julie and Carol had the golden touch.

Leslie and I packed our bags, closed the house, and headed off to Waikiki Beach for six months. It felt like a working holiday. Total bliss, and the experience cemented my relationship with one of the producing greats of television—Bob Banner. *The Don Ho Show* was a revolving door of great talent, including Lucille Ball, Tony Bennett, Redd Foxx, and other boldface names. And of course, Don Ho, who started his career as a recording artist with his hit "Tiny Bubbles." He was a terrific variety show host and spokesperson for his native Hawaii. He capitalized on this and attracted tourists as audience participants. He was definitely at the right place at the right time, and when the run of the show ended after ninety episodes, he continued to perform at the Beachcomber and other popular venues in Hawaii.

Two years later Bob Banner called me again, but this time he needed me in London for a short engagement—to direct Julie Andrews in her own special, *One Step into Spring*. I had never been to the city and had not worked directly with Julie, but I was over the moon at the prospect. This show helped set the stage for more than 150 specials I would later direct and produce beginning in 1978. You'll hear more about *One Step into Spring* in a later chapter.

~ ~

Becoming a father was going to be a real challenge for me given the demands of my career. The hours, the travel, and the requirement to be totally focused on whatever project I was immersed in. Leslie and I wondered how I would be able to juggle work and home life, knowing how demanding children are, especially in their early formative years. Could I even have a home life if I kept working twenty hours a day? I have often thought back to my childhood when I got to hang out with my cousins, parents, and grandparents to celebrate the holidays. Everyone treated me like a well-loved member of the family. How many directors, producers, and actors did I know who could truthfully say that family came first? It always did for me. I wanted the same thing for my children if I was lucky enough to become a father.

Many people I've met have asked me whether I became Hollywood-ized—sacrificing family for fame. As I got more and more offers, I was determined to keep my priorities straight. Family first—whenever possible. And I add that caveat because every now and then there are career situations that have to take precedence over family, but hopefully that's rare.

I'm reminded of the story in which a man is on his deathbed. He usually doesn't think about how many hours he spent at the office (or in my case, on a set). He's thinking about the people he loves and the regret that he might not have spent enough time with them. I never wanted to be that man who passed on without giving everything he could to his family and all the other people he loved who needed him, who made his life worth living. Happiness doesn't come from a big paycheck or your name in lights. It comes from the love you are given and the love you give!

I always tried to find a balance between career and marriage. When Leslie had something special that she wanted to do with another couple or a group of people, I almost always figured out a way to make the time. If I absolutely couldn't, I would ask her to change the date of the event, which she would try and do so that I could be part of it.

Eleven years after we were married, Leslie and I became parents to our first child, our son, Adam, who was born in 1982. I really had to adjust. I learned how to do in eight hours at the studio what used to take me twelve to fifteen hours. That way I could get home and be a good husband to Leslie and a good father to Adam.

I turned a couple of opportunities down toward the end of Leslie's first pregnancy and pretty much the first year after Adam was born. I just wanted to be home. But there was enough happening in Los Angeles that was offered to me, so I didn't feel as if I was making a huge financial sacrifice or jeopardizing my career.

Around that time, I realized that there were other people that I could rely on and trust to do the things that I had always felt I needed to do on my own. I found two editors, Pam Marshall and Kris Trexler, who thought the same way I did, had the same sense of comedy timing that I did, loved music the way that I did, and had edited so much with me that they knew my style. We developed an efficient way of working together. They would edit the first cut of a production and send it to me. I'd look at it, take notes, and call them with my comments and changes. Then they'd edit a second cut and send it back to me. I didn't have to go into the edit bay until it was time to add the finishing touches.

Limiting my time in the edit bay gave me the time I needed to be at home with Leslie and Adam. I learned to find other people—assistant directors and production supervisors—people whom I trusted to do the kind of prep work that I had always felt only I could do on my shows. I learned how to delegate: being a control freak and a family man are incompatible!

I was very confident with the people at Jeff Margolis Productions, and I trusted them completely, which made me feel comfortable enough to have a second child. Our daughter Erin was born in 1985. By that time, I learned how to do the greatest balancing act I'd ever done in my life—to be both a family man and a successful producer/director.

~ ~

You can read a hundred books that have been written by people in the business who talk about the fact that they were raised by nannies, or they never knew who their father or sometimes mother was until they became an adult and got into the business with them. I did not sacrifice my family or my career.

In case you are wondering if the apple does not fall far from the tree, I'm proud to give you a quick glimpse of my son, Adam, and daughter Erin. I used to take Adam with me into the control room. He'd sit with me from the time he was just a toddler and watch what I was doing. He was fascinated by all the pictures on the TV screens and all the buttons on the switcher and all the people moving around. Eventually, he'd join me on stage and kibbitz with the stars, who were happy to see him. Today he's one of the most sought-after camera operators in the entertainment industry, with his eye set on producing and directing. By the way, he has won eight Emmy Awards. I am so proud of him. But there is plenty of pride left over for Erin, who decided that the entertainment industry was not for her. Dr. Erin Margolis is a licensed clinical psychologist, with a doctorate, and she has a thriving private practice. (And on top of that, she's gorgeous.) Erin's mission is "helping clients connect with the truest version of themselves." So, Mom and Dad, there is a doctor in the family, even if it isn't me!

In 2010, I was blessed with another daughter, whose name is Samantha. Of course, everybody knows her as Sam. She is the sweetest thirteen-year-old on the planet. So smart, so sensitive, so thoughtful, so mature, and so beautiful inside and out. When she was around five years old, one night she said to me, "Daddy, you're my best buddy and I love you." Well, what can I say; she had me wrapped around her little finger. She's now studying for her Bat Mitzvah this year. And we just attended a father-daughter dance for the fifth graders at her school. I practiced the waltz, and we took to the dance floor for a short turn. And then I handed her a rose, and we had our picture taken, as a memento of a special evening. One day, I'm sure she also will be a producer and director, or a doctor.

I am filled with gratitude to have three incredible children.

In 1979, well before Leslie and I were parents, I received a phone call out of the blue. It was from the president of the editing company where I did most of my post-production work, Compact Video. He asked me if I wanted to direct my first film—a live concert with one of the decade's (if not the half-century's) most famous comedians. I practically dropped the phone but quickly answered with a resounding *yes*! And then of course I added my usual response at opportunities like this one with, "Are you fucking kidding me?"

CHAPTER 11

RICHARD PRYOR: SMOKIN' HOT

RICHARD PRYOR WAS ONE OF THE MOST FAMOUS STANDUP COMEDIANS OF ALL time. By the 1970s he had earned an Emmy and three Grammys for his trenchant humor. His titles included *Richard Pryor: Live and Smokin'*, *That Nigger's Crazy*, *Uptown Saturday Night*, and *Car Wash*. Pryor got himself in a boatload of trouble. He was arrested for crack cocaine use and for this and that, and he had to do something in exchange for avoiding jail time. I never knew the real story and never really knew quite how it all happened and how it all came about, and what went down, but he made some kind of deal with somebody high up somewhere to do a giant standup comedy concert for charity. And I was asked to direct it. Richard made me laugh out loud. I couldn't wait. I always admired Richard for taking on any and all sacred cows—poking fun at his father, suburban whites, or whoever popped into his insanely funny brain. Watching him work a crowd without taking a breath was incredible, and he carried the audience with him from the starting line all the way across the finish line. Every performance was a marathon of joke after joke and story after story.

The word was out that Pryor needed to redeem himself with a charity concert, and Bill Sargent, Jr., a well-known producer and technology guru, jumped on it immediately.

Sargent founded Electronovision with the forward-thinking idea of videotaping live events and distributing them in theaters. Videotape technology for this concept was still in its infancy. Later on, Sargent moved to Salt Lake City, Utah, and founded Theatrovision with the intention of continuing to tape or film live shows for television and theatrical distribution.

While Sargent was behind the scenes scrambling to put a deal together because *Richard Pryor: Live in Concert* hadn't been presold to a network or a movie distributor, I was busy with this and that. I used to do all my editing at Compact Video in beautiful downtown Burbank. When people started shooting shows away from the network studios and began editing and doing their music fixes and applause at facilities away from the network, Bob Seidenglanz opened the first non-network editing facility, called Compact Video. He later bought another company called Pacific Video. One of my best friends to this day, Steve Schifrin, ran Compact Video and later Pacific Video. I was one of their first and most loyal clients. I don't know how they got involved with Sargent, but he came to Bob and Steve and said, "Can you be one of my investors and put up some money for the Pryor film?"

They said, "We'll be your only investor, and we'll give you all the money you need."

"Oh, okay."

"On one condition. You have to use our director."

Bob and Steve called me up and said, "Hey, have you ever directed a movie before?"

"No, but I'd love to do one. One of these days I'll do a movie."

"Well how about now?"

"What are you talking about?" I asked. I had no idea I was their director! They didn't tell me until after they'd told Sargent.

"We're going to be the production entity behind a historic, ground-breaking motion picture: *Richard Pryor: Live in Concert*. Richard's going to do this charity benefit concert, and you're going to direct it, and it's going to be released as a movie."

"Okay." I might have said something more enthusiastic, but I didn't know Sargent and I wanted to hear the details directly from him and how he envisioned the structure of the film and if the whole project sounded feasible.

I met with Sargent, and he said, "Your friends at Pacific Video want you to direct Richard's concert movie. It'll include Richard preparing for the concert by doing comedy showcases around town, covering the concert, and then what goes on after the concert."

"That sounds good to me." Then I came up with an idea. "Why not shoot him in the limo also? He gets picked up at his house, and he's driven to Long Beach to the Terrace Theater where the concert will be filmed."

The opening footage of *Richard Pryor: Live in Concert* (1979) is a closeup of the headlights of the limousine pulling into the artist's entrance at the Terrace Theater in Long Beach. Holding a handheld camera, the camera operator followed the limo around and watched Richard get out of the car with his then-girlfriend, go into the theater, and on into his dressing room. When they closed the door to the dressing room, that was the end of the opening shot. The next shot was a wide shot from the balcony of the theater as Richard entered from stage right, and the concert started. It was spectacular.

I had all these 35mm film cameras, and I positioned them like I would position cameras for a television taping of a live concert. That means seven or more cameras are set up in a way to capture everything: a closeup of Pryor, a head-to-toe shot, a wide shot of the stage, a high wide shot from the balcony, a reverse shot across Richard's shoulder focused on the audience, and two cameras for audience closeup reaction shots. That's the basic setup if you are shooting a standup comedy show for television. Shooting on film, I had to have back-ups so that when Richard's closeup or head-to-toe shot cameras ran out of film, I had additional cameras with the same shot right next to them which would start rolling a minute before the film ran out on the first camera. That way I'd always have footage of everything. Or so I thought. We didn't have to stop to re-load, but at one point during the filming, a power strip that was operating the two center head-to-toe shot cameras blew out from being overloaded, and I lost that shot for two or three minutes. (If you don't have continuous coverage, you'll be in trouble in the editing room.) Nobody ever really noticed in the final edit except me. I was able to make it look good, anyway, but it was certainly an "oh shit" moment while it was happening.

I set up a control room backstage in the theater, and I had a technical director with me, plus an assistant director, a lighting director, and an audio director. I cut the show live, in the same way I'd cut a live comedy concert for television. I used a system called "video assist," which is where each film camera has a small video camera on top of its lens, and the show is recorded on tape so that I could edit it immediately afterward. Then we all looked at the show when it was completed, and the producers said, "There's nothing to cut out, really. It's a movie, and if Richard says 'fuck,' it's not a network show, so we don't have to bleep it out or cut it out." The standards and practices police weren't on duty as they would be if it were a network television show.

Richard was a gem. I had worked with him before, so he knew who I was. I only spoke to him once. He was in his own world, and he knew what the concept was, he knew what he had to do, and he didn't want to be bothered with what I was doing as the director. He knew he was in good hands. I don't know if he realized how big, how ground-breaking, how iconic the film was going to be. If he had, maybe he would have been more involved—or not.

Richard was shown the tape of the show to make sure he liked what he saw. I just got the message, "Good job." Once I had his approval and the producers' approval, I gave the tape version of what I had edited to a bunch of film editors, and they just followed my edits, cutting the film footage exactly as I had done on tape. That's how the movie was put together.

Richard was brilliant! It was the best comedy concert he'd ever done, and he did something that every comedian in the business would envy and want to emulate. And that's exactly what happened. Eddie Murphy did it, and Chris Rock did it, and then many other headline comedians wanted to do a standup comedy motion picture. Humble brag: in the Arts and Leisure section of the Sunday *New York Times* of June 13, 2021, Michael Che, of *Saturday Night Live* fame, is quoted:

> Richard Pryor Live in Concert *is the greatest piece of stand-up comedy ever recorded. I watch it and feel like a fraud every so often. It's the best at its best. It's so mature. It's so thoughtful. The stuff he is pulling off is seamless and effortless, to the point where I don't even know where the crowd work begins, and where the written word ends. It's so crazy good. I think it's also the direct line to what today's comedy is.*

Richard Pryor: Live in Concert was released in six hundred theaters nationwide for six weeks. I was offered more money by Bill Sargent than I'd ever been offered for anything I'd ever done in my career. The way the deal was structured by my agents at William Morris, I would receive three payments: the first upon signing the agreement; the second when the movie was released; and the final payment at the end of the theatrical run when the producers cashed in at the box office.

Bill Sargent (now deceased) turned out to be kind of a shady character. I didn't have much contact with him after I met him. He was never around. He was one of those executive producers that was a "send me a VHS and I'll look at it at home" guy. I don't think that he even came to the concert.

He trusted me, I guess. I never even saw any of the producers at the concert. There were two other producers that Sargent hired who were the lead producers—Hillard Elkins and Steve Blauner—I'm not sure what they did. And the night of the actual filming in Long Beach, I don't think any of them showed up to watch what was going on; at least I never knew they were there if they were. A lot of money was riding on that evening, and it would have been usual and ordinary to have a producer's pair of eyes on the event. Oh well.

I shot the show in one take, obviously—there were no stops and starts. No "Wait a minute, Richard, can you deliver that joke over again?" I followed him in from the limo. Once that was done, all the camera operators were ready to shoot what was happening on stage. I sat in the control room (if you could call it that), and a stage manager was backstage with Richard. When the door of his dressing room opened, the stage manager said to me, "Roll cameras." Richard walked out on stage, he started his routine, and that was it. He went for about an hour and twenty minutes, and the audience was with him for the entire ride. They came into the theater with high expectations and they were not disappointed (an understatement, for sure). They were in the presence of a genius comedian who did his high-wire act. And when he walked off the stage, I had one of my handheld camera operators follow him back to the dressing room. The dressing room door shut, and that was the end of the show. Cut to black! I have no idea who suggested that we end the film with a closeup of Richard taking his bows, instead of following him back to his dressing room. We rolled credits on that final shot. I was certainly willing to honor that one and only request.

I never received my second or third payments despite the best efforts of the William Morris Agency and the Directors Guild, who also got involved in what turned out to be a dispute. After the six-week run, I got a call from my agent, who said, "This is one of those Hollywood stories that you won't believe. Bill Sargent has disappeared off the face of the planet. And he's got all the money with him and you probably will never see another penny." (And I never did.)

I'm not sure how we all could have done things differently to ensure that I would have gotten paid. Fortunately, this was one of the only times in my career that I was stiffed. Oh well, it was a great experience working with Richard Pryor, and I was honored to be involved in such an historic event. Recently, Mel Brooks, speaking to Terry Gross on NPR's *Fresh Air*, said, "Richard Pryor is the greatest standup comic that ever lived and that's saying a lot." High praise from one of the funniest men in show business.[2] And to put the cherry on top of the cake, *Richard Pryor: Live in Concert* was just inducted into the National Film Registry of the Library of Congress. It's probably the most non-PC film to ever have received that honor.

2   If you want to hear an interesting discussion about this film, listen to Judd Apatow on the *Arts in Armed Forces* podcast with Marine veteran Phil Klay from 2021. Judd says that this film is a "perfect piece of comedy." He references a conversation with me about some of the plans for the film, which were jettisoned. "Film Q&A: Richard Pryor: Live in Concert feat. Judd Apatow," July 29, 2021, in *Arts in Armed Forces*, produced by Arts in the Armed Forces, podcast. https://blubrry.com/aitaf/79243846/film-qa-richard-pryor-live-in-concert-feat-judd-apatow/.

CHAPTER 12

DICK CLARK:
AMERICA'S STAR MAKER

If RICHARD PRYOR WAS THE MOST NON-PC TALENT I HAVE EVER WORKED with, Dick Clark was one of the most PC—at least in front of the camera. A couple of years before I directed Richard's movie, I got a call from a producer named Al Schwartz, who told me he was producing a television special for Dick Clark. He asked me if I was interested in directing the special. After I picked myself up off the floor, I said, "When do we start?"

Dick Clark was, of course, one of my idols as a teenager. How many hours did I spend in front of the television watching the teenyboppers twist and shout to the newest, hottest musical talent of the day? So many singers got their start on *American Bandstand* and so many viewers learned how to do the twist, the pony, and the shag, and I was certainly among them.

Laughing at me for nearly passing out at the prospect of meeting Dick Clark, Al invited me to meet with Dick to talk about *Dick Clark's Good Ol' Days*, scheduled to air in 1977. This would be my very first network primetime television special, and it meant everything to me. What a credit! What a way to celebrate being thirty years old!

Dick made me feel welcome from the moment we met. I learned very quickly that he knows what he wants, and he knows how to get it. I worked extra hard on this special because I wanted Dick and Al to be really happy that they hired me and even happier with my work. So, the icing on the cake was that Dick really liked the way I directed the special. Al Schwartz couldn't have been more pleased. I knew that this was the beginning of a long working relationship—and friendship. Dick was forty-eight years old, and with luck on his side, he'd have many productive years ahead of him in television, and I wanted to be right there with him.

Dick was the host of his show. Frankie Avalon and Annette Funicello co-hosted. The special was jam-packed with musical artists from the fifties, sixties, and seventies singing their hits. There were wonderful archival film packages that included references to world events and a couple of surprise guest stars, too.

Guests included the incomparable Bo Diddley, Captain & Tennille, Bobby Rydell, Lesley Gore, Dion, Fabian, the Kingston Trio, Martha Reeves & the Vandellas, Brian Wilson and the Beach Boys, and the list goes on. We shot the show on the beach in Malibu, California, for a number of glorious days and nights, as an homage to the beach party rock and roll music that dominated the music scene of the fifties, sixties, and early seventies. The song "Surfin' USA" was dropped in a number of times in case someone missed the theme. As the host Dick kept reminding us that music makes memories, and through music we can find a way to hold on to those memories. How true! As I was directing the show, I relived my own teenage years.

Four years later, I received another call from Al Schwartz. He had been watching my work on *Tony Orlando and Dawn, Cos*, and the America's Junior Miss pageant. The American Music Awards, produced by Dick Clark, needed a facelift; their ratings were slipping, and the Grammys were kicking their proverbial ass. Al and Dick knew they had to do something to bring the ratings up. Al suggested to Dick that they hire a new director, and my name came up. With the love of music in my DNA, and my admiration for Dick Clark, I was thrilled. Al set up a meeting for us. I crossed my fingers and toes that I'd pass muster with the maestro. I was thirty-five years old but I felt like a kid stepping into Dick Clark's office again.

Dick and I developed a good working and personal relationship from the first day we got together. We really bonded and understood one another. There was a real love there, all the way up until the day he passed away. He was a mentor, and he took me under his wing.

When I first got involved with the American Music Awards, Dick wanted it to look big and spectacular. That was one of my first challenges as his director: "big, big, big," because he was competing with the Grammys.

The show moved around a lot since its inception back in 1973, because Dick was never really satisfied with the way it looked. One year he tried doing the Awards at the Aquarius Theater in Hollywood, and another year at the Santa Monica Civic Auditorium. Neither worked out, so Dick moved the show to a sound stage on the ABC lot. The designer for the show put three walls of mirrors in the studio. The audience looked ten times bigger than it actually was. I don't think there were more than 250, maybe 300 people—if that—in the audience.

When I was hired to direct the show, Dick challenged me, "Okay, Mister Hotshot Director. Make me proud. I'm bringing you in here so that you can help make me a hero with ABC and bring our ratings up. Al Schwartz told me you could do it."

I did my research and ran my idea by Al Schwartz, who was not only one of my favorite producers to work with but had also become a good friend. He said to me, "Go for it." Then I went to Dick and said, "I think we should move the show from the ABC lot to the Shrine Auditorium."

"Are you fucking out of your mind? The Shrine Auditorium? Look, I'm in a studio at ABC. I got mirrors all over the place and two hundred people in the audience. It looks big enough. Focus on something else. You must have a better idea than that."

"Well, Dick, between you and me, it looks kind of cheap and cheesy."

"Cheap and cheesy?" I can't believe I had the balls to say that to Dick Clark, but he was paying me to give him my honest opinion.

"Yeah. The Oscars are at the Music Center—the Dorothy Chandler Pavilion. The Grammy Awards are at the Shrine. The AMAs are as big as those shows, and you're on Stage 57 on the ABC lot. Let's go big!" I argued.

By nature, Dick was not an optimist. He tended to focus on the worst-case scenario, while I'm an optimist even in the worst of times.

And of course, I was only thirty-five and had the brashness of youth on my side. Dick had been around for a long time. He grumbled, "We could never afford that, anyway. It's not going to happen. Forget about it."

"You asked me to come in and help you grow the show—make it bigger and make it better. I want to go to the Shrine Auditorium, and Al Schwartz agrees with me!"

"It's not going to happen."

"I don't want to think of anything else. I'm going to be like a little spoiled brat right now. I wanna go to the Shrine Auditorium!"

I got such a look, that scary Dick Clark "stop fucking with me" look, and then he said, "Well, find out how much it costs."

Al and I did some more research. We came back to him with facts and figures, and he finally said to us, "Okay. You guys win. I'll try it. But if it doesn't work, you're both fired!" In Al Schwartz's case that was an empty threat; in mine, not so much. I had a lot riding on this idea. I told Dick, "It's going to be great." This is something I say all the time to my crew and cast before every live show. I always try to get everybody up and excited so that they will do their best work and have a good time doing it. It also boosts everyone's confidence, including mine, and makes anyone I'm trying to sell an idea to feel that I know what I'm doing and speak from experience. There is nothing worse than to have a leader unsure of him or herself.

We visited the Shrine Auditorium. Dick looked around and said, "Oh God, I'm never going to fill this place up! It's got over six thousand seats. We're going to look foolish with an empty audience here and this giant stage." For a producer/impresario, an empty seat is the kiss of death, at least if the camera picks it up and broadcasts it to the home viewing audience. That's why there's a job in entertainment called a "seat filler." No empty seats!

"It's going to be fine, Dick. Worry about something else. I got this, and Al Schwartz and Larry Klein will help me." (Larry Klein was Dick Clark Productions' other major producer.) Larry was responsible for booking the talent on all the AMA shows with some wonderful talent bookers on his staff over the years, first Susan Abramson, and then later on Melissa Watkins Trueblood.

Dick was so worried about moving to the Shrine Auditorium that five days before the show was on the air, he had the stage crew put up a black curtain to cover the entire balcony so you couldn't see any seats up there. It looked as if part of the auditorium was in mourning.

"What'd you do that for?" I asked.

"We're never going to fill this place! There are over six thousand seats in this theater!"

USC is across the street from the Shrine Auditorium, and I had some relationships left over from my early days as a freshman there in the film department, so I called the school and said, "Hey, I'm going to send over some flyers for you to put around campus. Let people know the American Music Awards are here at the Shrine this year. It's free, and students can come and be part of the audience." What student wouldn't want to sit in on one of the biggest music awards shows on television? They'd get a chance to see all this music talent up close and personal, for free. And they'd get to see Dick Clark, who was a legend in the music and television industry.

We also invited the usual audience: agents, managers, publicists, and record company executives. The day of the show, we drove down to the Shrine Auditorium at eight o'clock in the morning, and there was already a line around the block with mostly USC students waiting to get in to see the show. Dick came into the theater and said, "What the fuck?"

"What's the matter, Dick?"

"What are we going to do? Where are we going to put all these people?"

"Take the black curtain down, and we'll fill the balcony as well."

Which we did. We filled the whole place.

The show was spectacular. It was giant, and we had great ratings. It wasn't just because we took the show to the Shrine. There were a lot of fabulous acts who were up for awards in 1981: Kenny Rogers; Diana Ross; Earth, Wind & Fire; Barbara Mandrell; Chuck Berry; Billy Joel; the Eagles; and more. But it didn't hurt to have a big audience for the acts to bounce off of. The energy in the auditorium was palpable, and everyone felt so excited to see such a large crowd all the way up to the nosebleed section in the last row of the balcony.

Mac Davis, a country music singer, songwriter, and actor who crossed over from his roots to mainstream pop, hosted the first year I directed the AMAs. He was a big name for Dick to get as a host. Incredibly personable, he was the perfect choice.

Al, Larry, and I pushed Dick to be innovative, not the same old same old.

We advised Dick, "Don't get the presenters that you usually get. Go for people who are sitting in the audience, who are nominated. Before their award, let them present something! You've got the artists there already! Put some of them on camera. They'll love it!"

"Well, they're going to be too nervous waiting to see if they've won. They're not going to want to do that," said Dick.

"You don't know how they're going to feel. Ask them if they want to present! We bet you that seventy-five percent of them will say yes!" And they did. The ratings went way up from the previous year. Even I was startled by the dramatic uptick.

The day after the show, everybody kind of unwinds and nobody goes to the office. But the following day—two days after the show— I'm sitting in my office at Dick Clark Productions, and one of Dick's assistants comes in. His assistant was his wife, Kari. (I love her, she's the best, and we are still friends today.) "Jeff, Dick wants to see you."

Nobody ever called him Mr. Clark in the office. He was Dick to everybody. "Aw, shit," I thought. "He's going to tell me he doesn't want to be at the Shrine anymore, or even worse, 'You're fired.'"

I went into Dick's office, and he said, "Close the door." I closed the door behind me, and he said, "Sit down." I sat down, and he looked at me and said, "Fuck you!"

I started laughing, and he started laughing, and he walked around his desk and said, "Stand up." He gave me a giant hug and said, "Goddammit, you were right. You little shit. You were right. Mister Hotshot. Mister New Director." Thanks to the support of Al Schwartz, I dodged a bullet and got an "atta boy" instead.

After that first year when we relocated to the Shrine Auditorium, everything about the AMAs was bigger and better. The sets were always bigger and better. The lighting was bigger and better. The stars who came to perform were so happy not to be going to that little stage on the ABC lot. It didn't seem like a second-class event anymore! Now it was a Big Event. It is only in the last few years that the AMAs moved to the Microsoft Theater/LA Live in downtown Los Angeles. (I recently watched the show, and there was Larry Klein's name still in the credits. Talk about longevity.)

You Can't Make This Up!

Dick was really impressed that I had so many industry connections, and he couldn't believe that I somehow would be able to get him in front of a camera to do something for Continental Airlines. (Continental Airlines has since been purchased and is now United Airlines.) Looking back, it all seems so easy.

Here's how it happened. I was directing a number of live event specials and network specials when I got a call from the television representative for Continental Airlines, Charles "Chuck" Lisberger. We met, and he asked me if I would be willing to make Continental part of my television family and use them on my shows to travel talent, staff, and crew. If I could get Continental Airlines to be the airline of a television show, they'd get a ten-second plug in first position before the end credits rolled on a show. Free advertising in exchange for flying talent around. (You're familiar with that announcement, "Travel provided by such and such airline" with a frame of the logo or one of their jets in the sky.)

All the out-of-town guests at the American Music Awards were flown to Hollywood on Continental. After one of the AMAs, Chuck Lisberger said to me, "Jeff, why don't you come up with an idea for a thirty-second commercial for Continental?"

I pitched them the idea that Dick Clark be the spokesman for Continental Airlines in the commercial. They bought the idea, but I then had to convince Dick to be on camera. He agreed. I worked out the content with Continental. They also asked me to be in the commercial. I don't even remember what I did; probably just a walk-by or something like that. When the day of the shoot arrived, Dick wanted to apply my makeup for me, rather than having makeup people do it. That was just how much he cared about me. That was one of the many up-close-and-personal moments in our working relationship that lasted for over thirty years.

Dick Clark Loved the Word American!

If I haven't said it enough, Dick and I were really close. He was always teaching me stuff and I appreciated him sharing his knowledge with me. He was so smart, and he knew so much. There was one lesson he taught me that I've taken with me throughout my career, and I'll never forget it.

"Jeff, one of the most important things you can ever do on any television show is come up with a good title. I found out years and years ago that for me, the magic word is 'American.' I've got *American Bandstand* and the American Music Awards and the American this and American that. It works for me. Always remember that when people go through *TV Guide* looking for something to watch, it's the title that grabs them." (Remember *TV Guide*? It was a weekly bulletin that listed all the television shows and gave an abbreviated description including a log line if it was an episode of a running show, and a list of stars if it was an awards show or a special or a series. Today all you need to do is go to the menu on your screen to see what's playing and when.)

After we had been working together for a few years, I gave Dick an idea for a show, and he said, "I really like the idea. What's the title?"

"I don't have a title yet."

"Remember I told you the title has to grab."

I came back to him with a title, and he said, "No."

"How about this," he suggested. "'America Votes the Number One Songs.'"

"Sounds good to me."

So, Dick sold the show, and that was the title. It was a year-end show and one of the first phone-ins where the American public voted for the winners. America picked the number one song in each of many categories like country, pop, rock, and so on. It was a two-hour show, with many different artists performing the nominated songs.

It was a great show, and it lasted for a couple of years.

Dick had production deals at ABC, CBS, and NBC, and he constantly came up with new ideas. His sense of the viewership was uncanny, and he turned out one hit after another to satisfy the networks looking for programs to fill their slate. *Superstars and Their Moms* was a 1987 special that Dick came up with. (Dick broke his rule about having "American" in the title.)

For this show, we picked a group of stars and simply asked them, "What do you like to do with your mom?" Robin Williams wanted to play tennis, and so we took him and his mom to a tennis court. They talked about Robin's childhood and how much he loved tennis and how she taught him to play. We shot them playing a match and when it was over, they hugged and kissed and walked off into the sunset.

Cher and her mom visited her high school principal together and shared some laughs remembering a few rules that the independent daughter might have broken. And then Cher and her sister surprised their mom by celebrating her birthday with a cake.

Carol Burnett's mom was no longer with us, but Carol really wanted to be on this show. She wanted to do something with one of her daughters, who was an aspiring actress and singer. Carol said, "I'll be the mom, and I'll have my daughter with me. We'll do something great."

Cybill Shepherd, John Ritter, Tom Selleck, and Debbie Allen were some of the other superstars whose moms we got to meet on this special.

The Apple Doesn't Fall Far from the Tree

Having Dick Clark as a father makes it understandable that his son, Richard A. Clark (known as Rac), would go into the television music business. I watched him grow up. When he was just in his twenties, one of Rac Clark's first forays into television was as producer of a new type of variety series, *Puttin' on the Hits*, debuting in 1984. It was a lip-sync contest for unknown singers, and the prize winner received $25,000 and a videotape of their performance. Dick was the executive producer, and I was in the director's chair and the co-producer along with Rac. The show ran for four seasons. Rac went on to have a tremendous career. Since 1999 he produced the Academy of Country Music Awards, Grammy specials, Oscar red carpets, Miss Universe, and Miss USA pageants, to name just some of his credits. It's gratifying to see Rac flourish.

I'll Be Seeing You in All the Old Familiar Places

One of the many pleasures of directing the American Music Awards— other than working with Dick Clark—was having the opportunity to spend time with some of the greatest musical talent in the industry— sometime year in and year out. For me—a kid that had little musical talent but loved music—it was a thrill to meet singers who I might have listened to as a teenager driving around LA in my VW with the radio on full blast and the windows rolled up so I had my own "sophisticated" listening room on wheels. Here are just some of the celebrities that I have been so fortunate to have worked with over the years on the AMAs.

Lionel Richie

Lionel Richie is a real gem. I directed a couple of Lionel Richie concerts for HBO and then he hosted the American Music Awards for a number of years during the time that I was the director. He's such a good guy, a real mensch. After the hugs, he would always say, "I'm here for you, I'm ready, I'll do anything you need me to do." I loved working with him. He was so very easy to work with. He wanted to be involved with everything he was doing and was very open to doing whatever you needed him to do. I believe that the magic he brought to the American Music Awards turned that show around. His production numbers were big and highly produced, with lots of dancers, great sets and lighting, and his hosting talents were spot on. The show was never the same once Lionel took over. He not only brought his incredible talent, but his warmth and engaging personality. He made the audience in the theater and at home feel like they were part of the event. In 2004, Lionel did the same brilliant hosting job for me when I executive produced and directed Motown's forty-fifth anniversary celebration, *Motown 45*, on ABC.

When he's not performing somewhere these days, I get to watch him look for new talent as a judge on *American Idol*. Wherever he is, whatever he does, he's great.

Stevie Wonder

I had the pleasure of working with Stevie Wonder numerous times, many of them at the American Music Awards. There was also Sammy's 60th, Motown's 45th, and Ebony's 50th, amongst the others. I would always greet him with a handshake and introduce myself and then I would tell him what he was going to do. I explained the whole segment to him so he would know what came before and after his performance. And I always thanked him for being there. Every year when he performed at the American Music Awards, and I would re-introduce myself to him, he always said, "Gee, it's great to see you again, Jeff. Now I know I'm in good hands." That was his response, which was so Stevie. I think he recognized my voice. It was always a delight to work with him.

Celine Dion

Celine Dion is one of the biggest recording artists in the industry today. She can draw thousands of people on her own and can fill an entire venue in Las Vegas night after night. Her records have sold millions of copies, and she has performed duets with some of the greatest singing stars in the business. But it wasn't always like that. One of Celine Dion's very first performances on American network primetime television was on the American Music Awards. She was in her early twenties, just a baby performer, and she was scared shitless. She was so very nervous, because she wanted to get it right. And she had the added burden of English as her second language. She is French Canadian, and at the start of her career she was learning to speak English. I tried to comfort her the first time she walked out onto the stage to rehearse, so I said, "Welcome to the American Music Awards. We're here at the Shrine Auditorium, a very famous and one of the oldest theaters in Los Angeles. Look out there and imagine that all the seats are filled with people, they're all your friends and you're going to have a good time performing for them. Make believe that this is your living room." Now that I say it, it doesn't sound very comforting. I myself would have been even more nervous. She answered, "But it's live on the air, and most of those people in the audience don't even know who I am. What if I make a mistake?" I tried to reassure her so I said, "You won't, but if you do, just keep going. You're the only person who will know you've made a mistake." She said to me, "*Merci beaucoup, je t'aime.*" Thank you so much. I love you. How sweet was that? She did not make a mistake; she was perfect, of course.

I worked with Celine many times after her first appearance on the AMAs. Each time, we would hug and kiss and she would whisper in my ear, "Make me look beautiful and sound great again, like you've done all the other times. *Merci beaucoup, je t'aime.*"

This is only one of the reasons that I love what I do so much. I am so sad to know that Celine has health issues today that prevent her from doing what she loves to do so much, and I only hope and pray that she will recover and will soon be back on stage performing once again for her adoring fans who only wish her the best.

Little Richard

Little Richard, now there's a treat. I worked with Little Richard on the American Music Awards many times. Our conversations were always about his performance: who was on before him and who was on after. I always knew what song he was going to perform, and I had listened to the track or watched a music video to familiarize myself with it. He always seemed to be very comfortable and ready to go to work.

Do you remember Steve Urkel from *Family Matters*? His real name was Jaleel White, and in 1992, he got to do his own special on ABC, *The Jaleel White Special*. Little Richard was Jaleel's guest on that special, so I got to direct him in comedy sketches as well as musical performances.

He was a bit nervous because he wasn't an actor. He was a singer—a performer, quite different from doing comedy. If my memory serves me correctly, in one of the sketches, Richard was a fortune teller who had his own shop where he read tarot cards and had a magic ball where he could see into the future. Jaleel just happened to stop by the shop to have his fortune told. Richard was really surprisingly funny. He did exactly what the script said and everything that I asked him to do, and then he ad-libbed a bit. It was okay, although I will say that we had to do several takes to get what we needed. But that's all right. He was always a pleasure to work with and always made it fun.

Whitney Houston

Whitney Houston was discovered by Clive Davis, then president of Columbia Records. Known as "the man with the golden ear" because of his ability to spot talent, he booked her first television appearance on Merv Griffin's talk show. She was a smash. Her second television appearance, which was her first network live primetime show, was the American Music Awards. That's where I met her. Her aunt, Dionne Warwick, came with her for moral support. She was so nervous. I mean, she was really nervous. She was actually shaking. But on the live show, her performance was flawless. It was hard to tell that it was her first live television appearance. Of the many times that I directed the American Music Awards, she probably appeared twelve times. So, I always made it a point to chat with her every time she was on.

Every time I worked with her, she was a guest on a music show. My contact with her was like any other guest on a music show. Doing a Whitney Houston special or a music video would have been a completely different experience—I would have had a lot more interaction with her. She always came on the AMAs just to perform a song. We always greeted each other with a giant hug and "I'm so happy to see you; how have you been?" In the beginning, she would always come for camera blocking, then after a while, only for the dress rehearsal and live show. She would send somebody in her place for camera blocking so that all the production folks who needed to see the set, lighting and wardrobe, and so on would be able to make her look and sound as good as we could. Her singing was always flawless.

I remember when she sang "Greatest Love of All." I got so emotional that I was weeping in the control room as I was directing. I was trying to say, "Ready camera three! Take...," and I almost couldn't get it out. That was when she was at the height of her career. That and singing "The Star-Spangled Banner" with the Statue of Liberty behind her at the Fourth of July celebration really got to me.

I had the opportunity to work with Whitney so many times because of the American Music Awards. I did do other shows with her, too. Once I had her as a guest on the very special *Opening Ceremonies of The Special Olympics* for ABC. That was some logistical nightmare because we did it from Notre Dame Stadium in South Bend, Indiana, and covering an entire football field, as well as featuring an amazing singer like Whitney, was a challenge.

She was one of the greatest singing talents of all time—as Clive Davis said, she was right up there with Lena Horne. And let's not forget her amazing performance with Kevin Costner in *The Bodyguard*. The camera couldn't get enough of her. And neither could her fans. It was heartbreaking when she passed away at such a young age. I will always miss you, Whitney.

I directed the AMAs for sixteen years on ABC, and all that time Dick and I maintained a strong relationship. For the first few years I worked on the AMAs, I always asked Dick what his vision was for the show that year. He finally said to me, "You don't have to come to me beforehand and ask me what my vision is any longer." I told him, "You're the executive producer; I'm the director; it's your show; I want to make you happy. I want to give you everything you want. So, tell me what your vision is." He used to get a look on his face, like "Get away, don't bother me," but he said, "I have nothing to say to you, Jeff. I don't need to tell you anything. Just do what you do because you do it so well!" I couldn't ask for much more than that.

Even after I left the AMAs in 2005, we kept in touch until the day he passed away at the age of eighty-two in 2012. Dick was a great innovator and a great showman, and he had his finger on the pulse of the audience. He understood what appealed to them, and his legacy lives on. I could not have been luckier than to have one of the greats as a mentor and friend for thirty years. He taught me so much. Even when he saw the glass half empty rather than half full, I'd find a way to fill it up for him and make both of us happy!

I miss you, dear friend.

My really good friend, Dick Clark. I loved working with him.

In the sound booth with Dick Clark and Gary Coleman.

Lionel Richie, one of the good guys.

Just finished explaining camera angles to Rod Stewart for
his American Music Awards performance.

Talking over the playlist with Stevie Wonder.

Discussing staging with Stevie Wonder.

Adjusting sound quality for Stevie Wonder.

The first time working with Celine Dion on the American Music Awards.

Serious conversation about a funny sketch with Little Richard.

One of the many times working with the great Whitney Houston.

CHAPTER 13

WHAT'S SO SPECIAL ABOUT SPECIALS?

SPECIALS HAVE BEEN AROUND SINCE THE 1950S, WHEN AUDIENCES WERE HUNgry for new shows. Of course, I wanted to watch whatever was airing, even if the programs were aimed at my parents' generation and not at a kid like me.

In a way, watching a special was like reading a Hallmark message.

Holiday greetings, birthday celebrations, memorials, and anniversaries can all be the impetus for putting together a special. What would Christmas be without a Christmas special? Or Thanksgiving? Or the Fourth of July?

They may not be wrapped in glittery paper, but every good special provides a powerful message to its audience or a walk down memory lane. There is usually a dynamic host who is a well-known celebrity. Specials can be made up of comedic sketches, or heart-felt performances by gifted singers. Or both. Sometimes specials are built around a celebrity to showcase their talent and build their following for a weekly series they might star in. Specials are particularly appealing to sponsors, and for that reason the per-minute cost of a special may be more expensive than for any other form of programming, other than sports events. From time to time, a special may have a single sponsor to increase their visibility; they don't have to compete with other sponsors for the audience's attention.

Maybe it's just for an hour or two, but specials are a way to encapsulate a collective memory. Specials can be shot in a studio, in a theater, in an outdoor arena, or at one or more eye candy locations.

They can be months in the planning stage or put together quickly in response to some newsworthy event or charity that is responding to a crisis.

Specials have always been the cornerstone of my career in television.

Here's How a Special Comes to Life

Specials are different from weekly variety shows, talent competitions, dramatic or comedy series, and regular music game competitions because they are just that—special. They are one-offs, which means that they only happen once. *Garth Brooks in Concert, Amy Grant's Christmas Special, Dolly Parton's Day at Dollywood, Julie & Carol: Together Again,* and *Jerry Seinfeld's Comedy Special* are one-time events. Typically, specials are produced as family entertainment—rarely are they salacious or titillating, at least not until recently. And, of course, they are usually shot before a live audience, which requires a special skill. Anything can go wrong, and you have to think on your feet. There are usually no "re-takes." A lot of directors simply don't have the stomach for this high-wire act. I thrived on it!

By the late seventies, I was on the list of go-to directors/producers who were in demand. I was asked to direct *Dick Clark's Good Ol' Days, Julie Andrews: One Step into Spring,* the Ringo Starr special, *Richard Pryor: Live in Concert,* and many more.

When I'm hired to direct a special, sometimes the producer will say, "Here is the star or here is the idea. What do you want to do, or how do you want to approach it, or where do you want to do it?" Then it's up to me as the director to come up with an overall concept and make it happen. Sometimes a producer will say, "Let's work together on this idea," and sometimes a producer will say, "Here's what I want you to do." Then that's what you start with, adding your own input as the chosen director.

For example, George Schlatter, the great television producer, called me in 1990 and said, "I'm producing a Frank Sinatra special. Part of it will include a concert being shot in the round at Meadowlands Arena in New Jersey. I would like you to direct it." What an opportunity! Now it was up to me to make Sinatra look and sound great. At seventy-five he still had the pipes to sing a song and hold the audience in the palm of his hand. And to do it in the Meadowlands Arena in his home state of New Jersey was brilliant. The boy from Hoboken live and in person. A once in a lifetime experience. The special was called *Sinatra 75: The Best Is Yet to Come.*

Sometimes the network would come up with an idea and call my agent at William Morris asking about my availability.

In the course of my career thus far, I've directed/produced more than 150 specials, many of which you can see in their entirety or excerpted on YouTube. I would like to write about all of them, but here are a few stories that will give you a glimpse into the world of specials that I love. Most of the stories are in chronological order so you'll see how I built my directing and producing career.

I'm not sure how many total hours of television specials I've directed, or directed and produced, but I'd guess that I'm credited with about 400 hours of television. Specials run between one to two hours including commercials. And by the way, a special, before streaming, used to have to appeal to commercial sponsors. Can you imagine the feeding frenzy over *Julie & Carol: Together Again*, which brought together two of the most popular and beloved women in the entertainment industry, or a Michael Jackson special, or *Happy 100th Birthday, Hollywood*, or Olivia Newton-John, or a Justin Timberlake concert, or *Garth Brooks Live in Concert*, or—well, I better stop here because you get the idea.

(I've included my IMDb credits in an appendix that includes all the television productions I've been associated with over my fifty-year career.)

Stepping into Specials: Julie Andrews (1978)

Thanks to Bob Banner, I got my first shot at directing a star showcase special, and what a special it was. *One Step into Spring* with Julie Andrews was a gift from the gods. Although British, Julie Andrews was America's darling, a bona fide stage and screen star appearing in *My Fair Lady, The Sound of Music,* and winning the Oscar for best actress in the 1964 film *Mary Poppins.*

It was the first time I had worked in London, and it was a difficult show because I had to adapt to the English style of television, and they had to try to adapt to mine. Bob Banner had introduced me to a wonderful and talented writer/producer, Stephen Pouliot, who became one of my stable go-to writers throughout my career. We have been friends and collaborators for over forty-five years. *One Step into Spring* fit Julie Andrews like Cinderella's glass slipper. It perfectly reflected her personality, her charm, her sense of humor, and her many talents as a dancer, singer, actress, and comedian.

In *One Step into Spring* rehearsals Julie would say to me, "What do you think about...? Do you think I should do it this way, or that way?" Or "Tell me what you want—how you want me to do it." This major, major star treated me like I was royalty, and I'll never forget that. She was the kindest, sweetest, most collaborative, giving person.

I love her.

The show included an appearance by the Muppets, and a star turn by Leslie Uggams. She and Julie did a few songs from *A Chorus Line,* which was the current hit on Broadway in 1978. Leo Sayer, the English singer/songwriter, also appeared in the special performing one of his many hit songs, "You Make Me Feel Like Dancing."

The opening production number featured Julie dressed in a white tuxedo and top hat, dancing with one, two, three, four, five, and then six men in black tuxedos, all ending up in a kick line generating huge applause from the audience. I used a few tricks to make the male dancers seemingly pop up out of nowhere in front of a white backdrop. It was a fabulous number. At the end, one of the Muppets sticks his head out of the floor and begs Julie not to do an encore, and out of "spite," she does it again. When the show wrapped, I hoped that I would have the chance to work with Julie again, and I did some ten years later on another special with her favorite sidekick, Carol Burnett.

Seeing Double: Ringo Starr (1978)

You might say I have a real affinity for the Brits. The same year I directed Julie Andrews in London in *One Step into Spring*, I was asked by NBC to direct Ringo Starr in his first solo special on American television. It was 1978 and *Ringo* was billed as a made-for-television comedy movie. Ringo was the first Beatle to have his own special on American television. You can only imagine how ecstatic I was to be asked to direct Ringo Starr. Remember how I had impersonated him in high school sitting behind a drum set and mouthing the words to a Beatles song? By the late seventies, The Beatles were still huge, and NBC was counting on their reputation to attract a viewership, even if it was just one of the Beatles in the TV special. (The band disbanded in 1970 and each of the Beatles went solo, producing albums and forming other groups, such as Paul McCartney and Wings.)

We shot this special like a movie at different locations all around Los Angeles. It was grueling because there was so much street inter-ference but a lot of fun at the same time. The script was written by Neal Israel and Pat Proft, two very talented and funny comedy writ-ers. Neal was a friend, and I had worked with him before. We are still good friends today; he is one of my favorite comedy writers/directors, and we are always looking for more projects to work on together.

The premise of the show was that Ringo was tired of being a Beatle and always being sought after, with the paparazzi chasing him and the like. He heard about a kid who lived in Hollywood who was star struck. Ringo was also told that this kid was his spitting image; he had a job selling maps to the homes of Hollywood stars on Sunset Boulevard, and his name was Ognir Rrats. In the special, Ognir Rrats was over the moon when he found out that Ringo Starr wanted to trade places with him. (Of course, Ringo plays both parts.) Ringo was less than thrilled about carrying a sign, "Star Maps for Sale," and being harassed by kids driving by in souped-up cars. Ringo was almost unrecognizable in a baseball cap, heavy beard, and mustache. A kid on a skateboard calls him a "nerd," and a group of nuns stopped him to ask where "Norm Crosby's house is," not recognizing that they were actually speaking to one of The Beatles; otherwise, they might have blessed him, crossed themselves, and said three Hail Marys.

The forty-four-minute movie—based on Mark Twain's *The Prince and the Pauper*—was narrated by George Harrison and executive produced by Ken Ehrlich (producer of the Grammy Awards) and included the musical numbers "I'm the Greatest," "Act Naturally," "Yellow Submarine," "You're Sixteen," "With a Little Help from My Friends," "Heart on My Sleeve," and "Hard Times." The song "Act Naturally" was reprised throughout the movie and we even put Ognir Rrats's name up on the Pantages Theater marquee and gave him a star on Hollywood Boulevard. If you catch some of the outtakes on YouTube you can see how much fun we had.

Ognir Rrats's father was played by the great comedian Art Carney (of *Honeymooners* fame). His character was a miserable drunk. Other cast members included Carrie Fisher (Ognir's girlfriend), Angie Dickinson, Mike Douglas, Vincent Price, John Ritter (as Ringo's manager), and George Harrison. What a cast!

All the scenes were on location, other than a scene shot in a studio with Mike Douglas, the talk show host. Mike Douglas was supposed to be interviewing Ringo, or so he thought. Douglas kept thinking to himself, "What the hell is going on with this guy?" because he couldn't answer any of the questions put to him. Ringo was such a good actor that Mike couldn't figure it out, until we told him what was going on.

Eventually Ringo (as himself) put a band together and ended up doing a concert at the end of the show. That's when I told him that I put a Beatles band together for a high school talent show. I played the part of Ringo on the drums. He loved hearing that and wanted to know if I had it on tape. But it was before the days of home video cameras. However, at one point when we were shooting a scene for the special in a recording studio, there was a drum set. Ringo said to me, "Okay, hotshot, you played me in your high school talent show, let me see you play the drums and look like me." I sat behind the drums, and he gave me two sticks. I never would have imagined back in high school that one day I'd be in a recording studio playing the drums for Ringo Starr. I was so bad, it was embarrassing, but that's show biz.

When I run into Ringo occasionally at a restaurant in LA, I usually ask him, "How's it going, Ognir?" and then we have a good laugh and hug.

The Man Who Invented Casual: Perry Como (1978–1984)

With his smooth voice and engaging personality familiar to television audiences from his years as the star of *The Perry Como Show*, Perry was the perfect choice to celebrate Christmas with his fans. Over the years I directed *Early American Christmas* (1978), *French-Canadian Christmas* (1981), *Christmas in New York* (1983), and *Christmas in England* (1984) with the crooner. All these specials were shot on location, which has its own set of challenges—scouting the location, scoping out any issues that might affect a shot, bringing in all the equipment, matching the location to the song, and praying that the weather will cooperate on the day that you plan to shoot. It's a very different experience than shooting a special in a single location such as a theater.

Traveling around the world with Perry was a thrill, but holy shit, what a lot of work. Perry was always willing to do anything unless it was really *cold*. Imagine traveling to a far-away exterior location in England somewhere, selected for its incredible landscape with castles and rivers and beautiful mountains, spending hours setting up and getting all ready for Perry's arrival and then....

Perry shows up ready to work, having been made up and dressed at the hotel. He is greeted by a stage manager, who brings him to meet me at the location spot where he will be singing his song. Perry and I hug each other. He holds my hand, looks around, and says to me, "This location is absolutely gorgeous. I love it."

Then he hugs me again, and I know I'm in trouble. He looks me in the eyes and says, "It's too damn cold out here to sing. Let's find somewhere else that's not so cold." We had spent all that time scouting the location, setting up the cameras and the lights, and the sound equipment, and everything. But he's the star and he was cold and he didn't want to sing in the cold. So what could I do? We went inside!

Here's another story that I can't resist sharing about Perry Como.

As part of our preparation for the specials, we always pre-re-corded the music in Los Angeles. Then we would send the tracks to Perry in Florida; he'd listen to them and rehearse the songs. Hopefully he would approve all the arrangements. (By the way, pre-recording the music is very expensive, but it's important to get everything right so that when Perry sings a song, he's comfortable with the arrange-ment and the sound quality is perfect.)

During the French-Canadian Christmas special, we were in the countryside outside Quebec with snow on the ground, a hundred miles from nowhere. I had picked the location because it had the most beautiful landscape in all of Canada. (It was like a travelogue for the countryside. Tour companies must have loved us.)

We'd set up all the cameras, lighting, and sound equipment, and made sure that everything was perfect before Perry arrived. He showed up in his car. Then the stage manager brought him over to me, we hugged, and then he looked around and exclaimed, "God, this is beautiful. This is breathtaking! This is going to be fantastic!"

I asked, "Are you ready to get on camera and rehearse?"

"Of course, I am; what do you want me to do?"

"Here's my plan. This is the area you can move around and per-form in, and this is where the cameras will be. We'll rehearse the song once to make certain that everything is good for you. And then we will shoot it." I usually didn't ask Perry to move. I let the cameras do all the moving so that he only had to concentrate on singing the song.

All of a sudden, Perry looked at me and said, "Come here." Oh shit, I knew what was coming. Putting his arm around my shoulder, he whispered, "We don't need to rehearse. I know the song. I know you'll make it beautiful; let's shoot."

"Okay, Perry, so why don't you go and get your hair and makeup touched up?" His people would be there, and they'd take him into the location trailer to get ready.

I was standing around in the freezing cold, stamping my feet to stay warm and clapping my hands together. The entire crew was standing by, at the ready. Suddenly I got a call over my headset from one of the stage managers. "Perry wants to see you." And I thought to myself this time, "Oh *holy* shit, we're fucked." It's been my experience that when a star wants to see the director privately, there's going to be a problem.

I went into the motorhome, and he sat me down. He would always give me a hug—an Italian hug from him, always. Then he looked at me and said, "I just don't want to do this song here."

"Pardon me?"

"I don't want to do it."

"Wait a second. Let me try to understand this. We recorded the music track. We sent it to you and you approved it. Now we're on location here in Canada. You just spent an hour in the limo to get out here; you're already in wardrobe, hair, and makeup; you said you loved everything about this location, that it was gorgeous. How can you not want to do it? What am I missing here?"

"I just don't want to do it."

"Okay, Perry, just hear me out." (I probably never should have said that.) "This will probably cost me...maybe sixty thousand to wrap and get everything out of here if you don't do the song. You've got to do it."

"I'll tell you what. Did you bring any other music tracks with you?"

"I've got the tracks in the audio truck for all your songs."

He said, "Okay then, here's the song I'll do up here."

And I thought, "Oy, God. I had such big plans for this new song he wanted to do." I wanted to do it in a different location, but I said, "Okay. Fine. We'll do the song." He was so sweet! I mean, how could I not accommodate him? I'll never know why he wanted to do one song instead of the other, and I thought it best not to ask. Sometimes, you just have to accommodate the talent and forget about the money going down the drain. You'll make it up somewhere else and move on.

Perry and I became like family over the years. I used to do two shows a year with him. He had a two-special deal on ABC—a springtime special and a Christmas special. The springtime specials disappeared after we did two of them because the viewers wanted to see more stars and different types of programming, and they wanted everything to move faster. ABC chose different artists to do a springtime show, but they wanted Perry for the Christmas show always. I mean, Perry Como was Christmas!

When I directed *Perry Como's Christmas in England* in 1984, Ann-Margret was his guest on the show. She was such a trooper and had so much fun with Perry. Everything they did together lit up the screen.

I brought my wife, Leslie, with me to London and our two-year-old son, Adam. In one segment, Perry was to sing "Silver Bells" on top of a double-decker bus riding through London. We were ready to shoot, and Leslie and Adam were on the bus in one of the seats as extras. They'd be in a couple of shots, but of course the focus was on Perry. A reverse shot captured what Perry was looking at on the street below.

We were just about to shoot, and I was up on the double-decker bus with him. I asked, "Everything good? You happy?" I got a thumbs up.

As I turned around to walk away, Perry said, "I'm going to surprise you with something. I want you to just shoot it, don't stop. I promise you you'll love it, and I want it to be in the show."

I said, "You know how I feel about surprises, don't you? I hate surprises!"

He said, "You're going to love this one."

I went into the little remote truck to shoot the number, and I got everybody ready, and I said, "Okay, roll tape." Then I said to the stage manager, "Tell Perry we're ready to go!" I got speed from tape, and I said, "Okay, here we go. In 10...9...8..."

During the countdown, Perry reached over and grabbed my son Adam off Leslie's lap, and he put him on his lap. He sang the song with Adam in the shot as we drove around London. And it went on the air just like that. My son had his official television debut!

Perry loved Adam. Jeez, he loved Adam. We stayed at the Grosvenor House Hotel in London—very posh—and it would be at the end of a long day of shooting, and he'd call me in my room. "Is Adam still up?"

"Yeah."

"Bring him over. I need a little Adam time." Then he would say to Leslie and me, "Listen, when we finish shooting every day, if you two want to go out to dinner, I'm your babysitter!" Who would make that kind of an offer? Perry Como, of course.

Perry Como was a meticulous performer who made everything look easy. Known as Mr. C, the title of his 1968 hit album said it all, *Look to Your Heart*, which was the way that Perry Como saw the world, and I was lucky enough to call him my friend.

Julie Andrews, one of the sweetest women in show business.

Ringo f---ing Starr.

In the recording studio with Ringo Starr.

Ringo Starr and George Harrison... Are you kidding me right now?!

My buddy Ringo Starr.

Perry Como, one of the kindest men in show business.

CHAPTER 14

THE CRAZY EIGHTIES: SPECIALS GALORE

THE NEXT DECADE FOR ME WAS KICKED OFF WITH A FABULOUS SPECIAL HOMAGE to Hollywood starring one of the loveliest young talents of stage and screen accompanied by a dance and song legend, none other than Gene Kelly.

May I Have This Dance? Olivia Newton-John and Gene Kelly (1980)

Olivia Newton-John: Hollywood Nights (1980) was Olivia's fourth television special and was ABC's lead-in to the Academy Awards on April 14, 1980. (I hadn't yet directed the Oscars, but I was inching closer, one special at a time.)

Olivia was known as a triple threat in the entertainment industry: she could dance, sing, and act. And the camera absolutely loved her with her beautiful blond hair, big blue eyes, and sparkling personality. Even though she was Australian, she was America's sweetheart (right up there with Julie Andrews). She rose to movie fame in *Grease* with John Travolta topping off a Grammy award–winning career.

Hollywood Nights brought together Dick Clark, Andy Gibb, Toni Tennille, Tina Turner, Karen Carpenter, Elton John, Ted Knight, and special guest star, the great showman Gene Kelly. The special was not only important to ABC, but it was important to Olivia. She had a record coming out and a movie that she was promoting at the same time, *Xanadu*. She wanted this special to be the best one she had ever done, and she counted on me to deliver.

The special was shot mostly out of doors in Century City, California, in front of an audience of enthusiastic fans. It was another one of those great, beautiful, sparkly nights. The viewer really got the feeling of being at a live concert. The opening number looked so magnificent with a special camera shot I designed that made Olivia look like she was flying over the shining skyline of Los Angeles landing in the courtyard of the Twin Towers in Century City. Appropriately, the song she sang was called "Hollywood Nights."

Her wardrobe was out of this world. In the opening number she wore a spectacular sparkling pink jumpsuit, and her costumes just got better from there.

One of my biggest challenges in directing this special was preparing for the number she was performing with famed dancer/choreographer/actor/director Gene Kelly, who had appeared with her in *Xanadu*. That would be the last film he made.

How did I prepare, you ask? I watched as many Gene Kelly and Fred Astaire movies as I could to learn the directing style that would be outstanding for both Olivia and Gene. I wasn't intimidated, but I was guided by the eighteen-minute, gorgeous dance number between Leslie Caron and Gene Kelly in *An American in Paris*. At the 1952 Academy Awards, it won six Oscars and became the third musical in the Academy's twenty-five-year history to win Best Picture. Kelly himself was given an honorary award "in appreciation of his versatility as an actor, singer, director, and dancer, and specifically for his brilliant achievements in the art of choreography on film." I also studied Gene's solo dance number, "Singin' in the Rain," in the movie of the same name.

Gene came to the ABC Studio lot, Stage 57, on the day of the shoot, where we constructed an interior set that resembled a comfy living room with a fireplace. We were going to camera block and shoot this segment with him and Olivia in five hours, start to finish. Everything had to be "in the can" in one day. There was no margin for error. We didn't have Olivia or Gene for any more time than was allotted. Talk about pressure.

I introduced myself to Gene, and he answered, "I know who you are; I did my homework. I watched a lot of your work."

"Is that a good thing?"

"Well, we will soon find out." If I wasn't confident, his remark might have made me a bit on edge, but I was fully prepared and I knew what I was doing. That's the only way to work with a legend—be prepared! We started camera blocking, and Gene stopped after the first run-through. He asked if it would be too much trouble for him to have a monitor (actually four or five monitors) on the floor so that he could see how I was shooting the number. (I'm not sure how you can dance and look down at the floor to check the picture, but I guess when you're Gene Kelly, it's not a problem. Who else would have been able to dance across a wet floor in *Singin' in the Rain* without a slip and fall?)

We set up monitors throughout the dance space in the studio. I didn't mind that he was checking what I was doing because I knew I was doing a good job. I had something in mind from looking at all the Gene Kelly movies. What I noticed was that every director that shot him, and even when Gene shot himself, he almost never went in for a close-up or a waist shot. He always stayed on a head-to-toe or full-figure shot so that you could see his entire body and you could see all the dance moves. What's the point of having the great Gene Kelly dancing, if you're on a close-up of his face during a dance sequence?

The segment with Gene Kelly opens with Olivia and him chatting on the couch when Olivia comments, "I love dancing with you so much, and I'd love to have another dance." She was referring to the dance number they had done together in *Xanadu*.

Gene said, "Well, why not?" They got up. I hit the music track, which was the great 1928 classic, "Makin' Whoopee," and the two of them started to dance. And at the end of the dance, they kissed and hugged and walked back toward the couch. We faded to black, and that was the end.

So, here's how I shot it. I followed them down from the couch in a head-to-toe shot. They were linking arms. As the music started, I cut to a high wide shot on the crane. (It was called a crane back then; now it's called a jib.) I gently floated down into a head-to-toe two-shot, and I never cut away. I followed them for the whole dance in that two-shot, and when the dance was over, as they turned around and walked away, the camera on the crane zoomed out and floated back up high into a beautiful wide shot. I never made a camera cut the whole time. I think it's exactly as Gene would have shot it.

We finished the final run-through, and before we taped, I spoke to Olivia and Gene over the PA system in the studio, and I said, "Is everybody comfortable? Are we ready to shoot?" And they said, "Yes, we're all set." Makeup and hair came in and touched them up, and then I rolled tape. We taped their conversation on the couch before the dance number and continued right on into the dance. We got it in one single take. (At least that's how I remember it.)

When the stage manager said, "Okay, cut!" Gene Kelly turned around to him and asked in a serious tone of voice, "Where's Jeff?"

The stage manager said to me, "Jeff, Mister Kelly would like to see you in the control room."

"Well, send him in."

He came in and said, "Where's Jeff?" I was sitting in front of the television monitors.

He walked over to me, and I thought, "Oh, Jesus, he's going to read me the riot act because he's not happy."

But instead, he gave me a giant hug and a kiss. Then he said, "Fucking perfect. I loved it. I'm going home. I've already kissed Olivia goodbye. Thank you very much. It's been a real pleasure."

He gave me another hug and walked out! Just like that, he was gone. That was it! He didn't make a single request. He obviously liked what he saw. And so did Olivia. And let's not forget the other people you need to please, Alan Thicke and Lee Kramer, who were producing the show for ABC. They were happy with everything as well.

Georgia on My Mind: John Schneider and Ray Charles (1980)

Born in Mt. Kisco, New York, John Schneider moved with his mother to Georgia, then Hollywood, eventually landing a starring role as

Beauregard "Bo" Duke in CBS's long-running action comedy series, *The Dukes of Hazzard*. In 1980 he earned his own special on CBS, *John Schneider: Back Home*, and I directed it. My good friend Ernie Chambers was the producer. What was so memorable about the show for me was being in the presence of the legendary Ray Charles, one of John's guests, along with the wonderful country singer Barbara Mandrell. Barbara had her own series on NBC at the time called *Barbara Mandrell and the Mandrell Sisters*. John was a frequent guest on Barbara's show, so for them it was like Old Home Week. John was not only a gifted actor, boyishly handsome with blond hair and blue eyes, but he also had a really good singing voice. At the same time as the special, John was launching his country music career. (He went on to record nine studio albums and eighteen singles, many of which reached the top of the *Billboard* country singles charts.)

CBS was happy to give him a special, counting on his legion of fans to tune in for this "one-off," one-hour show. The networks liked to create specials for their stable of talent. Their name recognition not only drew an audience but also loosened the purse strings of advertisers who were familiar with these stars.

I had worked with Ray Charles before on the American Music Awards. I didn't know if he remembered me, but I would soon find out. We came up with the idea of having Ray sing a duet with John Schneider, and—of course—the song we selected was "Georgia on My Mind," Charles's 1960 hit that was the first of his three career No. 1 hits on the *Billboard* Hot 100. We set the song in a beautiful old church located in a small town outside of Atlanta, about two hundred miles from Albany, Georgia, where Ray was born. It was also not far from where Ray had refused to perform when he learned that the auditorium banned blacks. Ray was sued by the producers, but the native-born son was declared a hero by civil rights activists.

When I walked into the church, Ray was already sitting at the piano next to the altar—noodling around softly on the ivories. I said hello, introduced myself, and reminded him that we had worked together many times before. He said, "Oh yeah, I recognized you when I saw you walking in." Then he chuckled that wonderful Ray

Charles laugh and said, "I'd recognize that voice anytime; it's good to see you, Jeff," then he chuckled again. What a gem! He continued to play the piano while I told him what was going to happen. He listened very carefully, and when I mentioned John Schneider's name he joked, "I watch *The Dukes of Hazzard* every week. When I see him, I'll know who he is." Looking back at some of the CBS promos for *The Dukes of Hazzard*, I wonder how he might have felt to see a Confederate flag on the top of the hog that Bo Duke, a.k.a. John Schneider, drove around his Georgia town. (Behind the scenes Ray was a militant civil rights activist, but he never showed his cards when he was working—there he was all business.)

I told Ray that we were going to shoot a portion of "Georgia on My Mind" in the church and that John would step in to sing with him; then we'd go out to the countryside to finish the song. I'd shoot the two segments and later edit them together.

Still noodling on the piano, Ray said, "Whatever you want me to do, just cue me when to start, and I'll do whatever you want as many times as you want me to do it." I couldn't ask for more. He seemed thrilled to be in the church. He said, "I don't often get asked to do something like this in the House of God; usually I'm on a stage in a theater, performing. I'm really glad to be here."

John Schneider had never met Ray Charles before, but he just idolized him. When he walked in, Ray stopped singing, and the two of them had a nice introductory chat. John was beaming. You could see the admiration on his face. I remember John saying, "Thank you for being here, Mister Charles. I can't tell you how much this means to me."

Ray's response was, "I'll tell you what, if I can call you John, then please call me Ray."

Then the two of them sang together; the duet was quite moving, and when it was over, John slow clapped with a smile on his face from ear to ear. His reverence for Ray Charles was genuine. Who doesn't worship Ray Charles?

Ten years later, Ray was on the *Ebony* magazine tribute I produced and directed. Ray has a phenomenal memory. He said, "I remember you. I recognize that voice. We were up in the mountains of Georgia together with John Schneider."

I said, "Yep, that was me."

He went on, "That was fun. I watched it when it was on TV. It was good!" There was that Ray Charles sense of humor, along with his special laugh.

Man, what a treasure.

How High the Moon? Bea Arthur (1980)

Bea Arthur was a tall handful, but boy was she good. A born and bred New Yorker, she gained attention in the movie *Mame*, starring Lucille Ball and Robert Preston, was cast by Norman Lear in *All in the Family*, and then earned her own Norman Lear television series, *Maude*, which ran for six seasons. She went on to join the cast of *The Golden Girls*, playing the part of a former Brooklyn school teacher and the daughter of Italian immigrant parents. She acted like a "tough broad," with a sharp wit that endeared her to her loyal fans.

In 1980 Bea Arthur was given her own special, which she described as "good times and having fun." Rock Hudson, Melba Moore, and Wayland Flowers and his puppet, Madame, were her guests. Like John Schneider's special, it was a showcase for her singing and acting talent. Once again, I got to work with my good friend and producer, Saul Ilson (Ernie Chambers's partner).

Bea was a force, and she was great to work with. This special was really the one and only time I had the good fortune to spend time with her.

She made me work for my money.

For example, Bea had a fear of heights. The way Ray Klausen, the set designer, designed the set, Bea was to begin the opening number high up in the air on a platform. As she introduced each of her guests, she would step down to a lower platform and perform a section of the number there. Every day in rehearsal, before we moved on to the set in the studio, Kevin Carlisle, the choreographer, and I would tell her about the platforms, where she'd start high up, and end the number on the lowest platform. We discovered that Bea was so concerned about her performance that she didn't really hear what we were saying. When she came into the studio for camera blocking and saw the set, she said, pointing upward, "Who's going up there because it's not me."

I said to her, "Bea, we talked about this every day in rehearsal. This is the opening of your special. Nobody else can go up there because," I repeated myself—this time more assertively, "this is *your* opening number!"

She said, "Well, who the fuck designed this set? How come I didn't know about it?"

"Bea, you did know about it. I showed you the drawings. I showed you all the sketches. We talked about this every day during rehearsal. You knew everything."

"Well, I didn't know how fucking high it is. You know I'm afraid of heights! I'm not going up there."

I gave her some kind of wise-ass answer like, "Okay, hold on. I'm going to call Betty White and see if she can come in and do it." When you are working with talent, from time to time, you have to "give" it as well as you "get" it. I thought maybe I'd get a laugh. No way. With Bea Arthur, an acerbic joke did the trick.

She looked at me, and it was another one of those "fuck you" moments. Then she had the choreographer take her up to the top platform to rehearse the number. She did it flawlessly and when she was comfortable, we taped the number.

The special was a variety show filled with lots of music and comedy. She sang and danced with Rock Hudson. She also did a very poignant scene lying on a king-size bed with him, sang duets with Melba Moore, and laughed with Wayland and Madame.

I look at the show now and remember that it was shot with only four cameras. I don't know of any director today, including me, who could direct a show with only four cameras, but that was the way it was done in 1980. Today it's not unusual to work with six, seven, or even eight cameras.

Bea Arthur was a big deal, and working with her taught me something. I never had another set built where I didn't specify the height and the number of steps that talent would have to walk up and down. And what's also true is that even if someone has a reputation for being tough, as Bea did, that doesn't mean that they don't have some hidden fear that a director needs to anticipate and address.

Hollywood Eye Candy (1981)

Sixty Years of Seduction was an ABC special that was very different from most specials being done in the eighties. Billed as an anniversary special and airing in 1981, it was mostly a clip show with wraparounds hosted by James Garner, Victoria Principal, Angie Dickinson, Robert Urich, and many more major stars. The clips were all from famous movies from the 1920s through the 1970s that were about love, scandal, and seduction. Once again, we shot on location all around Los Angeles. In one wraparound segment, James Garner notes that "while the East Coast may have its Statue of Liberty, the West Coast has Hollywood, urging the world to 'give me your young, your fresh, your wide-eyed beauties yearning to be stars.'"[3]

The producers, Scott Garen and John Brice, were very creative with the style of the wraparounds. They were all shot like scenes from a movie. Some of them were even choreographed like those wonderful Busby Berkeley or Gene Kelly movie musicals. This 1981 two-hour documentary-style show was totally put together in the editing room. I spent more hours in the editing room than I spent on location shooting the show. The material was organized around various themes such as "the kiss," "the male star," and "the female star." Arguing that, despite surface differences, Hollywood themes do remain remarkably the same, the program points up the similarity between a tuxedoed Rudolf Valentino tango and a white-suited John Travolta's famous disco number in *Saturday Night Fever*. One of the

---

3   From the Thomas Film Classics Catalog. You can buy this special, which is why you won't find it on YouTube or anywhere else. https://www.shop.thomasfilmclassics.com/product. sc?productId=2209&categoryId=-1.

funniest and most salacious clips is with Marlene Dietrich singing "What Am I Bid for My Apple" as only Marlene can deliver. This was not family fare, but it turned out to be a really entertaining retrospective with lots of "eye candy."

Do You Believe in Magic? David Copperfield (1984)

David Copperfield in my opinion is the greatest magician of all time. Executing some of his illusions (magic tricks)—designed for television—is especially challenging because the camera, or cameras, have to be positioned in such a way that no one can figure out how he does what he does, especially other magicians who would be apt to steal one of his secrets. David created a franchise for himself on CBS, delivering six specials, and I was selected by him to direct two of the six. What a privilege!

Working with David was a wonderful learning experience because David is an absolute perfectionist, and his illusions are brilliant, and his magic can't be beat. He gets involved with everything, and I mean everything—so much so that David and I shared co-director credit on *The Magic of David Copperfield VI: Floating over the Grand Canyon*, slated for 1984. More about that special later. Just suffice it to say that shooting in the Grand Canyon was a trip.

David's specials are always fascinating to watch and brilliantly put together. He brings a skill set to his performances and shows you how to pull off a magic trick without revealing the secret of how it's done. I may have a bit of magic up my sleeve but not the kind of magic that David Copperfield has at his fingertips.

Working with him was...difficult, but a thrill for me. He's probably the nicest, most difficult performer I've ever worked with because he invented himself. He is a Jewish kid from New Jersey who loves magic. He decided to reinvent himself changing his name from David Kotkin to David Copperfield.

While working on the special, I said to him, "David, I have an idea. You are concerned about camera cuts and edits. You're also concerned that other magicians might think that when there's a camera cut or an edit, it means that something needed to be hidden—or a mistake was made that needed to be fixed. Here's my idea.... There's a new piece of equipment called the Steadicam. Do you know what that is?"

"Tell me about it."

"It's a camera on a gyroscope. A guy wears a big harness around his upper body, the gyroscope is connected to the harness, and the camera sits on the end of the gyroscope. He can walk or move around anywhere with the camera, and it stays steady. It looks exactly like what you see through your own eyes when you're walking around. Does that make any sense?"

He said, "Sounds interesting and maybe even incredible, but I'm just not sold yet."

"I know the best Steadicam operator in the business. His name is Dave Eastwood. We should get him to shoot your illusions with his Steadicam, one single illusion, one single camera shot! That way nobody can ever accuse you of making a camera cut or an edit to fake a trick! We'll choreograph the camera so that we know where it needs to be and when it needs to be there to capture the illusion perfectly. No camera cuts, no edits. What do you think?"

He said, "I love it. I don't think it'll work, but I love the idea. And nobody's ever done it before in magic, right? I love that too!"

"Let's do it!" I brought Dave Eastwood in to operate the Steadicam. I had worked with him a lot. I'm almost certain that he might have been the first guy who did Steadicam in entertainment television. He was the best. We did almost the entire special on the Steadicam. It was brilliant. I'm always excited to use new technology that pushes the envelope of what can be accomplished in television. (Sound familiar? My dad was the same way—always after the latest gadget.)

After that special, I was David Copperfield's new best friend. But then he did his own personal magic act, and just like that, he disappeared from television. I've been trying to get him to do a comeback special. Maybe one day.

You might not know this about David Copperfield. He's very, very private. He's got his own museum in Las Vegas. I haven't been there yet, although I've seen photographs. I've been told that the museum contains the very first illusion that Houdini ever built. David obviously has every illusion that he's ever done and apparently lots of illusions that Houdini did as well, plus so much more from the world of magic. It's an amazing collection, so I'm told. I hope to see it one day.

His specials were great, especially the *Floating over the Grand Canyon* special. David took full advantage of the location and demanded a tremendous amount from me and my crew. I can't say how we did it because I signed a non-disclosure agreement. But the audience actually sees David Copperfield floating over the Grand Canyon. Not an illusion for a magician who is afraid of heights. The show was hosted by Ricardo Montalbán, of *Fantasy Island* fame, who introduced the Grand Canyon illusion: "It's the most incredible levitation trick in history. And why would anyone travel through the air for ten miles over the Grand Canyon? To meet a lady on the other side, of course." That lady was singer Bonnie Tyler, who sang "Holding Out for a Hero" as David floated through the air a mile above the canyon floor. The balance of the special was shot in a studio before a live audience. The final illusion required David to submerge himself in chains in a water tank with a huge knife-like instrument suspended above the tank. Just as two minutes passed, the knife plunged into the water, the blanket covering the tank was removed, and David crawled out, soaking wet but alive. The audience was speechless. The first people he acknowledged in the audience were his parents, Mr. and Mrs. Kotkin, who looked justifiably relieved that their twenty-seven-year-old son had tricked death. What an illusion!

Working with David was an experience that I will cherish forever. And I will never forget all the new directing "tools" he shared with me, and perhaps he'll remember a few that I shared with him. We made a great team! He is as obsessed with magic as I am with television, and between the two of us, we *really* delivered. David still performs in Las Vegas but not on television. He hasn't been on television in a long time but does sixteen shows a week in Vegas and is still going strong.

Winners All (1987)

Taped live for ABC at Notre Dame University in South Bend, Indiana, on August 2, 1987, created by Eunice Kennedy Shriver and members of the Kennedy family, the Special Olympics Opening Ceremonies was *ginormous*. The show included a parade into the athletic stadium of five thousand special athletes from all over the world, a huge marching band, music composed and conducted by John Williams, and a cavalcade of stars including Whitney Houston, Oprah Winfrey, Arnold Schwarzenegger, John Ritter, Jane Fonda, Don Johnson, Maria Shriver, Frank Gifford, Edward Kennedy, and co-hosted by John Denver and Barbara Mandrell, who announced to the packed stadium, "You are all part of this historical event." And they were. The band played "We're Lookin' Good," and it was my job to make sure they did just that. Think about the logistics of trying to cover an entire football stadium as well as a stage set up for individual performances at one end of the football field. When Whitney Houston sang "Didn't We Almost Have It All?" there wasn't a dry eye in the house or the control room. It took six hours to tape everything that would then be compressed into three hours of television time. We worked late into the night, and the show was to air the following evening on ABC.

This was a case of, "Oh my God, how are we going to get this show edited and on the air on time?" As soon as we wrapped, I jumped into a limousine with my producing partner (Lee Miller), my assistant director, and two production assistants. We had a police escort to the airport—sirens, flashing lights, and all—got on a plane, and flew from South Bend, Indiana, to the Burbank airport on the outskirts of Los Angeles, then went directly to the editing room at Pacific Video in Hollywood at three in the morning. It's a good thing that I don't need much sleep because we didn't even take a break. We had a total of fourteen hours before the first hour of the show was to air on ABC. That's not a lot of time to put together a three-hour show when you are working with six hours of taped material that needs to be cut down, sweetened, and made perfect for the network, the athletes, the stars, and, of course, the Kennedys, who considered this show an important family legacy. This was not a job that could be accomplished single-handedly. Fortunately, I had enough experience to take it in stride, surround myself with the best people possible to collaborate with, and make it happen. But to be honest it was still managed chaos.

There was a huge spread of lox and bagels and tons of coffee to fuel us so that we'd make it through the edit. My good friend Steve Schifrin was running Pacific Video at the time and certainly knew how to take care of a friend and one of his best clients. I was expected to deliver the first hour of the show over to the ABC network studios, not far from the editing facility, but I decided we'd never make the drive to ABC in time to get the first hour on the air. As necessity is the mother of invention, the editing technicians at the facility and the ABC studio technicians spoke by phone and decided to put up a satellite link between Pacific Video and ABC so that we were able to run the first hour of the show from the editing facility while I worked on the rest of the show. When the editor pushed the play button at 5:00 p.m. in Los Angeles, 8:00 p.m. in New York, everyone let out a partial sigh of relief because we only had two more hours to go. The second hour was almost finished, but we hadn't even begun to edit the third hour yet. Really, are you kidding me? Two more hours of show to edit? Holy shit! The pressure was, as I said, ginormous. At the end of the day, we had a hit on our hands without missing a beat. A million things could have gone wrong—the weather could have been against us getting out of South Bend, the tape could have somehow been corrupted, the traffic could have been backed up from Burbank to the editing facility, the communication between Pacific Video and ABC could have been interrupted—but none of that happened (thank God), and as I like to say, "It's going to be great." Just another day in TV land. I thrive on stuff like this, but it's not for everyone!

The Stuff that Dreams Are Made Of (1987)

Well, what can I say...? Every great star in Hollywood made an appearance on *Happy 100th Birthday, Hollywood*, a 1987 ABC special. It was so big. This was a once-in-a-lifetime event capturing the history of

Hollywood. I think there was more star power there on stage that night than at the Oscars. Here's a partial list of the nearly one hundred stars from across the generations who appeared: Bea Arthur, Carol Burnett, Sid Caesar, Tony Danza, Sammy Davis Jr., Katharine Hepburn, Whoopi Goldberg, Clint Eastwood, Burt Lancaster, Liza Minnelli, Gregory Peck, Bernadette Peters, Debbie Reynolds, Jimmy Stewart, Betty White, Henry Winkler, and Loretta Young.

The show's executive producer was Broadway legend Alexander Cohen, who was responsible for bringing Broadway's Tony Awards to television. Alex (as he is known to his friends) spoke with John Hamlin at ABC (one of the most creative and forward-thinking executives in television) with an idea: "Let's celebrate Hollywood's one hundred years. Let's do the biggest show that's ever been done in the history of television." And that's what we did. Alex was married to Hildy Parks, a well-known writer, who became his producing partner on most of his shows. The two of them were a team, and they never traveled anywhere without their dogs, two English cocker spaniels. They brought them to every production meeting we had (water bowls, beds, and all).

Alex knew Broadway a lot better than he knew Hollywood, so he asked Jack Haley Jr. to be his executive producing partner. Jack was Hollywood royalty—his father was the Tin Man in *The Wizard of Oz*, and Jack had tremendous street cred. Anyone he or Alex called to book on the show said yes, which is why we ended up with a cast of nearly a hundred stars.

The show consisted of gigantic musical numbers, clips from movies, and dance routines choreographed by some of the best choreographers in Hollywood at the time. The show opened with Liza Minnelli taking a train out of New York to California surrounded by dancers wearing porter uniforms that morphed into jackets decorated with palm trees. And, of course, out come the sunglasses and sunshine with everyone singing "California, Here I Come." That opening set the stage for a travelogue through time. Liza does a terrific imitation of a Charlie Chaplin routine that ends with a set representing the famous Grauman's Chinese Theater, the iconic movie palace on Hollywood

Boulevard. Jimmy Stewart steps out of the entrance carrying the Maltese Falcon, and we are off and running through outstanding film clips organized by genre. Sammy Davis Jr. and Debbie Allen perform a medley of Hollywood songs, and then there is a tribute to the great choreographer Busby Berkeley, with a cavalcade of actresses/dancers who wrap up this segment with a kick line. A segment of humorous scenes in Hollywood movies is introduced by Whoopi Goldberg, and then the show switches gears to illustrate that movies also deal with social issues such as racism, prejudice, the price of war, and the death penalty with clips from *Gentleman's Agreement, I Want to Live!*, and *The Best Years of Our Lives.* Imagine the hours that went into creating the film packages for the show. The show ends with Liza Minnelli coming out surrounded by Hollywood's handsome leading men and the entire cast that made it all happen.

It took three days to shoot this special, and we had three after-parties in the Grand Ballroom at the Shrine Auditorium where the special was taped. Talent always loves a good after-party, where they get to schmooze and learn about what might be their next gig.

It was, at the time, the most expensive special ABC had ever done—probably more than the per hour cost of the episodic *Roots.* The special was brilliant. If I remember correctly, the other networks didn't even want to put anything on against it—they knew they might as well just put on a rerun of an old movie out of the vault.

Maybe there will be another tribute to celebrate Hollywood's two-hundredth birthday, but I guess none of us will know. What I do know is that it was one of the most important shows—along with the Oscars—that I've ever directed. I mean come on, a hundred years of Hollywood. What a celebration.

Alex and I established a great working relationship. He was thrilled with the Hollywood one-hundredth birthday celebration, so he called me to work with him again, this time on *Night of 100 Stars III.* (I wasn't involved with the first two shows in this franchise which aired in 1982 and 1985.) Alex must like the words "one hundred" just as Dick Clark likes the word "American."

He sold the original *Night of 100 Stars* to ABC. It was a big three-hour deal, and there were a hundred stars—no false advertising with Alex. For his first special in this franchise, he made a deal with Continental Airlines and arranged for them to park a jet right on Fifth Avenue in New York City. The show opened with all one hundred stars coming off the plane. How's that for showmanship? I don't know how he managed to do this with all the red tape in New York City, but maybe Mayor Ed Koch liked the publicity, and Continental certainly did.

I was told that *Night of 100 Stars III*, which I directed in 1990, was the biggest and most spectacular of all three. Radio City Music Hall was the location, and I heard that the first two specials were shot over a couple of nights. I said to Alex, "Why don't we do it in one evening and shoot it like a live event?"

He said to me, "Are you out of your fucking mind? It's way too big. We could never shoot it like a live event!"

Well, guess what?

We shot it in one glamorous evening as a live event, and it was flawless. Every single star knew that it was going to be shot live—no second takes or pickups—so every star came to rehearsal, and it showed. Every introduction, every performance, every production number, and all the spectacular film clips made the evening unforgettable. Another one of those magical Hollywood nights.

What a Sport: Kenny Rogers (1988)

The personal manager Ken Kragen and I were very good friends. (He had been the executive producer of the *Smothers Brothers Comedy Hour* back in the day.) He had a stellar client list of musicians and songwriters that included Dolly Parton and Lionel Richie, both of whom I worked with. Kenny Rogers was also managed by Ken Kragen, and I had directed a number of concert specials for him including HBO's *Kenny Rogers Live in Concert*, so Ken brought me in to produce and direct ABC's *Kenny Rogers Classic Weekend* in 1988.

This special was very unique and different from anything that Kenny had ever done before, and it was quite spectacular. It was something different for me, too, and I learned a lot. Kenny was a sports fanatic; he loved basketball, and he loved golf. At the time, he lived on a magnificent 1,200-acre farm in Colbert, Georgia, named Beaver Dam Farms, about an hour and a half outside of Atlanta, where he bred Arabian horses and raised cattle. Kenny never wanted to fly commercially or drive between Colbert and Atlanta. He had his own jet, which he kept at the Atlanta airport, and a helicopter to ferry him back and forth from the airport to the ranch.

Kenny had the idea to do an on-location extravaganza on his property which had a nine-hole golf course, an NBA-sized basketball court, and a huge outdoor stage which was a mini-Hollywood Bowl. Kenny lived large, and he enjoyed every minute of it and wanted to share it with his television audience. He conceived of the ninety-minute special combining a music concert and competitions in basketball, golf, tennis, and fishing. The entire show was used as a local fundraiser with Kenny as the host. Some of the celebrities included Gladys Knight, John McEnroe, Lorenzo Lamas, Larry Bird, Kris Kristofferson, Tommy Smothers, and Michael Jordan.

When I went to do my location survey in preparation for this special, I got picked up at the airport in Atlanta in Kenny's helicopter. As we flew onto Beaver Dam Farms, I was inspired to open the special with a wide shot from the helicopter, flying over the ranch with Kenny doing a voice-over talking about how much he loved the land, his horses, his golf course, his basketball court, and everything this incredible estate contained.

We just had the best time on that show. It was a lot of hard work but so much fun at the same time. I got to direct so many things that I had never done before. I'd never shot a golf game, so I looked at some televised golf matches, and then I called a friend of mine who was a sports director, and I asked him to help me.

"How do you position cameras and what do you look for?" As he was telling me about it, I thought, "You know, I should let him direct this segment; I've got so much other stuff to do. There's golf and basketball to tape. I've never taped either, and then I've got a big con-cert to tape. Maybe I should be smart and turn the sports segments over to my director friends who know how to shoot sports." There wasn't enough time for on-the-job training for me. I decided to let the directors who know how to shoot sports do it. I was the producer of the special, but I only took credit as director of the wraparound and musical segments and gave the basketball director and the golf director credit for what they shot. Teamwork makes the dream work!

An important takeaway from this special is that I recognized my limitations—I was not going to become a sports director in twen-ty-four hours. I knew when I needed outside help to make the show the best it could be—and it was.

Another side story. Remember I told you about that spectacular opening wide shot I thought about from the helicopter flying to the ranch? Well, we rehearsed it one time, then while we were still up in the air, I asked the stage manager, who I was communicating with on a walkie-talkie, to bring Kenny out because we were ready to tape it. I said, "Roll tape." I counted down 5...4...3...2...1, and we were on our way. I was watching everything on a small monitor in the helicopter, and I was pleased with Kenny's performance and how everything looked on camera.

The helicopter was small, so the camera operator was also operat-ing the tape machine. We didn't have room for a tape operator. When we landed, and I said, "Great job, everybody; thank you." I then turned to the camera operator and said, "Let's make sure we got everything and it looks good on tape."

I looked over, and my camera operator was ghost white. (I won't mention his name because I would never want to embarrass him.) He said, "I am so sorry, Jeff. I forgot to push the record button." Oh, shit! Take a deep breath, count to ten, and figure out a solution.

Kenny didn't want to do it again, so there went that idea. I thanked the helicopter pilot, sent him on his way, and started to think of a new opening shot. Oh well, sometimes you do have to go to Plan B. Other than that little hiccup, the show was still another great experience, and we raised a lot of money for a children's charity affiliated with J. C. Penney, and the show got good ratings. A win for all!

British Royalty: Prince Charles and Princess Diana (1988)

To be asked to produce and direct an ABC special for Prince Charles and Princess Diana—really, are you kidding me? I was packed and ready to get on that jet to London right away. As you know by now, as the director/producer you always need to do a survey of the location so that you can see where you will be taping the special, schedule meetings with everyone on the local production staff, and speak to the representatives of the royals. Then come home, put it all together, and you're now ready to go back to London and make magic. And even when we speak the same language, there are differences in the way things are done. Fortunately, I had enough experience working in England (with Julie Andrews and then Perry Como) to recognize what most of the differences are.

Gary Pudney was an executive at ABC, and he loved Charles and Diana. I'm sure that he and ABC executives John Hamlin and Ted Harbert came up with the Royal Gala idea. Gary kept saying, "Charles and Diana. Charles and Diana. There's nobody bigger in the world. We've got to do something with them. We've got to be the first network to do a special for them." It would be quite a coup, and the ABC execs were on board and determined to make it happen. Princess Diana was the world's darling, and everywhere she went cameras followed her—to see what she was wearing, what she had to say, and to admire her. The wedding of Prince Charles and Lady Diana Spencer had commanded a television viewership of over 750 million people worldwide in 1981, so the show *ABC Presents: A Royal Gala* was sure to be a hit in 1988.

ABC had an overall deal with David Frost, the producer, writer, and host, so they figured, "David's got an in with Charles and Diana; he practically lives next door to them in London; he'd be the perfect guy to partner up with Jeff to produce this thing."

Off to London I went, and I met with David Frost. I spent a week with him. Oy! What a week that was. As a matter of fact, David used to have a satirical show on the BBC that poked fun at political figures and other celebrities called *That Was the Week That Was*. It certainly was a week for me.

I met Charles that week and Diana later. *Wow!* What a thrill. I produced the television show for two years in a row. And then I flew to London to do my survey to prepare for the third year, as I did every year. I arrived in London, and one of David Frost's people met me at the airport. The first words out of his mouth were, "Charles and Diana are getting divorced. There's no show."

I said to them, "You couldn't have made a phone call? Before I took the fuckin' eleven-hour flight from LA for you to give me this news? What the fuck?"

Well anyway, the other two years working with David Frost were interesting. He woke up in the morning, and I think he lit a cigar before he took a shower. He smoked more cigars during the day than you can imagine. Never had a cigar out of his mouth. I would go to his house and meet him after he'd showered, and we would have coffee together and work all morning. Around two in the afternoon he'd have a nap and be ready to go back to work again at three thirty. While he was snoozing, I'd use that time to first call home and make sure my family was okay. Secondly, I'd check in with my assistant to get filled in on the day's activities at the office.

Charles and Diana loved Hollywood and many of the American performers, so we always designed a wonderful evening of entertainment for them. We shot the special at the London Palladium, which was the Queen's theater, and Charles and Diana sat in the royal box.

John Ritter, may he rest in peace, hosted with David Frost. We had wonderful performers on the shows, including Phil Collins and Elton John and pretty much every other English performer you can think of. Then we introduced some new American talent each year with some performances that we knew Charles and Diana liked. We didn't know how they knew about a group called Gloria Estefan and the Miami Sound Machine, but they did. The group had never performed on television in England before, but Charles and Diana knew who they were and wanted them, so we booked them.

Listen to who else was on the show that evening. Besides Elton John, Phil Collins, and Miami Sound Machine, there was Art Garfunkel, Amy Grant, James Taylor, and Belinda Carlisle. It was also the year that we booked Robin Williams. Oh my God, what a memorable moment in television history his performance was.

I worked out a deal with Robin's terrific manager, David Steinberg, for Robin to come to London a week before the show so that he could try out some of his comedy in the local comedy clubs. Of course, word got out, and soon you couldn't find a seat anywhere. The night of our show, we told Robin that he had six minutes for his routine. He was happy with that much time, which was very generous for a standup comic on a one-hour variety television special. Well, sixteen minutes later, he finally finished to uproarious applause and a standing ovation from the royals. He was genius. The audience started laughing from the time he opened his mouth and they never stopped. And by the way, I had no idea what Robin was going to do. I was seeing it for the first time just like the audience. I love to direct comedy that way because it's real.

Charles and Diana couldn't have been more gracious. When I met them after the show, it was always, "What a great show. Thank you so much for putting it on for us," and "We couldn't be happier." They were so kind and generous. It always took me a bit longer in the receiving line than anybody else because they wanted to spend more time with me to say thank you. That's how genuinely appreciative they were.

Princess Diana was stunning! There was just something about her. Here was this innocent-looking, naturally beautiful young woman, who all of a sudden was a princess. She was royalty, but she always had that look of innocence and shyness about her.

Looking back on Elton John's performance of "Candle in the Wind," performed during the second year of *The Royal Gala*, is strangely eerie. Who would ever have imagined what happened to that beautiful princess, but the words of the song say it all: her candle did, indeed, burn out long before her legend did—or ever will. Elton sang that song once again, changing some of the lyrics, at the memorial to Princess Diana who left us long before her time.

So now I was back in Los Angeles editing the show, and Robin Williams's sixteen minutes was brilliant. Why would I want to edit it down to six minutes? I wouldn't, but that meant that there was no way I could turn in a one-hour special to the network. My good friend and ABC executive John Hamlin came to the rescue. He knew that Robin couldn't be cut; he pulled whatever strings he needed to pull, and our one-hour special became a ninety-minute special. The network had to rearrange the day's schedule to accommodate the additional thirty minutes, go back to the advertisers, and do whatever was necessary. But it paid off. Robin Williams won an Emmy Award for his performance on that show. Bravo!

Not long afterward, *The Royal Gala* would be the inspiration for eight specials with President Bill Clinton and First Lady Hillary. You'll read about that later. Let's just say that no great idea goes to waste.

Olivia and I had a special bond.

Ray Charles with me... Did this really happen?

David Copperfield explaining the illusion to me.

I'm scouting a location at the Great Wall of China for the next David Copperfield magic special.

Telling Kenny Rogers where to look for his close-up.

I loved working with Oprah, every time I could.

John Ritter, one of the most beloved stars.

CHAPTER 15

THE NONSTOP NINETIES: BACK-TO-BACK SPECIALS

Except for time out for family vacations, I was turning out what seemed like one special a week during the 1990s to satisfy the ever-growing demand for this genre of television entertainment. I loved what I was doing so much and I had so many great people working with me at Jeff Margolis Productions that I was able to keep up with this schedule. And all of it would not have been possible without the love and support of my wife, Leslie, and the sweet smiles of our two children, Adam and Erin.

Tea for Two: Julie Andrews and Carol Burnett (1990)

Twelve years after I first worked with Julie Andrews in London in 1978 on *One Step into Spring*, Julie told ABC executive Gary Pudney that she wanted me to direct *Julie & Carol: Together Again*, because we had such a great experience previously. Carol Burnett agreed with her and we were off to the races. The special was about friendship, and in case you don't know this, Julie and Carol had long been best friends— twenty-five-plus years of friendship even then. They had appeared in two previous television specials together: first at Carnegie Hall in 1962 and then again in 1971 at Lincoln Center. These two shows were spectacular, and the bar was set very high for me to deliver a special that could top the success of its predecessors. But I was up for the challenge and thrilled to be working with Julie again—and with Carol.

I had a great meeting with the ladies. I suggested, "Instead of going into a studio and doing all of your musical numbers with an audience of two hundred fifty, three hundred people, let's make it big. Let's go to some famous theater somewhere in Los Angeles. What about the Pantages? Everybody knows the Pantages Theatre in Hollywood just like the Brits know the Palladium in London."

They loved the idea, and we did all of it there: music, comedy, everything. We never went into a studio. The show was mostly musical numbers, but there were also comedy sketches. We used a live orchestra on stage, and they earned every note—Julie and Carol are the great ladies of musical theater. Julie made her name on Broadway in 1956 starring in *My Fair Lady* as Eliza Doolittle opposite Rex Harrison after a successful London run, and Carol Burnett caught the attention and adoration of theater audiences in the off-Broadway musical comedy *Once Upon a Mattress*, which moved to Broadway in 1959. Both of them transitioned to television, and Julie went on to a huge career in film as well. So did Carol, but first, she earned her own variety comedy show on CBS. The show was a staple of many American households, including mine, back in the day.

The theme for this third collaboration was to celebrate old friends, best friends. Carol Burnett was close with the talented team of writers/composers/producers Ken and Mitzie Welch, who worked with her on *The Carol Burnett Show*. Mitzie and Ken came up with the material, and then Carol and Julie would pick and choose what they liked best. It was a real collaboration. The music was all, but for one song, popular songs from the 1970s and '80s and familiar to the audience. All of the sketches reflected the show's theme; some even harkened back to sketches from their two previous shows together.

In *Julie & Carol: Together Again*, their friendship and love for one another were palpable, but nothing was off limits for an honest laugh—not age, not gray hair, not baggy pants, not rap music, not bosoms, and definitely not pies in the face. At one point Carol says to Julie, "We've always been brutally honest with each other. We know how old each other is. I lied when you asked me how old I was. I was barely in my teens. I just looked a lot older."

Julie says serenely, "You still do."

With these two women, comic timing comes naturally—especially when they decide to talk about the Boston Tea Party, which Julie considers "a childish prank that happened well over two hundred years ago. You Americans are so simple," she tells Carol. "You even use those dreadful teabags."

Carol adds, "We were forced to dress up like Indians and we dumped the whole thing into the Boston harbor. It's too bad we didn't have those dreadful teabags in colonial times. It would have been a lot easier to clean up, I'll tell you."

Then, out come the cream pies and a beautifully iced cake on a tea caddy, and the chums couldn't resist throwing desserts at one another. Then they remember they have been friends for twenty-five years and they have a medley to do. It's more important to maintain their friendship than argue about age and politics with one another.

One day in the middle of rehearsals, Julie and Carol called me over for a chat. They wanted to talk to me, and we sat down and just schmoozed a little bit. "How's everything going? Are you guys happy with the show?" I asked. As their producer and director, I wanted to be sure they were comfortable with everything that was being asked of them to make the show the best it could be (although it's hard to mess up when you are working with two consummate pros).

Julie said to me in a very caring, loving, respectful way, "Darling, listen. I hope you don't take offense to this, and I hope you understand. You're here because we want you to be here. We admire your work. We love your work. Would you mind if we had Blake—my husband, Blake Edwards—come in and help stage the comedy? You can do all the camera work. He doesn't want to do any of the camera work, but he wants to help stage the comedy for us."

I was in shock. The ladies looked uneasy. They did not expect to hear good news, but I surprised them.

"I would love that!" I told them. "Blake Edwards! I can watch Blake Edwards staging comedy! Peter Sellers and all the *Pink Panther* movies! Absolutely!"

"Really?" Julie looked at me. "I thought I'd have a fight."

"Julie, you know me better than that. When I put together the call sheet for rehearsals, I'll put his name on, and I'll give him the time when he will need to show up."

"Well, when I show up, he'll show up."

Blake came in and looked at everything I had done with the choreographer, a good friend of mine, Kevin Carlisle. Blake was there every day of rehearsal, taking the reins for the comedy sketches and weighing in on some of the songs and how they were being staged. I sat back and learned from the master. I had no ego about this. I was eager to learn what Blake Edwards had to offer. After he staged a sketch and the ladies were happy with it, he'd say to me, "Do you have any problems shooting anything? Is there anything I need to fix for you?"

Most of the time, I had no problems with the action on the stage, but occasionally I would say, "Well it would help me if...." I'd suggest something so that I'd get a better angle for the camera, and he'd usually accommodate what I wanted to do. For the show, I used seven cameras, and we taped the show straight through in one day with a dress rehearsal in the morning and the show before a live audience later in the day!

Blake looked over the choreography, which, as I said earlier, was designed by Kevin Carlisle. If he felt he could add something, he would say, "Well, if you want this part to be more effective, Julie, why don't you jump up on the piano? Do the line from there. Sing that part of the song to Carol down on the floor. It'll just be funnier." He would do that kind of stuff. There was a little bit of Blake in everything.

The tea party scene was just one of the hilarious moments in the show. In it, Julie and Carol came out on stage in beautiful ball gowns, Julie served tea to Carol and mayhem ensued—of course there was pie in the face, and Julie milked it for all it was worth, using the whipped cream like shampoo, shaping Carol's hair into ears and stuffing an apple in her mouth so she looked like a stuffed pig.

And that was just one of the sketches in the show. The show opens and closes with Stephen Sondheim's "Old Friends." In addition to the Boston Tea Party sketch (which you can watch in its entirety on YouTube), there is a sendup of *Phantom of the Opera*, retitled "Phantom of the Oprey," with Carol playing a Minnie Pearl–type singer for all she was worth, and Julie dressed in a sweet Swiss maiden costume who ends up stepping into the spotlight and getting rid of Carol. Of course, it brought the house down. And then there was a sketch in which they delivered a medley of 1970s and '80s songs dressed as janitors. At one point Julie stands up on a piano and holds up a toilet plunger in the style of the Statue of Liberty as they sing "New York, New York." If you blinked you might have missed that comedic choice, but it was perfect in every way.

Of course, Carol and Julie had some wonderful ideas, which they wanted to incorporate, and Blake said, "Okay, Carol, we'll do that. Why don't you do this beat first? Then we'll get to that, and it'll make it funnier."

Blake could play off their ideas and make them even funnier (and that's not easy because both Carol and Julie have fabulous comedic chops). He would say, "Don't throw the pie in her face. Let's figure out another way to get Julie's face covered with pie."

When I direct comedy, do I remember the things that Blake did? Probably. They're in the back of my head somewhere, and maybe they helped me. We're two different types of directors. Blake's experience is mainly in directing comedy feature films, and I'm in my element directing live television, both music and comedy.

I camera blocked all the numbers a few days ahead so that everyone was ready to go on the day we taped. It was not intimidating for me. I was completely prepared, and by this time in my career—in my early forties—I knew exactly what I wanted to do. I loved what I was doing, I was honored to be asked to work with these two women, and I just wanted to do the best job I could.

The show was a huge success, and it reflected the very special friendship that Carol and Julie had. They both admired one another immensely. The reviews were glowing and the ratings were high. It was a lovefest. Carol and Julie are still going strong. Blake Edwards passed away at the age of eighty-eight in 2010. I've had a couple of other experiences with Julie Andrews since then. In 2007 she appeared on the SAG Awards, which I directed and executive produced. Dick Van Dyke presented her with the Screen Actors Guild Life Achievement Award. (She and Dick Van Dyke had appeared together in the feature film *Mary Poppins* years earlier.) I hadn't seen her in a while. When she came to rehearsals, I was outside waiting for her. Of course, there were hugs and kisses. What a reunion!

Taking Care of Mother Earth (1990)

How did I get so lucky as to work with a bevy of talented women and Robin Williams in *An Evening with Friends of the Environment*? This 1990 ABC special was taped as a live event on a beautiful summer night at the outdoor Greek Theatre in the Hollywood Hills. The show was the brainchild of Jane Fonda who was married at the time to the politician Tom Hayden. As a representative of the beach town of Santa Monica, California, he was very concerned about the environment, and he and Jane probably discussed the idea of doing a special to raise awareness about the threat to our environment and to raise money for environmental causes. Part of the deal for getting the special on the air was that ABC allotted ten seconds between each commercial break to solicit contributions from viewers.

How did I get called in to direct and produce this show? Bottom line, Jane Fonda somehow connected with Olivia Newton-John, who had a friend in the entertainment news business. Her name was Nancy Gould Chuda, and Nancy and I were old friends from junior and senior high school. Olivia asked Nancy who she thought might be the right director for the special.

Nancy said, "I've got just the guy who should do this—Jeff Margolis." I'm told that Olivia responded, "Of course. Jeff directed my last special, and I've worked with him many times on the American Music Awards." Nancy set up a meeting for me to meet everyone and that was it! That's what friends are for.... Thank you, Nancy. And thank you Olivia.

Jane, Olivia, and Nancy brought together some amazing women: Meryl Streep, Bette Midler, Cher, Goldie Hawn, Lily Tomlin, and of course, Olivia, most of whom are mothers, which was emphasized in their remarks throughout the special. And then there was Robin Williams, who added a note of hilarity to the evening. And by the way, Robin managed to tip his hat to my eight-year-old son, Adam, who was sitting in the first row with my wife, Leslie. I'll tell you about that in a minute.

The entire production was a love letter to Mother Earth, and the audience at the outdoor Greek Theatre grabbed on to the message. It was really a call to action since not enough people were paying attention to the threat to our beautiful planet back in 1990.

The ninety-minute special opened with the fireball performer and comedian Bette Midler singing "You Gotta Have Friends." With her bright red hair, dressed in a khaki pantsuit, her smile stretching from ear to ear, she minced her way across that enormous stage of the Greek Theatre with the spotlight following her. Backed by a live orchestra and a trio, she held the audience in the palm of her hand. After singing the opening song, she told a few spicy and sarcastic jokes including one with a self-deprecating remark, "I am a living example of recycling." She followed up with "Wind Beneath My Wings," which earned her a standing ovation. She really set the tone for the show, which ended with Meryl Streep calling all the ladies on stage to sing the song "What A Wonderful World"—"that is an anthem of love to our beautiful, beautiful planet." And it was a lovefest wrapping itself around an important message without being preachy—the magic of a special doing its job.

What was it like working with Bette and Meryl on this incredible special? Many women are formidable, and then there's Bette Midler. She's one of a kind.

Before the show Bette wanted to rehearse at the home of Marc Shaiman, her musical director. He called me and said, "Bette's coming over to rehearse. Maybe you'd like to join us." Of course, I got in my car and drove right over. She was very friendly. But she also knew what she wanted. She said, "This is what I'm going to do."

"This is how long I'm going to perform."

"This is probably what I'll be wearing."

JEFF MARGOLIS with LOREN STEPHENS

"I need the lyrics on a prompter or cue cards."

"How far am I going to be from the camera?" She told me all the information that she needed me to know and asked me all the questions that she wanted answered. That was fine with me! I had all the answers.

Bette wanted to know if she was going to be performing at dusk or when darkness had set in. I told her it'd probably be dark because we decided to open the show as the sun was setting over the Hollywood Hills. Then she wanted to know what the lighting was going to be like, what the set was going to be behind her, and how close she was going to be to the audience.

Bette was very particular about how she was introduced, where she was going to stand, how far away her closeup camera was and where the prompter or cue cards were going to be. (In fact, she starts singing off stage and then comes out into full stage lighting—who doesn't recognize that voice?) She told me how long her musical numbers were going to be, and she said, "Don't edit them. If they're long, find somewhere else to get time out of the show. Do not edit my numbers."

"All right, Bette. I hear you loud and clear." I knew I was going to need Marc's help to get Bette to shorten one of the songs.

After she left Marc's house, I said to him, "That second number that she's performing is a little long for television. Can you cut at least a minute out of it? Can you talk her into it?"

"Well, you saw what you just saw, but she listens to me. I'll try." And he did. He got her to cut it so that I wouldn't have to. She was amenable to doing that and a team player.

And then there was Meryl Streep.

Meryl Streep became heavily involved with how we were going to get *An Evening with Friends of the Environment*'s message across. But I never expected that would include having a glass of wine at my house.

When we spoke on the phone, I told her, "It would be much better for me to get together with you. I'm happy to come wherever you are."

"Okay. What's your schedule look like tomorrow, and where do you live?"

"I'm in Beverly Hills," I told Meryl.

"Oh! I'm going to be in Beverly Hills tomorrow. What does your schedule look like in the afternoon?"

"It's open now."

"Just give me your address, and I'll come to your house." And she did!

She stayed maybe for an hour, and she said, "It sounds like it's going to be great. Tell me what time I have to be there to rehearse."

She left, and I watched her drive down the driveway, and I said, "Holy fuck, Meryl Streep was just at my house." (By that time, Meryl had already starred in *Silkwood*, *The French Lieutenant's Woman*, *Out of Africa*, and *Kramer vs. Kramer*, to name just a few.)

During the show Meryl delivered a personal monologue. She was funny, emotional, spectacular. I set up the shot to capture her beautiful face and her hand gestures. That bone structure—the camera loves it. A single flute underscored her words. She pointed out, "Here we are, and it's 1990." She reminisced about what life had been like for her ten years earlier—she had just had her first child and her first hit. Mentioning *Kramer vs. Kramer*, the audience erupted in applause. She went on with an anecdote illustrating her naivete back in 1980:

> *"Every Thursday I'd put all my garbage into a plastic bag and leave it on the curb for the garbage man to pick up. I didn't think about where it went—New Jersey, maybe? I wonder how things will be ten years from now. Will I be able to tell my daughter that she can take gulps of clean air; drink fresh water from the river?"*

In true Meryl Streep fashion, she filled the stage of the Greek Theatre with her heartfelt message.

Meryl also appeared in the finale when all the ladies—Bette, Cher, Olivia, and Lily—came out for the wrap-up song, "What A Wonderful World." Who knew that Meryl Streep could sing? She did, and she had the time of her life—at least it looked that way to me sitting in front of all the monitors in the remote truck.

My wife, Leslie, and our son, Adam, were sitting in the front row of the Greek Theatre, and Robin Williams had a straight shot of both of them.

He came out to applause and started his routine. Then he noticed my son, Adam, and he went over to him and said, "Tommy, how come you're sitting in the front row? I have to change my whole entire routine now! I didn't expect to see some eight-year-old kid sitting there." He did a whole bit off the cuff with Adam, calling him Tommy for some reason. It was a really cute way for Robin to open his act. And by the way, he changed nothing in his routine. Robin was hysterical, and as usual, the audience loved him.

Leslie called me when they got home and said, "In the car on the way home, Adam asked me what the word 'fuck' meant." I laughed for a good five minutes.

Robin wasn't about to clean up his act—not even for an eight-year-old. That was Robin. I loved him. He will be missed forever.

Mr. Bo Jangles: Sammy Davis Jr. (1990)

George Schlatter was the producer of the *Sammy Davis, Jr. 60th Anniversary Celebration* in 1990 to benefit the United Negro College Fund. (He and I had worked together many times before.) Billed as a tribute to Sammy's multifaceted career in show business, the evening, and the television special on ABC, turned out to be so much more than that. To this day, it is still considered to be one of the greatest evenings in television history, and one of the greatest television specials ever. At the start of pre-production, George and I went to Sammy's house to discuss the show with him. It was at that meeting that Sammy revealed he had throat cancer, and that he wouldn't be able to sing on his own anniversary special.

When we heard the news about Sammy's health, we were shocked and saddened, but George had a plan. He knew what he needed to do to get Sammy up on that stage to perform. George asked Sammy's wife, Altovise, to sneak a pair of Sammy's tap-dance shoes from his closet and give them to us. We didn't explain what we needed them for—it was going to be a huge surprise!

Because Sammy wasn't performing, we built a "queen's royal box" for him on the main floor of the stage at the Shrine Auditorium. That way all the performers could walk over and touch him—shake his hand, hug him, or kiss him. He sat in that royal box with his family and a couple of his closest friends.

The tap shoes that Altovise had given us were hidden under Sammy's chair. Gregory Hines performed on the show, and at the end of his performance, during the applause, he went over to give Sammy a hug and a kiss. After he did, he put his finger up and said to Sammy, "One minute." He got down on his knees and reached under Sammy's chair. Sammy couldn't figure out what he was doing. He pulled out the tap shoes and said, "Put them on, Sam. We're going to dance together."

Gregory held Sammy's hand and walked him on to a special tap floor we had installed on the stage. They just improvised a number. Gregory said to the band leader, who was a young man named Glen Roven, "Glen, give me a percussive beat." The drummer started and then the band joined in. Gregory and Sammy improvised for about a minute. It was brilliant, and oh so sad to think that this might be the last time we ever saw this incredibly gifted and talented artist perform. You can watch it on YouTube and see for yourself.

I received my first Emmy Award for producing and directing *Sammy's 60th*, and George Schlatter, who was the executive producer, received an Emmy for Best Variety Special of the Year. ABC had originally bought it as an hour special. Before we shot it, we knew how good it was going to be, and jam-packed full of stars, so George talked them into a ninety-minute special. It was in the day when the networks were still doing ninety-minute entertainment specials. Today, specials are traditionally one hour; on special occasions, two hours, and in the case of award shows, such as the Oscars, Grammys, Emmys, AMAs, and Tonys, three hours plus.

When we finished editing the show, it was so good, and so moving, and so entertaining, that we delivered a two-and-a-half-hour show to ABC. The executives said, "Wait a minute! The show's supposed to be ninety minutes!" George and I said to them, "Yeah, we know. Take a look at it, and you tell us what to cut." They looked at the show; of course, they couldn't cut and they didn't cut. The show aired exactly as we delivered it, all two and a half hours of pure gold. Every one of Sammy's friends who showed up for him was on the special. Nobody ended up on the cutting room floor.

The show was hosted by Eddie Murphy and opened with Frank Sinatra singing a song directly to Sammy and his family. There was one incredible performance after another—they never stopped: Michael Jackson, Liza Minnelli, Whitney Houston, Goldie Hawn, Ella Fitzgerald, Clint Eastwood, Debbie Allen, Bill Cosby, Gregory Peck, Dean Martin, Bob Hope, Richard Pryor, Stevie Wonder. Nobody wanted the evening to end. All who were there at the Shrine Auditorium in Los Angeles had so much love and respect for Sammy. You could feel it in the room all night long. It's hard to pick out a stand-out performance but a few come to mind: Whitney Houston singing "One Moment in Time"; Goldie Hawn delivering a short monologue to thank Sammy for making her feel so special, not once but twice in her career; Stevie Wonder at the electronic keyboards playing a song made famous by Sammy, "I've Gotta Be Me" followed by "Light of the World," a gospel song backed by a choir singing thanks and praise to Jesus (Sammy was a converted Jew, but what the heck); and Dionne Warwick singing the most passionate rendition of "Who Can I Turn To (When Nobody Needs Me)?" Throughout the show there were incredible film and television clips of Sammy's performances, beginning when he was just a little boy on the Chitlin' Circuit. Then in Las Vegas with the Rat Pack and to a performance on his own television series of "Mr. Bojangles," a song that haunted him throughout his life. In a famous interview with Dick Cavett, he admitted that he always wondered if he would end up like Bo Jangles. He also talked about his limited education and only being able to read at the fourth-grade level because he was always on the road, making money to support his family. Talk about the odds stacked against him, and yet he had this legendary career.

Michael Jackson wrote a special song for Sammy (along with Buz Kohan) called "You Were There." People knew that Sammy was dying of cancer. I think by the time we went to the Shrine Auditorium to shoot the show, the word had gotten out.

When the announcement was made to the press that Sammy Davis Jr. had throat cancer, George Schlatter's phone started ringing off the hook with people who wanted to be on the show and pay their respects to Sammy. He had broken so many barriers in the entertainment industry and had survived so many slights large and small. He had made it through a terrible automobile accident that took one of his eyes and suffered the slings and arrows of terrible prejudice. And yet he never forgot why he was put on this earth—to share his God-given talent as a singer, dancer, and actor.

Of course, Michael Jackson's song was the moment that stole the show when he came on stage and told Sammy that he wrote a song called "You Were There" especially for him and that he loved him.

The song paid tribute to Sammy, pointing out that because of his bravery, he opened the doors to other performers who had been barred from the fame that was their due. It was so heartfelt and meaningful, and a true celebration of Sammy's greatness, from one of his biggest and most appreciative fans, Michael Jackson.

Sammy passed away a few months after we taped the special, and the world was a poorer place for his passing. The special turned out to be Sammy's last public appearance, and I am sure that everyone who was in the Shrine Auditorium that night will never forget this incredible evening.

One last story to share. I've already mentioned what a great relationship George Schlatter and I have. So, we finished taping this incredible live event for television, and it was definitely *live*. No stops, no pick-ups from the first to the last moment.

The first person I saw when I left the remote truck was George, who was waiting for me so he could congratulate both of us for such a successful evening, or so I thought. He gave me a hug and then looked straight into my eyes and said, "Nice job, but don't worry, we can fix it all in editing." I was speechless, and for a moment, I actually believed him. Then I got that big George Schlatter "gotcha" laugh, another hug and a kiss, and he told me that I was brilliant, and that this night might have been the highlight of his television career. Coming from a man like George Schlatter with all his credits, those words meant everything to me.

Chairman of the Board: Doing It His Way: Frank Sinatra (1990)

As long as we're talking about George Schlatter, here's another collaboration.

George approached Frank Sinatra to do a CBS special on the occasion of his seventy-fifth birthday, and he agreed. Once Sinatra was on board, George asked me to direct this 1990 special—coproduced with Frank's younger daughter, Tina. The special would include a live show, which was to take place in Sinatra's home state of New Jersey at the famed Meadowlands' Brendan Byrne Arena. *Sinatra 75: The Best Is Yet to Come* was conceived of as a retrospective of Sinatra's monumental career from his beginnings in Hoboken, New Jersey, singing with a quartet to working with Jimmy Dorsey's band, and on and on. He was not only a crooner, but a great actor, and every now and then he put on his dancing shoes. And guess who taught him how to dance—none other than Gene Kelly.

The special included the live performance at the Meadowlands Arena, as well as film and television clips (two amazing clips included Sinatra performing with none other than Elvis Presley and joking around with Michael Jackson), and an interview with Sinatra at his home in Palm Springs with his wife, Barbara, his dogs, and a feisty parrot by his side.

The television special was introduced by the smooth Roger Moore, and then numerous other celebrities who stepped in front of the camera, all wishing Ol' Blue Eyes a Happy Birthday and reminiscing with a special Frank story, including Tony Bennett, Rosemary Clooney, Vic

Damone, Ella Fitzgerald, Whitney Houston, Gene Kelly, Sophia Loren, Shirley MacLaine, Paul Newman, and Sidney Poitier, just to name a few. Even Luciano Pavarotti made an appearance, as well as Quincy Jones, who called Frank Sinatra "the greatest pop singer of all time." Many agree that his phrasing was like no one else. Only Fred Astaire's phrasing is admitted to hold a candle to Frank Sinatra's. (Yes, Fred Astaire is not just the smoothest dancer to ever grace the floorboards; he was also an incredible singer.)

The concert at the Meadowlands' five-thousand-seat arena was packed with celebrities and Sinatra fans lucky enough to get a ticket. The show was intended to kick off Sinatra's Diamond Jubilee world tour, which would take him as far away as China. There was no risk of Frank slowing down anytime soon at seventy-five. The opening act was the married team of Steve Lawrence and Eydie Gormé. They were to kick off the show, then there would be a fifteen-minute intermission followed by Frank's appearance on stage. The only other person who appeared on stage with Frank was Liza Minnelli. He called her up from the audience and invited her to sing (wait for it) "New York, New York" with him.

So, we're at Meadowlands in New Jersey, Sinatra's home state. We're all set up to shoot the show. His son, Frank Sinatra Jr., is the orchestra's conductor. The concert was set up in the round, which is great for the audience but not so much for the director—me. You're always trying to avoid picking up another camera in the shot, because there are cameras covering all 360 degrees of the stage. My advice to other directors is don't accept a gig to shoot a special in the round if you can avoid it. But when your star wants it, and you want the gig, so be it. But be aware of the challenge!

Frank never came to rehearsals. We just shot the show as if it were live on the air. I had no insurance against a major mistake. This was walking on a tightrope without a net to catch me. I kept reminding myself, "It's going to be great!"

The morning of the concert, Frank showed up with his right-hand man, Jilly Rizzo. (Anything you wanted from Frank, you went through Jilly.) Frank was not happy because he wasn't feeling well.

Not a good way to start the day with a live concert in front of him. He wanted us to change the event and do it at another time. George Schlatter had to have a "come to Jesus" meeting with him. He told Frank, "Sorry. We're here. We've built the stage. The crew is here. It's costing a fortune to do this, and we've got to do it tonight."

Frank said to him, "Well, I'm not going to be at the top of my game. I'm sick." They called in doctors, and they gave him I don't know what to boost his energy, and it worked. The consummate pro that he was, he walked out on that stage and sang his ass off. Nobody had a clue that, earlier in the day, he felt lousy.

Steve Lawrence and Eydie Gormé came out to open the evening as planned. I directed it as if it were going to be the opening of the television special. After they finished their set, applause, applause, applause. I instructed the lighting director to turn the house lights up, and I asked the announcer to make his announcement: "Ladies and gentlemen, there will be a fifteen-minute intermission. Mister Sinatra will be out in fifteen minutes. Please be back in your seats by that time." At this point I was hit with what seemed like the worst stomachache I have ever had. I said to my assistant director, Allan Kartun, "Please give everyone a quick five-minute break. I've got to run to the bathroom. I'll be back as soon as I can." I also told my stage manager, David Wader, "I'm going off headset for a minute. I'll be right back. Whatever you do, don't let Sinatra come out until I get back." Where was my father's cork when I needed it? Although to tell the truth it wouldn't have solved my problem in this situation.

The bathroom seemed like a mile away from the remote truck where I was directing the show. I couldn't get there fast enough. I finally found the bathroom in the basement of the arena. I'm sitting on the toilet in this giant bathroom. I figured, "Okay, it took me five minutes to get here, five minutes to do whatever, and five minutes to get back."

Suddenly, I heard my stage manager David Wader down this long, echo-y hallway, yelling, "Jeff! *Jeff!*" I thought, "Oh my God, what's wrong?" And his voice kept getting closer and closer and finally he came in, and I said, "*What*, David? I'm taking a shit."

He said, "Sinatra said he's walking out in two minutes. He doesn't give a shit, pardon the pun, about the fifteen-minute intermission." He repeated himself, "He's walking out in *two minutes!*" I knew it was going to take me five minutes to get back to the truck. I quickly washed my hands and started running back to the truck. I heard Sinatra singing his opening number. He's out there singing, and I'm on my way back from the bathroom! Holy shit, are you kidding me right now?

I rushed into the truck, and Sinatra was already about a minute into his opening number. My assistant director, Allan, was really good, and he knew how I wanted to shoot the opening number. We had rehearsed with stand-ins, so Allan directed the first minute until I got back in my chair and put my headset back on. It was all great.

So much for the power of the director. When Sinatra is ready to start, that's it. Fortunately, I have a great team who can swing into action when I'm MIA for an unavoidable emergency.

After the Meadowlands performance, Sinatra continued on his Diamond Jubilee tour with a schedule that would challenge someone half his age. He filled arenas around the country, patterning each show after the Meadowlands performance. In the *Los Angeles Times* review of his appearance in San Diego in February 1991, he earned a rave:

> *"Trim, fit and rod upright, the silver haired star resembles a septuagenarian Caesar in whom sage authority has supplanted youthful vigor... He said, [toasting the audience with] a glass of Chivas Regal (the tour's sponsor), 'May you have a long life, and the best of life, and may the last voice you hear, be mine."*[4]

I have one more Sinatra story. I was directing another show with him a year later called *Welcome Home America*, to celebrate the USO's fiftieth anniversary, which my dear friend, George Schlatter, also pro-

4   John D'Agostino, "Music Review: Sinatra Covers Wear of the Years with Style, Charm," *Los Angeles Times*, February 11, 1991, https://www.latimes.com/archives/la-xpm-1991-02-11-ca-800-story.html.

duced. There were a number of sitting presidents in the audience including then-president George H. W. Bush.

The show was taped at the Universal Studios Amphitheater. The amount of time spent dealing with the Secret Service and FBI personnel to protect the presidents was mind-boggling.

On the day of the show, it was a nightmare getting to the theater even though we all had special passes. Traffic clogged the LA freeways and the surface streets. (Nothing unusual for those of us living in the film capital of the world.) Universal is right off the Hollywood Freeway on Lankershim Boulevard and up a long hill. Anyone going to the theater had to pass through numerous security checkpoints.

Sinatra was slated to open the show with a patriotic song. The military meant a lot to him. He had won an Oscar for *From Here to Eternity*, playing a soldier in World War II. As the son of Italian immigrants, he loved and appreciated everything that the United States gave to him. (At least that's what I've read about him, and I believe it.)

Meanwhile presidents had been arriving in the last hour on helicopters that landed and took off on the Universal lot, or they drove up the hill or through a backroad in a long line of limousines. It was like a military operation.

I went into the remote truck, and I touched base with my team. Cameras were covering the arrival of the presidents. The audience, who had passed through metal detectors, was already seated.

I was poised to start the show. In front of me at the director's spot on the console, I have a regular phone that's got two lines on it, and then there's an emergency phone. The only person who had that number was my wife, or once my kids were old enough, they would have access to that number as well, but absolutely no one else. God forbid it should ring! It probably meant that something was wrong. (Obviously this was before cell phones were commonplace.)

I was sitting in front of the monitors setting up my shots for the opening, and my emergency phone alerted me that there was a call. It's got a red flashing light on it, and the light started flashing.

I thought, "Oh God, I've got this big show to do. Please, God, don't let anything be wrong." I picked up the phone and said, "Hi, Honey, is everything okay?" thinking it must be my wife.

Somebody on the other end said, *"Who the fuck is this?"*

I said, "I'm Jeff, the director. You must have the wrong number because nobody's got this phone number."

He said, *"I've got this phone number. This is Sinatra.* I'm in my limousine, and I can't get to the fuckin' theater." And then he handed the phone to somebody—probably his man, Jilly. I heard Sinatra yelling and screaming in the background, "I'm supposed to open the show, and I can't get to the goddamn theater!"

The city of Los Angeles, the police department, and traffic control had closed a lot of the freeway off-ramps into Universal. The audience had been there for two hours before the presidents arrived and before the show started.

Sinatra was running late because he was stuck on the Ventura Freeway, and he was going ballistic. How he got my phone number, to this day, I can't figure out.

I said to the person on the phone, "You're talking to the wrong guy. I'm the director; I can't do anything about the traffic. Let me get somebody who might be able to help you. Give me a number, and I'll have somebody call you right back." I called George Schlatter and said, "Your friend Frank just called, and he is having a shit fit because he's stuck on the freeway and can't get here. Here's the number." I hung up and George took it from there.

Frank didn't make it on time. The presidents were sitting there, and we couldn't keep them waiting any longer. We had to start, so somebody else opened the show. Frank did show up, and man was he pissed off! Holy shit! And it wasn't because he was feeling sick this time. My stage manager (Dave Wader again) said he couldn't even talk to him. But Frank went out on stage as if nothing happened—he was the consummate performer as he always is, and he had a job to do. Frank said, "I'm here and I'm singing my song," and "Mister Presidents, I'm glad you're here. Welcome, and this is for you." He sang "The House I Live In" perfectly, smiled at the audience, and took his bows. It was an emotionally fitting song to express Sinatra's patriotism and love for this country. Then he walked off stage, got back in his limo, and left. I never said a word to him other than that brief telephone call, but I'm sure that George said thank you and goodbye on his way to the limo. I just carried on with the business at hand and delivered the show.

Extra! Extra! Read All About It (1996)

Ebony magazine was the first large-circulation African American magazine in the United States. Founded in 1945 right after World War II by John H. Johnson, the monthly magazine carried stories about African American personalities in the arts, news, culture, and sports for over fifty years. Modeled after *Look* and *Life* magazines, it reflected the successes of the African American community. (*Ebony* is still going strong with a monthly circulation of over one million.) In 1996, it was an honor for me to put together this special for ABC. *Celebrate the Dream*: *50 Years of* Ebony *Magazine* portrayed its history through music, dance, readings, and film clips. As you can imagine, when *Ebony* magazine calls to ask you to appear on a show paying tribute to its pages, you say yes.

The show took place at the Shrine Auditorium in Los Angeles, which over the years became one of my stomping grounds, for sure. Some of the celebrities who took part in the show were Whitney Houston, Michael Bolton, Debbie Allen, Halle Berry, Quincy Jones, Will Smith, Patti LaBelle, the Four Tops, Cicely Tyson, Smokey Robinson, Luther Vandross, and Stevie Wonder. There were thirty-two performers, sports figures, and speakers in all. There was also archival film footage of Lorraine Hansberry, the playwright of *A Raisin in the Sun*, and a film package of sports and political luminaries. The anniversary celebration was produced under Ted Harbert's chairmanship at ABC, and two heavyweight advertisers—Coca-Cola and Ford—sponsored it for airing on Thanksgiving to capture the largest audience possible.

And who better to host this television event than Oprah Winfrey? Oprah and I worked together on a number of specials. The year that

Quincy Jones produced the Oscars, we featured Oprah greeting all the stars on the red carpet, making it the opening of the show. And she also participated in the tribute to Quincy Jones (which I'll talk about later).

Oprah was a delight to work with, as always. "What do you want me to do? What time do you want me to be there? Where do you want me to stand? Yes, I'll come to rehearsal."

She is the consummate professional, but if Oprah doesn't like something, she will tell you! A couple of times she said, "I read the copy, and that really isn't the way I speak. That doesn't work for me, Jeff, so I've already talked to the writers, and they're going to change it for me, so you'll be seeing some new copy."

Everything else I asked her to do she did, and she did it perfectly.

When we were finished shooting the show, and I was sitting in the editing room the phone rang. My production assistant picked up and said to me, "Excuse me, Jeff, Oprah Winfrey's on the phone for you."

"What? It's got to be a joke." So, I picked up the phone and said, "Hi Oprah; how are you doing?" (Very matter-of-factly.)

"Hey Jeff, how are you doing?" Oprah's got that voice. I've never heard anybody impersonate Oprah. It was definitely her.

"I've been thinking about a couple of things I did in the *Ebony* special that I'd like to point out to you, and maybe you can help me look better before it airs." Or she might have said, "I didn't like the way I said something. Maybe you can look at the dress rehearsal, and—I don't know, edit something together that I did on the live show with something that I might have done better in the dress rehearsal since you've got it on tape."

She had some really good suggestions, so I made her fixes. Nothing gets by Oprah.

When we were taping *Ebony*'s fiftieth, everything that Oprah did was spot-on. She didn't make a mistake that I ever saw, but obviously she made a couple of mistakes in her mind that bothered her. For a star of her magnitude to call me in the editing room—to track me down and call me personally rather than to have her "people" do it—that was special, and I did whatever she wanted. For somebody to care that much is really impressive to me…that's Oprah.

One of the many highlights of the evening was a pregnant Whitney Houston singing "I Love the Lord" with the Georgia Mass Choir, and then she sang "Joy to the World." She took everyone to church. The evening was a full two hours of music, comedy, and fifty years of great film clips. Needless to say, it was spectacular, and this anniversary celebration garnered an NAACP Image Award for Outstanding Variety Series/Special.

But this special was not without controversy. *Variety* summed up what happened behind the scenes and how some of the ABC affiliates refused to carry the show:

> GOOD MORNING: *Howcum ABC's Atlanta and Detroit affiliates, WSB and WXYZ respectively, did not air the network's two-hour Thanksgiving special, "Celebrate the Dream: 50 Years of Ebony Magazine"? ABC Entertainment chairman Ted Harbert admitted to me the web is investigating fully, adding, "I am so upset. I went crazy when I learned about it. It was the local stations' decisions." But he can't imagine why. Two of the sponsors are also maddened: Coca-Cola, which h.q.'s in Atlanta, and Ford, in Detroit. Why any station would fail to air a show of such pride is insulting and baffling. Also awaiting word is John Johnson, publisher, chairman and CEO of Johnson Publications (Ebony). Jeff Margolis, who exec produced the special, told me, "ABC didn't know about it (the absent affiliates) until the ratings came out (lowest in its network timeslot, with 4.6/9) and the breakdown sheet showed eight (!) stations did not carry it. The show boasted a powerful list of hosts, performers and live sports legends plus a filmpackage (by Doug Stewart, who will ditto on the Oscars for the 15th year) of sports figures including Satchel Paige, Jackie Robinson, Joe Louis, Willie Mays, Arthur Ashe, Wilt Chamberlain, Kareem Abdul-*

Jabbar, Florence Griffith Joyner, Michael Jordan and O.J. Simpson. Margolis admits, "I fought using the O.J. Simpson clip. I didn't want it in there. I felt strongly to get rid of it. But 65% of my staff was African-American and they felt strongly about it. After all, he was a Heisman winner, and a great African-American athlete. I understood their reasoning. So I used it. But a number of people were offended that he was included." Margolis next directs Dick Clark's "American Music Awards" (for the 16th year). Jan. 27 on ABC.[5]

Star Power: Elizabeth Taylor (1997)

Elizabeth Taylor! Talk about a superstar. Wow! And what a way to celebrate her sixty-fifth birthday. It was 1997, and there were more than thirty major stars invited to this party at Hollywood's Pantages Theatre billed as *Happy Birthday Elizabeth: A Celebration of Life*, including Michael Jackson (who escorted her), Madonna, John Travolta, Carol Burnett, Kevin Bacon, Cher, Alec Baldwin, Rod Stewart, Whoopi Goldberg, Hugh Grant, Drew Barrymore, Roseanne Barr, Lily Tomlin, David Copperfield, and Shirley MacLaine, just to name some of the guests. (Yes, these are just some of the guests.) Some performed, and some came by just to "kiss the ring" and say happy birthday. The evening was most notably a way to give Elizabeth Taylor all the accolades she deserved, not just for her legendary career as one of Hollywood's most iconic film stars, but for her tireless work to bring AIDS into the forefront of America's consciousness. Since 1985 she has raised millions of dollars and pressured Congress to do more to fight against the scourge of this disease and put a human face on its victims with bravery. This special was the quintessential example of marrying a birthday celebration special to an important cause, and Elizabeth Taylor was the ringleader.

---

5   Army Archerd, "Affils shock ABC, don't air Ebony spec," *Variety*, December 11, 1996. https://variety.com/1996/voices/columns/affils-shock-abc-don-t-air-ebony-spec-1117862999/.

The job of organizing and coordinating all these stars and their entourages and their security details on these big specials is a challenge to say the least. But hats off to the talent departments and production coordinators, who always pull it off.

So just a quick side story. Michael Jackson participated in this special because he had a very close relationship with Elizabeth. He wanted to make sure that his performance to celebrate her sixty-fifth was magical and memorable. Michael pre-recorded the tracks and rehearsed the song on his own for weeks. The day of the show, he arrived early in the morning in his "studio van." He actually had a small van with a complete state-of-the-art recording studio built in. He parked right next to the remote truck, where I was.

On our first break from rehearsal in the theater, Michael sent for me to come to his van so that I could hear the song he was going to perform. He wanted me to be familiar with the music before he came on stage to rehearse for cameras. When I walked into his van, I was completely blown away. Only Michael Jackson could have something this unique. He had pretty much designed it on his own, and it was spectacular. (Would you expect anything else?) He played the track for me once, then a second time where he sang along with the music. The sound was better than almost anything that I had ever heard in a real recording studio.

When Michael Jackson took to the stage to sing his original song "Elizabeth, I Love You," the audience went wild. With the wind machine blowing, and the lighting making Michael's white shirt glow, his words expressed not only what Elizabeth had endured as a child star but the similarities in their experiences. He also expressed his gratitude for Elizabeth's loyalty to him, "Remember the time when I was alone/You stood by my side." Michael was referring to all the trauma around the allegations against him two years earlier. I worked with him during that period, and you'll read about the night that never happened later.

Q (1998)

Quincy Jones... The First 50 Years (1998) was a two-hour ABC tribute to Quincy's multifaceted career as a musical arranger, composer, producer, and all-around gentleman. It meant the world to me because Quincy was a good friend and such a wonderful man. I love him and I wanted this evening to be really special for him, and I wanted this television special to reflect that.

The first call inviting celebrities to participate went to Quincy's best friend, Oprah. "Where do I need to be, and when do I need to be there?" That was her response, and every person we asked to be on the show had a similar response. This man is one of the most beloved men in all of the entertainment industry, and one of the most powerful.

I have so much to say about Quincy Jones. Talk about a mensch. If you look in the dictionary under *mensch*, his picture will be right next to the definition. He always says to me to this day, "You're my brother from another mother." That's the relationship I have with him. I had worked with Quincy a number of times. One of the most important specials we did together was *The Kennedy Center Presents: Concert of the Americas* in 1994, celebrating the cultural diversity of the region. Quincy was the executive producer, and I produced and directed. Leaders of thirty-four nations from Latin America, the Caribbean, and Canada were there. It was an absolute nightmare because of all the secret service and security issues that we had to deal with before we could concentrate on the show itself. There were also so many stars there with their entourages and security, plus an audience of about four thousand people at an auditorium in Miami. The concert featured performances by Celia Cruz, Jimmy Smits, Daisy Fuentes, Paul Anka, Liza Minnelli, and CeCe Winans, among many others. The executive producer along with Quincy Jones was David Salzman, a television veteran of Lorimar and Warner Bros. What a blast to have so many international stars to spice everything up and showcase music of the region.

JEFF MARGOLIS *with* LOREN STEPHENS

Oy, talk about pressure to get everything done on time, in one take. When you're dealing with all these world leaders and their security teams, you start when the schedule says you're going to start, and you stop when the schedule says you're supposed to finish. *No* adjustments or changes. We followed the schedule down to the second. The show was to air two weeks after taping on PBS, so I had plenty of time to edit.

The entire show was put together in under nine weeks from start to finish, and it was only because of Quincy Jones and his telephone calls that everything came together so quickly.

Anyway, back to Quincy's special, which we shot at the Pasadena Civic Auditorium. It was my idea to do the Quincy Jones star-showcase celebration, but I had to convince him to do it first. I said, "You've worked with everybody from Michael Jackson to Frank Sinatra, and just about every other singer in the business. You've scored movies. You came up with *The Fresh Prince of Bel-Air* on television. You've worked with all these artists, so many who have had their own television specials...and you've never done your own! You need to do a special. It's time!"

His first response to me was, "Well, I think that when people like me do a television special, it's usually because their careers are just about over or they're about to die."

"No, no, no, maybe I can convince you with the right title. Let me think about it for a day or two." Benn Fleishman and I were at a meeting at ABC and they asked about titles. We threw out a few ideas, and then Benn came up with a great title that everyone agreed set the right tone: *Quincy Jones... The First 50 Years.* (Remember Dick Clark's advice to me? Titles are important!)

"I love it; you got it. I'm in." That was all it took to convince Quincy and we were on our way. That was the title of the special which aired on ABC in 1998!

Quincy and I worked very closely because it was his show! He is Quincy Fucking Jones. This was his first time celebrating himself—he was always producing shows and celebrating other people. Listen to some of the people who showed up to celebrate with Quincy: Stevie

Wonder, Halle Berry, Gloria Estefan, Ray Charles, Patti Austin, Beau Bridges, Little Richard, Smokey Robinson, Bernadette Peters, Nancy Wilson, Jolie Jones (Quincy's daughter), Lesley Gore, Savion Glover, and Maya Angelou—and those are just some of Quincy's guests.

The show opened with Stevie Wonder at the piano playing "We Are the World," and we were off and running. In the middle of the song Tap Dogs came out and put down portable metal plates so they could do a rabble-rousing tap routine, and then Stevie wrapped up the number. He came back later to sing "One Hundred Ways" and played the harmonica.

It seemed as if most of the songs were focused on the theme of love, or love lost. Bernadette Peters sold "I'm a Fool to Want You" like nobody's business from the American songbook. And then James Ingram and Patti Austin performed the duet "How Do You Keep the Music Playing" from the movie *Best Friends*. Quincy said that this was one of his very favorite songs, and Patti and James did the song proud.

There was a montage of some of the film titles that Quincy scored—over forty—and a clip from the Montreux Jazz Festival where Ray Charles sang "My Buddy, Quincy Jones." The camera caught Quincy with tears in his eyes. It wasn't the only time during the evening for tears as each performer sang or danced something special to honor their friend, Q.

The evening ended with Oprah and Dr. Maya Angelou on stage. Dr. Angelou summed up the role of the composer as expressed by the great American composer and orchestrator Aaron Copeland: "A composer gives us himself."

I'll tell you, that was an evening to remember. There was so much love and emotion in the theater; no one will ever forget this night. And I'll never forget a quote from Quincy himself, "A song should have all the beauty and color of a rose." *Wow*! That is my friend, Quincy Jones.

To Israel with Love (1998)

Every Jewish performer in Hollywood and more came to wish Israel a happy birthday in 1998, on *To Life! America Celebrates Israel's 50th.* I can't believe how the Shrine Auditorium in Los Angeles could become a synagogue, church, town hall, award show venue, and concert hall, all at once. We had satellite feeds from Israel with some of its biggest music stars performing live and best-loved stars paying tribute to Israel's special birthday. I think it was something like three o'clock in the morning there. Setting up all these satellite feeds between Los Angeles and Tel Aviv and Jerusalem in Israel was extremely complicated. The engineers who put this all together were amazing. Our control room looked like the control center at NASA right before a rocket takes off. So exciting, but so complicated. For me, as the director, coordinating the back and forth to Israel and directing a live television special at the same time was quite a chore. Needless to say, I loved every minute. I knew it was going to be great!

Look at who was there: Steven Spielberg, Stevie Wonder, Natalie Cole, Harry Connick Jr., Fran Drescher, Michael Douglas, Dustin Hoffman, Richard Dreyfuss, Mili Avital, Kathy Bates, Ted Danson, Kirk Douglas, Sid Caesar, and once again, the list goes on. And once again, an unforgettable, memorable evening.

We Need Another Christmas Right This Very Minute: Amy Grant (1999)

It seems that Christmas and I have a real affinity for one another. Perry Como once said to me. "You're Jewish and Jews do Christmas better than anyone, because you don't know what you can and can't do; you just do it, and that's why your Christmas specials are the best. And don't forget, Irving Berlin, who was Jewish, wrote 'White Christmas,' one of the best Christmas songs ever written." It was a match made in heaven to put Amy Grant and me together for her own Christmas special in 1999. *Amy Grant: A Christmas to Remember* was one of those magical experiences that doesn't come along very often, and I was thrilled to be chosen as the director. Amy Grant is one of the sweetest people I've ever had the pleasure of working with. She has the voice of an angel, a strong spiritual core, and a lovely gentleness that the camera picks up and embraces. And that subtle southern Georgia accent—*irresistible.*

Oh, and did I tell you how sweet she is? The special was timed to the release of her album of the same title, giving it an extra push up the charts for pop and Christian music.

Listen to this for a Christmas special: a snow-covered frozen Lake Louise in Banff, Canada, freezing cold weather, nonstop snow, fireplaces inside a majestic ski chalet, and Amy Grant singing with Tony Bennett. How much better than that can it get? Add CeCe Winans singing "Silent Night" and the hottest boy band at the time, 98 Degrees, and we had a recipe for a totally amazing one-hour Christmas special on CBS. I couldn't wait to put the show together as a gift tied up in a bow for all our viewers. By the way, it snowed almost the entire time we were shooting. I promise you I didn't engineer that, but it added to the magic and beauty of the show. And the hotel we shot in was already dressed up spectacularly for Christmas. There were Christmas trees, lights, bulbs, angels, sparkling stars, and—well, you get the picture.

I worked with Amy Grant when I directed *ABC Presents a Royal Gala* in London for Prince Charles and Princess Diana at the London Palladium. The royals wanted Amy to be on the show, so I called her, and she gladly accepted. She was a big hit that night—her first time performing in London and, of course, the first time for Charles and Diana. They loved her performance. And after that, I worked with Amy numerous times when I was directing the American Music Awards for Dick Clark. She appeared regularly as a nominated artist.

Okay, now back to Christmas in Canada. At Lake Louise, we created a family together for this Christmas special. Amy and I became very close, and she relied on me a lot to take good care of her and make sure that she looked and sounded as good as she possibly could. The show meant a lot to her. As a Christian and pop singer with a number of Christmas hits to her credit, she wanted to be sure that the special properly showcased her talent and her devotion to her faith.

She incorporated a number of gospel songs into the show, which she sang with CeCe Winans. Amy is known today, amongst other titles, as the queen of Christian pop. (She released a feature film in 2021, *The Jesus Music*, highlighting songs that crossed over from the world of Christian music to a wider audience.)

Although Amy was very involved in the creation of her show, she left it up to me to pick all the locations for all the songs, but we worked together to select which songs in her catalog would be featured in the special. At the time, she had a friend who was managing her, so she was also involved in the song selection too. Surprisingly, Amy never asked to see a rough cut of the finished show before it aired. She said, "Jeff, I trust you. I'll watch it the night it's on TV." That made me feel great—for her to have so much trust in me meant an awful lot.

By the way, just a side note but very important to me. This special was a huge undertaking, just like shooting a small movie. I knew that with the time and budget constraints, I wanted some insurance for myself. I called my friend Alan Carter, who is a brilliant editor/director. Alan responded, "Christmas, Canada, Amy Grant, I'm in." I don't think I could have done it without him. For the first and only time ever, I shared a director credit with Alan. He really contributed a lot and deserved it. (If you want to see more of Alan's directing chops, watch *The Voice* on NBC; he has been there since the premiere for its entire twenty-three-season run.)

Now, back to the show once again. I keep getting sidetracked. Oh well! The first guest I booked on the show was Tony Bennett. Amy said, "Oh, if you could only get Tony Bennett...I don't know why he'd want to do my show, but oh my gosh, if he would...."

I had some history with Tony so it wasn't entirely beyond the realm of possibility to book him—and it was Amy Grant. I had worked with Tony a number of years before on a special that he was a guest on. Tony was a dream to work with then. He didn't make a fuss about anything. He and his son, Danny, who was his manager, just hopped a cab from his Central Park West apartment—no limousine requested—and arrived the day of the show at 30 Rockefeller Plaza in

Midtown Manhattan. He hadn't participated in the camera blocking the previous day, which was fine with me. I met him at the curb, and it was freezing cold. We said, "Hello, so good to see you," we hugged, and I walked him to his performance spot in front of the Christmas tree above the skating rink, showed him where the cameras were going to be positioned for his segment, and told him to feel free to move around the space. We rehearsed on camera, and it was freezing outside. I was in the control room at 30 Rock eight floors up, which by the way was the same control room used by *Saturday Night Live*. What a thrill that was! I communicated with Tony through my stage manager, who was on set. We rehearsed Tony's number, and I wanted to do it again, to make it even better for Tony. I said to my stage manager, "Could you ask Tony if we could do it one more time?"

Tony's response was, "Did I do something wrong? Do I need to change something?" I assured him that he had done everything perfectly. I just wanted to give the lighting director and camera operators the opportunity to make minor adjustments. After the second take, he asked, "Was I better?" How could Tony Bennett be any better than he was? He was the best. I put on my heavy coat and gloves and told the stage manager that I wanted to talk with Tony. Down the eight flights and out into the freezing cold. "Is everything okay with you?" I asked him.

"Yeah, it looks like everything is going to be beautiful." I assured him that he didn't need to change a thing. I told him we had a dressing room that he could hang out in until the show, or he could go back to his apartment. "No, I'll just stay here. It's fine. Don't worry about me."

I told him I probably wouldn't see him again because I was going to be upstairs in the control room. I said, "I just want to thank you for being here. It's such a pleasure to work with you and have you on the show." And I gave him a big hug. He put his arms around me, and I almost started to cry. Here I was in Rockefeller Center in front of the Christmas tree in the freezing cold, hugging the great Tony Bennett. It was too much—he was the guy my dad listened to on his record player when I was a kid. Despite his fame and fortune, he is so humble. Sometimes the bigger the star, the more humble, and that was especially true of Tony. He always wanted to make sure he gave the director what they needed. He is a consummate artist and one of the nicest guys on the face of the earth. How lucky was I to have worked with him?

So back to the Amy Grant Christmas special. I called Danny Bennett, Tony's son, and said, "Listen, I'm doing an Amy Grant Christmas special for CBS, and it's going to be really spectacular. We're doing it in Alberta, Canada, in and around Banff and at Lake Louise, which is in Banff National Park. Amy and I would really like for Tony to be on the show. You can come up to Banff and stay for a week if you'd like to. I'll do everything I need to do with Tony in one day. Work one day and stay for a week, what do you say?" I held my breath hoping for a resounding yes. (I'm a pretty good salesman, but I didn't get an immediate response one way or the other.)

Danny said, "Let me talk to Tony about it, but I think he'd love it." Danny called me back the same day and said, "Tony loves working with you, and he'd love to meet Amy Grant, and he'd love to be on the show." I was over the moon and couldn't wait to tell Amy.

He came to Canada with us and stayed for a while. I only needed him to work for one day, as promised, and he was a delight. I did one interior setup with him singing a solo song, then he did a duet with Amy in the most beautiful interior setting at the lodge, and then we did one exterior setup with both of them.

The show was so much fun that Amy and her guests really didn't want to leave Banff. What a great time we all had. I was up there for two weeks with the production staff and technical crew prepping and scouting location shots for the songs as well as scenic panoramic shots that would be intercut with the performances. I wanted to make the viewers feel as if they were spending Christmas with all of us. The hotel looked magnificent. It was all decked out in its Christmas splendor with Christmas trees everywhere, candles, pine boughs, and crackling fireplaces—all a backdrop to gorgeous interior shots. The exterior was the magnificent terrain of the Canadian Rockies and Lake Louise.

We all had dinner together the nights that we could, and then we'd sit by the fire and just talk and sing. We had a pianist with us who casually went over to the piano, and one night, Tony and Amy started to sing just for us. I wished I had a camera to cover that impromptu moment, but it was probably better that I didn't because it would have changed the feeling in the room.

Amy was so comfortable around her guests. We did a number of vignettes with her talking about family and faith with CeCe Winans (they are both mothers) and a roundtable with 98 Degrees sharing how they formed their group. These moments were intercut between the singing numbers, which were spectacular: 98 Degrees singing "I'll Be Home for Christmas" a cappella; and CeCe Winans singing "What Child Is This?," a beautiful version of "O Holy Night," and a duet with Amy on guitar, "Count Your Blessings (Instead of Sheep)"—their voices blended together so beautifully.

And of course, there were the numbers with Tony Bennett. First, he sang "The Christmas Song (Chestnuts Roasting on an Open Fire)" and then a duet with Amy, "I've Got My Love to Keep Me Warm."

We created an impromptu theater inside the hotel for Tony and Amy and invited all the hotel guests so we had a built-in audience. Can you imagine the excitement the guests felt having a surprise performance with Amy Grant and Tony Bennett? What a way to spend an afternoon on vacation. I'm sure anyone who was there talked about it for years afterward. I know I did.

The segment begins with friendly banter between Tony and Amy when she admits that she first saw Tony performing when she was just thirteen years old. She recounts that it's twenty-five years later (if you do the math, you'll realize that Amy was thirty-eight, and wow, did she look good). Tony can't resist flirting with her, and she actually blushed on camera. What woman wouldn't be flattered when Tony Bennett sings to her, "I've Got My Love to Keep Me Warm"? Tony oozes charm. He can't help himself. Ever since he broke on the scene in 1951 singing "Because of You," he's made women's hearts beat just a little faster. And he is so sincere. There isn't a phony bone in his body, which makes every word he sings sound true.

Tony couldn't have been nicer, and he couldn't have been happier to be with us in Canada. Before he left to go to the airport and back to New York, he sent for me. I remember driving back to the hotel from one of the exterior locations to say goodbye to him. We hugged and kissed, and he said, "I always have so much fun working with you, and it always seems to be at Christmas time [referring to the Rockefeller Center Christmas tree lighting show], so I guess I'll see you next Christmas!"

I said, "I hope to find something in between for us to do together, and if not, then next Christmas it is." We hugged again, and he was off to the airport.

Before the special ends, Amy and her guests sing a beautiful song called "Grown-Up Christmas List," which we shot on location at numerous exterior and interior locations all around Banff. The show's final number is Amy Grant standing all alone at an altar in a small wooden country church that we located somewhere in a village in the Canadian Rockies—too picturesque for words. She is wearing a red velvet dress, surrounded by poinsettias and candles and sings "Silent Night." At the end of the song, she simply looks straight into the camera with that beautiful face, those sparkling eyes, and that soft, gentle voice and says, "May the peace and joy of the season be yours. Merry Christmas, everybody." She just makes you smile, and you have to fall in love with her. (I certainly did.)

When I returned to Los Angeles with all the footage and went into the editing bay with my editor, we made some creative decisions. I intercut some very funny outtakes into the special: Amy with whipped cream on the tip of her nose from the cup of cocoa she is trying to sip; CeCe Winans holding up a thermometer that reads zero degrees; a wide shot revealing all the lighting and sound equipment, cables and cameras, and the small army of people that it takes to create all these beautiful shots. We added sound effects such as a crackling fire (the quintessential sound of Christmas); rushing water; and a lot of split screens, especially in the 98 Degrees number, "This Gift."

And before I drop the mic, you can watch the credits roll, which included Jeff Margolis Productions, Amy Grant Productions (a star who was now running her own production company), and, as the names roll by, there is Peter Margolis, my brother whom I hired as the associate director. Always fun to work with family when you get the opportunity. And now, my son, Adam, who is a brilliant camera operator and has already earned eight Emmy Awards, works on every one of my shows. That's the best, when your child grows up around the business, gets the "bug" at a young age, and follows his or her dream. (The apple really doesn't fall far from the tree, does it?) I'm so lucky. I'm sure that one day soon, Adam will be producing, and I know he will hire me to direct for him. I can't wait. In the meantime, he's working on *Dancing with the Stars*, *America's Got Talent*, and *American Idol*. We speak every week to compare notes on the shows, and I always tell him what a great job he's done! And it's true.

I was so happy I got to work with Julie once again.

About to rehearse with Carol.

Carol and Julie, two of my favorites.

Lily Tomlin, Cher, Goldie Hawn, Meryl Streep, Bette Midler, and Olivia
Newton John. Imagine directing all of this talent in one special.

Michael Jackson and I at the Sammy Davis Jr. special.

Gregory Hines trying to teach me to tap. It didn't work.

This was a really special "Special."

Who doesn't love Oprah?

With Amy Grant trying to keep warm in the freezing Canadian mountains.

One of my personal heroes, Tony Bennett.

On location with Amy and Tony in Canada.

Toni Tennille and I got to work with Ella Fitzgerald, what a thrill for me.

Even when you're as sick as a dog, no matter what kind of
show you're directing, "the show must go on"

When you have to make script notes, you have to find the only available seat on the set.

189

CHAPTER 16

THE NEW MILLENNIUM: THE LIGHTS STAY ON

As THE BALL CAME DOWN IN TIMES SQUARE MARKING THE BEGINNING OF THE 2000s, we all breathed a collective sigh of relief that televisions didn't go dark, that computers didn't malfunction, and that we were all still standing the next day. There had been so many warnings of doom and gloom but fortunately it was a case of "Chicken Little, the sky is falling." And as for me, the first decade of the new century was slated with one award show after another (the Daytime Emmys, the Screen Actors Guild Awards, the TV Land Awards, and the Academy of Country Music Awards, to name a few). Everyone wanted an award of one sort or another, and I was right there to produce and record these events for posterity. Many of the specials we produced were wall-to-wall music with celebrities from previous decades who were thrilled to reprise some of their best hits.

Dancin' the Night Away (2002)

My friend John Hamlin at ABC and his wacky ideas for specials! They always worked. *The Disco Ball* might have been by far the most fun of all the specials. Disco music was making a resurgence in 2002. The show featured so many hit songs and so many colorful artists performing their hits. I was lucky to hire Tisha Fein, who was a talent booker on the Grammy Awards, and she booked the hell out of this special. She got everyone to come and perform, including Paula Abdul, KC and the Sunshine Band, Village People, Gloria Gaynor, Usher, the Pointer Sisters, Aaron Carter, George Lopez, Mýa, Ryan Seacrest, Whoopi Goldberg, and so many more. The Shrine Auditorium in Los Angeles was turned into a giant disco club, mirror ball and all. Performance stages were built in the opera boxes, in the balcony, and everywhere else that they could be constructed throughout the house, and the music never stopped, from Village People's "YMCA" to a surprise performance by Whoopi Goldberg of "Last Dance"—to end the evening, of course. From the start of the show until we had to kindly ask them to leave, the audience never sat down. I mean, really, they were standing and dancing in the aisles until the music stopped. It was a ball.

We taped the show on October 12, 2002, and ABC aired it right away. The ratings were great, and John Hamlin and I are still talking about doing *Disco Ball 2*.

Who knows, it could happen!

"Ain't No Mountain High Enough" (2004)

Ten years before Berry Gordy founded Motown Records in Detroit, the RCA Victor record label introduced the 45 rpm single, "a format that would revolutionize pop music." Featuring a major song on Side A and a secondary song on Side B, the 45 sold for sixty-five cents in the 1950s. Jukeboxes all over the country played 45s, and their popularity grew through the early 1970s when more than two hundred million sold. And then their popularity started to die out, making way for long-playing 33s, tape, the compact disc, electronic formats, and now back to single-release format through Spotify and other streaming services.

Capitalizing on the popularity of the 45, Motown released many of its greatest songs on the 45 format, creating a home for some of popular music's iconic talent with the likes of the Supremes, the Temptations, the Jackson 5, and other group and individual artists. And at the helm through forty-five years was the father of Motown, Berry Gordy.

The ABC two-hour special *Motown 45* (May 2004) paid tribute to that history and referenced the 45 format in its set design that had a floor labeled "45" in the shape of a record, stairs and scaffolding for artists to perform on, and the big stage of the Shrine Auditorium, which was filled with singers, dancers, and a band performing on three levels at the back of the stage. It was big, big, *big*, and there even were flame twirlers in the aisles of the audience and on stage just in case the singers weren't enough to hold your attention. And of course, great lighting and scenic moves so that the television audience would not miss a beat.

I produced and directed this two-hour special with more than twenty-five artists, including my friend Lionel Richie, as host and performer; Cedric the Entertainer as his co-host; and Mary Wilson, Cindy Birdsong, Nick Lachey, the Backstreet Boys, Macy Gray, Smokey Robinson, Gladys Knight, the Temptations, Brian McKnight, and Michael McDonald among the many featured singers through- out the evening, as well as talented backup singers, and, of course, the band delivering "wall-to-wall music." And Dick Clark made an appearance as well.

Lionel Richie opened the show singing "All Night Long" and then got the audience involved in the theme of the evening: mar- rying the classics with the contemporary. Many of the songs pre- sented were written by the original stable of Motown talent (such as Marvin Gaye) and performed by the next generation. For example, Nick Lachey sang "I'll Be There" with Jermaine Jackson—their voices blended seamlessly and showed off their talent. Raven-Symoné sang "Superstition," one of Stevie Wonder's greatest hits, and on and on— all night long.

And then there was Smokey Robinson, who made "Just to See Her" famous. (Listening to him, I wonder how many babies were con- ceived to that sultry tune?) After his performance he gave a shoutout to Berry Gordy sitting in the first row, center, of the audience: "We are standing here because of the dream of one man, Berry Gordy," who was one of the first Black record producers in the industry and remains a presence in the record industry today.

One of the many highlights of the special was Brian McKnight singing "What's Going On," originally sung by Marvin Gaye. If you listen to the lyrics, they are relevant today, telling a story of violence and strife, riots, and restlessness in America.

Berry Gordy put his finger on the pulse of this country through music, and to give him his due with this special was particularly important. The evening ended with all the talent coming out on stage singing "Ain't No Mountain High Enough," and we are still climbing it. I am really proud that Jeff Margolis Productions has its banner on this special. What an honor.

"Pow...Right in the Kisser" (2002)

Aired on CBS, the home of the original *Honeymooners*, and hosted by Kevin James, *The Honeymooners 50th Anniversary Celebration* paid special tribute to this long-running family sitcom that ended its run in 1978. The special starred Carol Burnett, Tom Hanks, John Ritter, and Dennis Franz. Kevin set up all of the historic *Honeymooners* film clip packages, and he also re-enacted some of the most famous and memorable sketches from the show. If you were a Jackie Gleason fan or a die-hard *Honeymooners* groupie, this special checked all the boxes. It showcased Jackie and his cast executing some of the most amazing physical comedy and jokes—most of which were scripted but some of which were improvised. As Jackie Gleason said, "If you can go out in front of an audience and do something to make them laugh, or induce them to laugh, there is no greater thrill."

I remember when I used to watch *The Honeymooners* years ago, and while I was working on this special, I was reminded of some of the greatest episodes that kept audiences like my family coming back for more.

While live television specials were my bread and butter, I also had a chance to direct a number of series. Some of these experiences were great fun, but in all honesty, there is nothing like the excitement of a live special. Nevertheless, there were a few experiences that are worth sharing.

CHAPTER 17

SERIES-LY: KEEP THE AUDIENCE COMING BACK FOR MORE

THE GREATEST TV SITCOM SERIES OF THE 1950S WAS *I LOVE LUCY* WITH THE husband-and-wife team, redhead Lucille Ball and Cuban band leader Desi Arnaz. The series ran for six seasons, and after it ended, there were three one-hour specials that were produced for die-hard fans like my parents and me.

Every week we'd tune in to the antics of this comedic couple and their sidekicks, Fred and Ethel Mertz, played by William Frawley and Vivian Vance. There was a lot of physical comedy on the show and lots of cuts to Desi leading his orchestra with Lucy always trying to get in on the act. The sitcom was shot in black and white, and it is available for viewing to this day, mostly on YouTube. Another series that commanded my undying loyalty were *The Honeymooners*, starring Jackie Gleason who threatened to "take us to the moon" with a punch in the gut. I also was a fan of Norman Lear's *All in the Family*, with the lovable racist Archie Bunker and his dysfunctional family led by his long-suffering wife, Edith, played by the great stage actress Jean Stapleton. In addition to these family-friendly comedies there were popular Westerns like *Gunsmoke* and *Bonanza*, as well as weekly variety shows starring Milton Berle, Mel Tormé, George Gobel, Jack Benny, Red Skelton, and Danny Kaye, which were all successors to earlier variety shows like *Your Hit Parade*. And who could forget *The Ed Sullivan Show* with its cavalcade of exciting new talent?

With the introduction of color television in the mid-to-late fifties, television attracted more advertising dollars, and the selection of series shows greatly expanded. Inventors and technical engineers figured out a way to increase the size of the television screen and the sharpness of the image so that viewers were delivered a better picture. Series programming was crafted to appeal to a family audience in the early evening hours, while more adult shows were aired after the kids went to bed. Advertising agencies responded to this idea, knowing that they could target their commercials to a particular audience. Thank you to Alka-Seltzer, Bayer aspirin, Chevrolet, and Ford for priming the series pump!

Here are some of the series with the Jeff Margolis stamp on them, along with stand-out anecdotes that I hope will give you an appreciation for the differences between television specials and series and the challenges that a director/producer comes up against.

Just Be-Cos: Bill Cosby (1976)

Fred Silverman, who was president of ABC, wanted to create a show starring Bill Cosby that would go up against CBS's news show *60 Minutes* on Sunday evenings at 7:00 p.m. In 1976, Cosby was hot, hot, hot. A few years earlier he had starred in the television international thriller *I Spy,* a series in which he was an undercover agent. After that series, he had his own show, *The Bill Cosby Show,* playing a gym teacher who spun lessons about growing up to high school students. The show garnered huge ratings for NBC and was nominated for Primetime Emmys for its two seasons on air on Sunday evenings.

Fred decided to call this new show *Cos.* And he conceived of it as a thirteen-week variety series showcasing Cosby's brand of humor and appeal to kids and their parents. The show had a standard opening each week. Bill would come out and sit in a comfortable chair on a small stage and he'd deliver a monologue that would appeal to the adult viewers as well as the kids—he knew how to talk to kids, telling them personal anecdotes that had some sort of a message wrapped in humor, things like a trip to the dentist or a family vacation, stories like that. To enhance the show and make it a true "variety show," we added musical numbers and sketches with other great comedy stars.

Fred asked me to direct the series; I was thrilled to accept his offer.

Bill Cosby was not so easy to work with. I dreaded going on the set some days. He was usually late, and he would always come in his tennis shorts smoking a cigar, making guests like Tony Randall, Valerie Harper, Nancy Walker, and even Mary Tyler Moore wait. Not a good thing to do.

When I first met Cosby, we hit it off very well. As our first meeting was wrapping up, he said, "I just want to tell you one thing. When I walk on that stage for the first show, I want to see as many black technicians as I see white technicians working on the set."

I said, "I don't think that's possible, but I'll do my very best." I knew it wasn't possible because in September 1976, there were just a handful of minorities and women working in television on the technical side at ABC. There were no cameramen that were black, but there were a couple of sound guys and a couple of stage-crew guys who were minorities.

At our first production meeting, I asked the tech manager at ABC to "assign every person of color you've got on staff or there's going to be hell to pay with Cosby."

He said, "I'll try."

The first day on stage, we were all waiting for Cosby to show up. It was the first day of rehearsal and camera blocking on the set. He came in wearing the signature tennis shorts, smoking a cigar, and he stood offstage, looking around at everything. Then he said to one of the stage managers who was with him, waiting to bring him onstage, "Get me the doctor." He called me the doctor because he thought I could make everything better.

The stage manager talked in his headset to the other stage manager, who I was standing with, and said, "Cosby wants to see Jeff."

I walked over to him and said, "Hey, Bill, welcome; how you doing?"

He said, "Doctor, I've got a problem."

"What's the problem?"

"I told you that when I walked on the stage for the first time, I wanted to see as many black faces as I see white faces. And you didn't do that."

I thought for a moment and responded, "Bill, oh my God, I'm so sorry. I forgot to tell you that I'm colorblind!"

He stared at me for a minute and before he could respond, I jumped in, "Listen. I want your show to be a success, so I hired the most *experienced* people. And as much as I'd like to see more diversity behind the camera, I can't control the labor pool."

That's when he turned around and walked away and went and changed out of his tennis outfit and into a shirt and pants ready to rehearse. I never heard another word about it. Thinking about this moment in light of today's efforts to bring more diversity in front of and behind the camera, it's embarrassing. But that's the way things were.

Oy. The way that series ended, oh my God. We didn't even make a season, only nine shows. Bill was impossible. He fired the first producer, my friend Chris Bearde, and demanded another one. Fred Silverman hired Alan Thicke, a late-night talk show host, and asked me to produce with Alan and continue to direct.

"Okay, I'll direct, but I don't want to produce *and* direct. It'll just be too much." Alan was a very talented guy, but I was afraid for him—really afraid. I thought to myself, "This is never going to work. Bill Cosby will fucking eat this guy up and spit him out," which is exactly what happened. But with Fred Silverman's support, Alan did make it through six episodes.

The show ended shooting when we still had two shows left to put on the air. I remember going into an editing room and taking pieces from everything we had taped but never used. We always over-taped every week. I put together two shows with all those pieces, comedy sketches and musical numbers. Those were the last two shows that aired. It ended ugly, and it was still quite an experience. We only taped seven episodes, but nine had to go on the air. I got paid for thirteen because I had a pay-or-play deal, which means that even if a show is canceled, I am still paid for the number of shows I was contracted to deliver—in this case, thirteen. (A full season used to be thirteen weeks; now it is up to twenty-six.) Thank you to my agents at the William Morris Agency at the time. (This is an important clause for a director in any contract. You are being asked to clear your schedule to accommodate a specific number of episodes, and if they are canceled, you should not be penalized, especially if you have turned down other work. Remember this!)

Cosby went on to do other things, but unfortunately, his bad behavior off-stage took him down. It's sad to see how some people in the world of entertainment, as in other fields, think they can do anything they want and get away with it, abuse their power, treat people badly, and fly under the radar. But not always. No one is that important to be unkind and disrespectful.

Hello and Goodbye, Dolly (1987)

There was a lull in weekly variety series in the late 1980s. To revive the genre, ABC and Dolly Parton asked Nick Vanoff to be the executive producer, and Don Mischer to produce and direct her new variety series, *Dolly*. The network gambled on the star power of Dolly Parton, and the opening episode had one of the highest ratings in the history of variety television series, but the series ran for just one season.

Don and I were friends and had worked together on other projects. After the first couple of episodes, he decided that he wanted to concentrate his creative efforts on producing the show for Dolly, so he offered me the chance to sit in the director's chair until he was ready to return. I felt like the adopted child because it wasn't my show, but I understood why I was there. Don had set a style for the show, and I had such a great deal of respect for him both as a producer and director, that I just carried out his plan each week. Dolly is the ultimate professional and knows exactly what she wants. The subtitle of the show was "Dolly's Way." There was a lot of pressure on everyone involved to try to bring weekly variety series back to television. I did everything to try and make that dream become a reality for both Dolly and Don. When Don decided that the show was in good shape, he came back to the director's chair, and I was off to the next project.

Saying No to Roseanne: Roseanne and Tom Arnold (1993)

I got my first shot at directing a series sitcom in 1993 from Roseanne (Barr) Arnold and her husband at the time, Tom Arnold. They both liked the job I had done directing Roseanne's one-hour standup special for HBO. In television as in life, people like to work with people they know and trust, and Roseanne and Tom trusted me.

I was originally linked up with Tom and Roseanne through my agent at William Morris, John Ferriter. Tom was one of his clients, and together they sold a Roseanne Arnold special to HBO. It was her first one-hour standup comedy special in front of an audience, shot live. Tom wanted to be the producer, and he wanted to do everything on the show including direct, but he didn't have the experience. It was just too much for him. The agents at William Morris thought he was fuckin' crazy for wanting to do everything.

Tom needed help, and the William Morris people thought that I would be a good match for him. I had already gained a reputation for being able to handle difficult talent.

I met Tom and then Roseanne about the HBO show. She asked me to meet with a young comedy writer, whom she thought was going to be a huge success in the industry. His name was Judd Apatow. I hired Judd (because Roseanne told me to) to write material for Roseanne, which might have been his first big break. I can't swear to it, but isn't that a story? Jesus. Judd Apatow! Just look at him now, umpteen movies later and one of the hottest comedy film producers/directors in Hollywood.

Tom, still trying to do everything, wanted me to teach him how to direct by letting him direct some of the camera blocking, but it didn't work out, and he gladly relinquished the director's seat to me once he realized what was involved. It might also have been difficult directing his wife, although Judd Apatow has done very well with Leslie Mann, his wife of twenty-four years, and Blake Edwards and Julie Andrews got along famously. I'm sure there are other examples.

Tom came into the editing room after we taped the show. We edited it together and then showed it to Roseanne, who loved it. It was all sugar and spice and everything nice, and the show received great ratings for HBO and was a feather in Roseanne's cap and mine. You work for your money when you work with Roseanne though.

Roseanne has a reputation for being difficult, but she wasn't difficult with me. At least, nothing out of the ordinary. She just wanted to make sure that she looked great and was funny. I don't mean that her face looked great and her makeup and hair, but her overall appearance and the way she presented herself in this standup comedy special. Her jokes about being a domestic goddess were hilarious, and her in-your-face delivery totally worked. She just wanted to be taken care of and protected, which is understandable. I can hardly think of an actor or actress who doesn't ask the same of their director. I always try to provide a safety net for the talent. Any talent who works on a Jeff Margolis production knows I will have their back, and I think that is one of the reasons that talent likes working with me. I don't mean it as a humble brag—it's just something I do—and it's a reflection of my respect for talent. Just try standing in front of a camera someday, and you'll learn to appreciate how nerve-wracking it can be! Some of the greatest stars in the business have a case of the nerves, so it is comforting to see someone like myself, who stays calm and gives them the assurance that "everything is going to be great."

After I directed the HBO special, I got a phone call from my agent at William Morris, who said, "Tom and Roseanne called here, and they want you to direct Roseanne's sitcom."

I said, "Pardon me?"

"They want you to direct her sitcom."

"I've never done one before, but I've always wanted to. I'd love to give it a shot. Let's go for it."

"We'll set up a meeting for you with the Carsey-Werner Company."

Tom found out about my meeting with Carsey-Werner, the producers of the *Roseanne* sitcom, and he said, "No, I don't want Jeff to have to meet with them. He's directing the show. That's it. There's nothing else to discuss. Roseanne and I decided he's directing the show."

I directed the last two episodes of a season. What a totally different atmosphere from directing any kind of entertainment special, series, or event. I tried to direct the show as if I were shooting a live play on Broadway. I went for no second takes and no pick-ups. I think it worked. We finished earlier than they had ever finished on a tape day. I remember everyone being in shock when Roseanne came into the control room after the show to see me. Apparently, she had never done that before.

She shouted, "Where's Margolis?"

I thought, "Oh shit, it's my ass."

Instead, she came up to me, hugged me, and said, "Thank you, good job. I've never been out of here this early on a show day; now what the fuck am I supposed to do for the rest of the evening?" Everyone in the control room had a good laugh.

A couple of weeks later, while the show was on hiatus, Tom called me and invited me over to their house in Brentwood. They had something to discuss with me. They asked me if I would consider directing *Roseanne* the following season. Oh my God, I really wanted to do it, and I thanked them profusely. But I had numerous other commitments—the Oscars, the American Music Awards, and the Miss America Pageant as well as other one-offs. I just didn't have time in my schedule. Who knows what twists and turns my career might have taken had I done an entire sitcom season on *Roseanne*, but it was not meant to be. And truthfully, I like the excitement of constant change, which is the hallmark of specials.

Fridays with Dennis Miller (1994)

Dennis Miller Live was one of the first-late night weekly series on HBO (1994). We did it live to air on the East Coast every Friday night from Los Angeles. It was a ballbuster because Dennis wouldn't rehearse, and he was always making last-minute changes. With all that going on, I got the show on the air, live every Friday night, and no one watching was ever aware of what was going on behind the scenes. I only directed the first season because I had prior commitments and could not continue due to my insane schedule. The show ran from 1994 to 2002. I'm fairly certain that it led the way for shows like *Real Time with Bill Maher* on HBO.

Looking for New Talent (2003)

There was a new series on Fox called *American Idol*, created by Simon Fuller, which was introduced in 2002–2003. It was a talent contest for unknown singers to compete for the grand prize, a recording contract. The American public voted on the contestants. The show was a huge success on Fox and ran for fifteen years, then went on hiatus and came back again. It now airs on ABC.

America loves talent competitions, so there was room for one more at the time. *Fame*, named after the feature film and television series with talented high school kids aspiring for a shot at stardom, aired on NBC in 2003–04 a year after *American Idol* debuted. It was a talent competition for contestants who were "triple threats." They had to sing, act, and dance. The American public voted for the winner, who earned an acting audition for a soap opera or a sitcom and the opportunity to make a demo recording for a major record label. Pretty good grand prize, right? The show was an instant success as well. *Fame* was executive produced by David Stanley and Scott Stone, and Debbie Allen and I served as producers, and I directed the series. Debbie and I had worked together on numerous Academy Awards shows over the years, so it felt like old home week to be working with her again on *Fame*.

Debbie and I each brought our own bag of tricks to the task of producing the show, and we shared them to make *Fame* a ratings hit. Every once in a while, she would say to me, "No shit! How come you knew that and I didn't?" I would say to her, "Holy shit, all these shows. I've never done that before." That's the way we taught each other. It was really fun to work together and create. I love her. She was a great, great, great partner to work with. Did I mention how much I love her?

We produced *Fame* in Los Angeles, and we had to deliver the show by five o'clock to air in New York on NBC at 8:00 p.m. every week. It was intense. There were three parts to the show: each contestant had to sing with a live band conducted by Rickey Minor (who was the great Whitney Houston's conductor during her career), then do a group song and dance number, and the final segment was to appear in a short comedic scene, most of the time from a famous movie or play. The scene ran two-and-a-half to three minutes. We brought an actor in to work with the contestants in the scene. Same actor, same scene, different contestant each time.

We would shoot the show in front of an audience at two o'clock here in Los Angeles (which was five o'clock in New York). I would then have to run to the editing room and edit the show down to time and have it ready to go on the air, being broadcast to the East Coast from Los Angeles, by five o'clock LA time. It was a one-hour show, weekly. Luckily, our stage and the editing facility were on the same studio lot, next door to one another.

I would finish taping the show, which always ran a bit long, then I'd have to run into the editing studio and cut the show down to fit the time allotted. I had an hour to deliver the show to New York to go on air. I never delivered the entire show by five o'clock LA time. Usually, I sent New York the first half of the show, and while the show was on the air, I'd finish editing the second half.

Oh, God! The stressed-out AD at NBC in New York was a wonderful woman. She was always sitting on pins and needles. She had a stand-by show in a tape machine and was ready to push the play button if I didn't make delivery of the second half of the show to her on time. It never happened. I always made it. It would have been so much easier if we just could have done the show live on air. No editing, no near–nervous breakdowns.

All the final episodes on all the talent competition shows today are done live—*American Idol, The Voice, America's Got Talent,* and all the rest.

Sadly, *Fame* only ran for one season. And then it was on to other projects for me.

Debbie Allen and I remained steadfast friends through all the frenzy of *Fame*. Years earlier, when I won a Directors Guild of America Award for the Oscars in 1993, I had invited her up on stage to accept it with me. We did six Oscars together, and she had been so instrumental in so much of the show that I wanted her there with me.

Her choreography brought the Oscars that I directed to a whole other level of glitz and glamour, and she deserved to share the DGA award with me, for sure. That's what friends are for.

Debbie was recently presented with the Kennedy Center Honor for her incredible career as a choreographer, director, producer, teacher, and inspiration to so many kids with stars in their eyes. Well deserved, Debbie. Congratulations.

"In Search of the Partridge Family" (2004)

The original *Partridge Family* starring Shirley Jones and David Cassidy was a huge hit in the 1970s. It ran for four seasons on ABC. In 2004, the executives at VH1 came up with a series idea for a talent competition to recast the characters of the Partridge family with unknowns. Nothing like this had ever been done, and it was a huge challenge to create an entertaining series that would capture the audience's attention. The American public would watch these unknowns act a scene from an original episode of *The Partridge Family*, and then they were asked to vote on who they thought would make the best Danny, Laurie, Keith, Shirley, and so on. Jeff Margolis Productions produced the show. Gloria, Mick, and Benn, part of my team, were invaluable, and I brought in my friend Alan Carter to direct all the episodes. It was just way too much work in such a short amount of time for me to try to be both director and producer.

~ ~

As much as I enjoyed the world of directing and producing series, there is something magical about being part of a big production like the Miss America pageant that you get to reprise from year to year. It was one of the tentpoles of my career beginning in 1993. I couldn't wait for the allure of cotton candy, the Atlantic City Boardwalk, the ocean, all those talented ladies vying for the Miss America crown, and the bouquet of roses.

CHAPTER 18

HERE SHE IS, MISS AMERICA (1993–2000)

THE MISS AMERICA FRANCHISE WAS ONE OF THE MOST POPULAR PROGRAMS IN television history. First introduced in Atlantic City on the boardwalk, it was designed to attract tourists to this seaside playground in 1921. It had its ups and downs in response to the Great Depression, and, by the 1940s with newsreels covering the event, Miss America became a national figure. By 1945, after World War II, the event producers introduced a scholarship program supporting women's desire to go to college and pursue a career. This was a very popular move and showed that the pageant was not just about a pretty face and a lovely figure—but that those women were aspirational and the pageant was in a position to help them fulfill their career goals. Another milestone in the history of the pageant was the crowning of the first Jewish Miss America, Bess Myerson, Miss New York, in 1945, reflecting the diversity of the contestants, which has continued to this day.

In 1954, the Miss America pageant was televised live for the first time, and it became a big hit with family viewers across America. Fast forward to the 1970s when a law student was crowned the next winner, a doctoral student, and the idea that Miss America was not just beautiful but also smart was the pageant's subliminal message, but most of its audience still tuned in to what they perceived of as a beauty pageant. Some of the later firsts included Vanessa Williams, who broke the color barrier as the first mixed-race winner. Unfortunately, her crown was taken away when nude photos of her surfaced, which was against pageant rules, obviously. There have been other momentary goofs, too many to mention, but to this day through all its trials and tribulations, Miss America endures, brains and beauty.

I was one of the millions of Americans who watched the Miss America pageant growing up. I was always excited to see the amateur talent on stage and watch the show as Bert Parks sang "There She Is, Miss America" and the winner took her stroll down the runway, crown on her head, and carrying a beautiful bouquet of long-stemmed roses to the rapturous applause of the audience, who came from all over the country. Each contestant had their fan club—of course, I always wanted Miss California to win (being loyal to my home state), but I was happy for whoever ended up with the crown. For the rest of the year, Miss America appeared at various public events throughout the country, promoting her platform and representing the pageant organization. Many of the winners went on to careers in television broadcasting, such as Mary Ann Mobley, to name just one, and of course there was Bess Myerson, who made a career for herself on *The Big Payoff* and *I've Got a Secret* in the 1950s and '60s.

I liked that it wasn't strictly a beauty pageant. In the entertainment business beauty pageants are referred to as "tits and ass competitions." Miss America didn't seem to be one of those, like its two major competitors, Miss Universe and Miss USA.

Miss America had judges pose interview questions as part of its competition for the five or ten finalists. For a while, it was also the only pageant that had a talent competition, which set it apart and gave it a bit of gravitas, even if the talent was not always up to professional standards. It was great to see these women in serious performance mode, whether playing the piano, baton twirling, tap dancing, or pulling out a surprise act. The judges' interview questions included, "If you are crowned Miss America, what will your platform be?" Every young lady had to have a platform, which was a cause or a charity, or some organization that they represented, usually an organization that was doing something to make the world a better place. If a contestant stumbled and fumbled, it wasn't likely that they would be the winner.

When I got the call to produce and direct the 1993 Miss America pageant, I couldn't have been happier. I knew if I got the gig and made all the improvements that were asked of me, it could be a yearly commitment for me. I would just need to slot it into my already-busy schedule, but it would be something that I could count on year in and year out.

Leonard Horn, the CEO of the Miss America Organization, and previously its attorney, contacted me about giving the pageant a fresh look. It was already heading into its seventy-fourth year, and in the years since it had begun broadcasting live on network television, not much had changed. I had lots of new ideas about what we could do. Leonard lived and breathed Miss America, and by the way, he lived in Atlantic City.

Leonard brought me in because NBC said to him, "The show is tired. People have other ideas now about what they want to watch. They are looking for different kinds of programming. Although Miss America has been one of the highest-rated shows ever on broadcast television, it's not anymore. The ratings are starting to fall, and we're losing our younger audience. The pageant doesn't have the relevance it once did. It's your job to get the ratings back up. Make it relevant." When someone says they want you to give a long-running show a "new look," be careful. Don't go overboard in the beginning. Turning an ocean liner around can't be done with one quick adjustment of the rudder. Old habits can be hard to break. Test the waters before tearing up the rulebook (forgive all the metaphors!). I already had the experience of trying to make the American Music Awards more modern and relevant for Dick Clark, so I knew the drill.

I met with Leonard almost a year before I was to produce and direct the pageant, and I came back to him about a month later with some ideas. As I read each idea, he said, "Nope. That's not going to happen. Nope. Nope. You can't do that. Nope!"

I got a no to everything I wanted to do. I said to him, "Well, what do you need me for, then?"

"Because you're Jeff Margolis, and you've got a reputation."

"Yeah, but you're not going to let me change anything!"

"Okay. Leave me your list and let me rethink some of your ideas. I can't make any decisions on my own. I have to go to my board."

"Who's on your board?"

"Well, there are men and women from all over the country who represent the state pageants."

"What's the average age range of those state pageant directors?"

He started laughing.

"Listen, Leonard; you hired me to make changes. You've got to work with me, and you've got to convince those state pageant directors that it's time for a change! Just show them the ratings. Viewership is going down. This trend will continue unless you do something. Talk to your board and get them to buy in. Otherwise, the network may drop the pageant."

I treaded very lightly the first year, not wanting to alarm anyone. I pointed out that Miss America was really a scholarship competition. I wanted to make sure that the message was loud and clear: "If you had no tuition money, competing in the Miss America contest might solve some of your financial problems." Young women didn't realize the opportunities open to them. Any young woman could apply to the Miss America organization to secure a scholarship to go to college even if she wasn't competing in the pageant. All the state pageant directors loved this approach. I had to make sure that this message wasn't lost amidst the swishing of taffeta and silk ball gowns, swimsuits, glamour parades, and pretty smiling faces.

My plan was to give the Miss America pageant a new image— one that would appeal to young women *and* their families. Times were changing. More women were going to college. The Women's Movement of the early 1970s supported the idea that today's young women should have the freedom to follow their dreams. It was a message that angered some but inspired many others. I wanted to be part of something worthwhile. Could Miss America become the model for the modern young woman? The idea of the scholarship was perfect for the times, as more and more women were launching their careers and needed the advantage of a college education to compete in the workforce.

It was the age of *Ms.* magazine, Gloria Steinem, and other female trailblazers.

By the time I took over Miss America in 1993, Miss Universe and Miss USA had already been on the air for years, and they were definitely "tits and ass competitions." The best-looking young girl with the nicest body and the prettiest face always seemed to win. Somebody made a comment that the Miss America contestants weren't as beautiful as the girls on the other pageants. So what? Miss America wasn't really about beauty on the outside, but more about inner beauty, brains, and talent.

I modernized the look and brand of the Miss America pageant by changing the graphics, lighting, and scenery, and I rebuilt the famous Miss America runway. I slowly altered everything about the look of the show in the seven years that I directed the pageant, but let's just call it "cosmetic surgery" the first year.

The second year I produced and directed the show, I asked Leonard, "Tell me the last time you went to the beach or a swimming pool and saw a young lady wearing a one-piece bathing suit in nylons and high heels? If you've actually seen that, then we can discuss doing the swimsuit competition that way.

"Otherwise, no more high heels, no more nylons. I think the ladies (never call them girls) should have the opportunity to wear a one-piece or a two-piece suit, their choice, and be in their bare feet, no nylons, no high heels!"

I got the high heels and the nylons off my second year; all the ladies were in their bare feet, but I didn't get any two-piece bathing suits. They all wore one-piece bathing suits. The Miss America Organization still had a promotional tie-in with a bathing suit manufacturer who wanted to showcase their one-piece bathing suits. I was finally able to change that the next year.

The third year I continued making changes. I asked the choreographer to create a production number so that all fifty-one contestants could be on stage at the same time. I shot that part of the number so that the audience saw all the contestants parading on stage, before the ten finalists were announced and later were highlighted in the swim-suit, evening wear, and talent competitions.

I hired three different choreographers. We started with Dee Dee Wood, then Anita Mann came in, and finally Barry Lather, who I think still does the show to this day. Each one of these choreographers brought their own style and good work to the pageant. The contestants had no idea how fortunate they were to be working with these three brilliant artists.

The talent competition became an increasingly important part of the pageant. Many of the contestants were very serious about their performance skills—some were studying opera, music, and dance, and patterned their segment after the style of variety show performances that were popular in the 1990s. The bar was set higher and higher from one year to the next, and the talent competition was no longer an afterthought but a sincere measure of a contestant's skill. The television audience came to expect real professionalism.

Then I had an idea to make the show more interactive. If America sits in front of their TV sets—as they have been for forty years—watching this show, why not let America have their say so and vote? Let the whole country be the seventh judge. You have to have an uneven number of judges on any of these contest shows because if there's a tie, somebody has to be able to break it. Why not bring in six big-name stars to judge and let America be the seventh judge?

The board liked the idea. The Miss America pageant in 1996 was the first time the American public phoned in to cast their vote. Through NBC we made a deal with AT&T. AT&T predicted how many phone calls they thought that they would get from all across the country. They grossly underestimated the response to this idea. When we opened up the phone lines right after the Parade of the States, which showcased each of the fifty-one contestants, the number of calls within the first five minutes blew up the AT&T phone-in system.

When they calculated the number of calls that didn't get through, they were absolutely astounded. The next year AT&T had a whole new approach because the phone-in vote became such an integral part of the show. I hired a co-host, Steve Kmetko, an entertainment reporter on the E! channel, to anchor the activity at the AT&T phone center. Before every commercial break, we cut to him for a voting update! It made the voting more exciting for the viewer and gave them the feeling that they were involved with what was happening on stage.

I wasn't done making changes. I revised the evening gown competition so that you could see all fifty-one contestants in their evening gowns at the same time before the competition of the finalists began. There was a beautifully choreographed production number for the women to model their dresses and gowns.

Eventually I was given (almost) free rein by Leonard Horn to do what I wanted because the ratings had improved and the reviews were a lot more favorable. He still had to run all my ideas by the board, but he was so pleased with the changes that I had made thus far, and the uptick in ratings for the show, that he was really supportive and became my biggest cheerleader. I continued to come up with new ideas to make the show more relevant.

I brainstormed with my production staff. "The ladies come to Atlantic City; they're there for two weeks, and we work them to death. Maybe we take 'em out to dinner once or twice and let them have a night off and let them dance at a club. That's it. Why don't we do something special for them? Before the ladies get to Atlantic City, let's take them someplace fun so that they can get to know one another before they start competing against each other. I know; let's call our friends at Disney."

We ended up at Disney World in Florida, and Disney hosted the fifty-one contestants, their chaperones, and the production staff for five fun-filled days and four nights in Orlando. The ladies got first-class treatment. They never had to wait in line for a ride at Disney World, or to get into a restaurant...and I got everything on camera. By the way, I don't think that I ever got to thank Disney publicly, so thank you so much, Disney, for helping change the face of the Miss America pageant.

My go-to editor, Alan Carter, eventually directed all of these B-roll segments at Disney World.[6] He did such a good job that I soon had him directing other shows for me that I was too busy to direct but still produced under the Jeff Margolis banner. We worked together a lot. Today Alan is the director of *The Voice*. It's so gratifying to see people I have mentored become successful. Always pay it forward...it's one of the most rewarding aspects of the entertainment business—when you can help someone else climb the ladder of success. It doesn't cost you anything, and it can make you feel like a million bucks when you are thanked.

When we got to Atlantic City after a few days at Disney World in Orlando, I took all the contestants out on the famous boardwalk with its arcade, which featured a Ferris wheel, bumper cars, cotton candy, popcorn stands, the famous salt-water taffy, and the smell of the ocean. We shot everything and edited it into a short fun film. My staff and I picked a current piece of music that was appropriate to put under the visuals when it was all edited together. It was a three-minute segment that we dropped into the television show. This had never been done at the pageant before. The ladies had a ball, and the audience loved the segment. (The Atlantic City Chamber of Commerce probably loved it too!)

My relationship with Continental Airlines was exceedingly valuable because they picked up the airfare for the production staff and crew to travel from Los Angeles to Disney World in exchange for a couple of ten-second plugs during the live broadcast. I also arranged with Continental to send a private jet to pick up the contestants in Orlando and fly them up to Atlantic City. These ladies had their own private jet. They were beside themselves. I shot them getting on and off the plane and made it part of the Disney World package. Continental loved all the publicity, and it saved the production a lot of money.

---

6   B-rolls are the cutaways from the main focus of a show. For example, when a contestant is introduced on a competition show, there might be a cutaway to a B-roll with a behind-the-scenes look at a contestant's home life. This is done frequently on *America's Got Talent*, *The Voice*, and *American Idol*, and we did it on the Miss America pageant.

The ladies felt comfortable together after their week at Disney World. They had a chance to feel like they were part of a production together, rather than meeting on day one in Atlantic City. It was a bonding experience, and they developed strong relationships and supported one another. There was a real esprit de corps even though the pageant was fundamentally a competition. As I said earlier, we edited together a wonderful three-minute piece for the show and gave Disney a pretty spectacular three-minute commercial for Disney World. I don't have any proof, but I suspect that it made a positive impact on Disney World's attendance in the long run. It was product placement to the nth degree. (Whenever you can do product placement or barter airtime for services, it's a great way to keep the budget in check.)

I had exactly two weeks in Atlantic City to rehearse the fifty-one contestants and shoot the show. Choreographers, the live orchestra, the hosts, moving the sets around—it was managed but fun chaos, and a lot of hard work. We didn't sleep much while we were there. My entire team and the other professionals had to be at the top of their game because we were mostly dealing with contestants who had not had much, if any, stage experience. But I knew it would be great, and if there were some minor goofs, the audience would either not see them, or they'd pick them up and enjoy that it was all part of putting a pageant together. There was no fixing anything in the editing room because the show was *live*. Never expect perfection when producing live television; just know that "it's gonna be great" if you keep your cool, your sense of humor, and most of all you are kind!

Putting the Miss America Pageant Together

Orchestrating the Miss America pageant was a huge assignment. I was dealing with contestants/ladies with no television experience, most of whom had never been on a giant stage like Atlantic City. They all were required to do some dancing to show off their evening gowns and bathing suits in the competition. When I hired a choreographer, I always said, "Remember, these ladies are not professional dancers.

They're not professional singers. They're not professional actresses. They're college students who may be studying all of the above, but they certainly aren't used to performing live on television before millions of people."

I really relied heavily on the choreographer to help me produce the opening Parade of States, the evening wear and swimsuit competition production numbers! Every time the women were on stage, they had to be choreographed somehow so that they looked like they knew what they were doing. Usually, they did. They worked so hard to look like professionals. And again, usually they did.

Then there was the final competition, which was the interview questions handled by the hosts. Donny and Marie Osmond, who came on board in 1999, were so good at this; they would have made Bert Parks—the suave host of the pageant telecast for twenty-four years—proud.

The show began with the Parade of States, where the ladies all came out and introduced themselves and you see them for the first time. (Watch the 1999 or 2000 episodes of Miss America to get a real flavor of what a pageant should look like. Those shows were so good.)

In the old days, long-time host Bert Parks always sang "There She Is, Miss America" during the parade. When I took over the show, Regis Philbin sang that song, and Kathie Lee had her moment in a big production number where she sang with all the contestants. They were amazing co-hosts. There was a real easiness between them from hosting the *Live with Regis and Kathie Lee* morning talk show for so many years on ABC.

After the first year I decided to change the style of the Miss America theme song. It felt tired and old to me. I thought it might work better just to have the music and forget about the lyrics. Everyone knew them anyway. I asked the musical director, a genius lady named Diane Louie, to take the Miss America theme, and make it today. I also asked my brother, Peter Margolis, an incredible musician, to take a crack at rearranging the theme as well.

They both did a brilliant job, so I had two versions to choose from, and neither version needed the lyrics. The music stood on its own for the opening and the final runway walk when the crowned Miss America took her bows.

We had our share of bloopers. Occasionally a few of the ladies got confused during the parade or during some other segment of the show. Someone would go in the wrong direction, and it would mess up the whole look of the production number. But it's a live show, and I would say, "Oh shit," and cut to a different shot so that I didn't make anybody look bad. Before every show I used to repeat my mantra to the production team and crew, "It's gonna be great (no matter what happens)."

The choreographer would come to me every year after a rehearsal with a warning, "Oy, look out for Miss So-and-So. She's a problem. Just be prepared because if anybody is going to screw it up, it's going to be her."

I had a couple of ladies trip during the Parade of States or during some other segment of the pageant, but I never had a contestant actually fall over or fall off the stage. I'm sure if you were sitting at home watching and you saw one of the contestants make a mistake, you would love it; it's live television. But most of the time, the viewers didn't even notice. They'd be so wrapped up in the excitement of the event and would be cheering for whoever came from their state or whoever they hoped would be the winner.

In rehearsals, I had to make sure that all fifty-one ladies were treated equally and that all of them had an opportunity to rehearse all the competitions, because we didn't know who was going to end up being one of the ten final contestants.

I told Leonard Horn at one point what the rehearsal schedule was going to be and how each of the fifty-one contestants would have the opportunity to do everything. He said, "Well, no producer or director has ever done that before."

"Well, you're lucky you haven't been sued." We could have been accused of favoritism.

"You know what, Jeff, you're right."

The Miss America pageant was a four-month commitment for me—June, July, August, and September. As soon as I faded to black on the pageant, I was on a plane back to Los Angeles from Atlantic City, and it was prep time for the American Music Awards. Pre-production started at the end of September, and the show aired live in January. The Academy Awards pre-production started in December, which meant that in December and January I was actually doing double duty working at the same time on the AMAs and the Oscars for a couple of months. I loved every minute.

After the Oscars each year, I took my wife, Leslie, and our children, Adam and Erin, to Hawaii for a two-week, much-needed family vacation. I always left two days after the Oscars. I was outta here, on a plane, on my way to the islands. Gone. Man, did I need that. If I didn't have such a great production team, I could never have double booked—high energy also helps.

When the contract was up between the Miss America Organization and NBC, Leonard Horn went in to negotiate a new contract with the network. He and the head of NBC at the time didn't agree on much of anything, especially a cut in the budget. Leonard asked me, "Hey, remember telling me about your buddies at ABC? You said ABC has always been looking for a pageant, and if I ever had any trouble I should go to ABC? You want to make a phone call for me?"

The Miss America pageant, believe it or not, started on ABC, as a segment of their nightly news in the early fifties. Then it was carried by NBC as a standalone televised live event, and it was on NBC forever. Then just like that, however many decades later, the contract was up, and it was time to renegotiate.

I'll never forget this. I called my friend John Hamlin at ABC on a Sunday. John Hamlin called Ted Harbert, who was head of ABC Entertainment at the time. Ted Harbert called Michael Eisner, who was head of Disney and ABC. I put this call together for Leonard, so Michael Eisner, Ted Harbert, John Hamlin, and Leonard Horn got on a phone call, and after what seemed like about fifteen minutes, the deal was done. I know because I was waiting by my phone to hear from John or Leonard; I didn't know who would call me first. While John Hamlin called me, Leonard called his friends at NBC and said, "Thanks anyway, guys. It's been a nice forty-year relationship, but it's time to move on." We had a new home for the Miss America pageant—signed, sealed, and delivered! I don't imagine that a deal like this is made on a Sunday afternoon very often. And of course, the fact that we had a tie-in with Disney World didn't hurt: Disney owns ABC.

So now we were on ABC. The year was 1996, and that first year was very interesting. John Hamlin and Ted Harbert were really instrumental in bringing Miss America to ABC. The pageant was always live on TV on Labor Day weekend—and we were still a year away before the show was to air. In the interim, Ted Harbert left ABC and went to NBC, and Jamie Tarses became president of ABC after moving over from NBC. (It felt like musical chairs.) Jamie was the first woman and one of the youngest people to hold this position on an American broadcast network. (While at NBC Productions, she helped to develop the hit series *Friends, Caroline in the City, Frasier,* and *Mad About You.*)

It's not so unusual for the person who gave you the green light to leave the network and go elsewhere; but then you have to establish a new relationship with someone else. Hopefully, it is someone who sees things the way you do. If not, it usually means you're going to have problems.

On his way out, Ted said to Jamie Tarses, "Hey, we've finally got a beauty pageant." We were still calling it a beauty pageant. Even though it was a scholastic competition, it was still thought of as a beauty pageant. "This beauty pageant is really important to ABC, and you've got to do whatever Jeff wants. Please make it work."

I met with Jamie right after Ted left, and said, "I'm here to tell you about this year's pageant and everything that I would like to do on the show."

The first words out of her mouth were, "Well, let me tell you, Jeff, I like you and I'm a big fan of your work, but I hate beauty pageants."

"Oh shit." (Remember I told you there were going to be problems?)

"Since you've already started production on this year's show, carry on and we'll meet again to talk before you start next year's show." I knew that this first year she was in charge was a test and if I didn't pass with flying colors, the following year would be a nightmare.

We got through the first year on ABC with good ratings and happy sponsors, and the critics even liked the changes I had implemented. And then there was Jamie. "Okay, Jeff, let's talk about next year. The first thing I need you to do is replace Regis Philbin as the host." Regis Philbin had taken over from Bert Parks in 1991 and was very popular. He was also the co-host of the ABC morning show *Live with Regis and Kathie Lee*, with its legion of fans.

"But Regis has a couple of years left on his contract and besides, he's like the new Bert Parks. Everybody loves him."

"We need to attract a bigger, younger audience, and new hosts will help."

"But…"

"I'm sorry, Jeff. Figure it out."

OMG, how was I going to tell Regis? Well, I did, and he was actually kind of relieved. I think he knew that he had done all he could to help lift the ratings, and that it was time to move on. He made it so easy for me. What a nice man.

Okay, now it was time to talk about the 1997 pageant. Jamie's first words to me were, "You're really going to have to sell me on *everything!*"

Which I eventually did, or so I thought.

Jamie told me, "You can do whatever you want on the show because I like your ideas, but I'm going to pick the new hosts."

"Oh, shit. Really?"

"Yes. I want Meredith Vieira to be the female host, and I want Boomer Esiason as the male host. I want to get the daytime audience with Meredith since she's on *The View*, and the men who watch sports will know Boomer Esiason. I want to put those two together, and those are your hosts."

"All right." (I knew that there was no point in discussing it any further. Jamie had made up her mind.)

They turned out to be great. We did get viewers from daytime and the sports world, so Jamie was pleased. I told her that I really thought it was a one-time stroke of luck and that we needed to bring in some new hosts. She agreed and made another suggestion (or rather a demand), and my hosts were daytime stars Eva LaRue, and her husband, John Callahan, from the soap opera *All My Children*. They were also good and continued to get the daytime viewers to watch the Miss America pageant. Then for the 1999 show I was more or less given free rein to select the hosts and I knew the perfect pair to bring in a large audience—brother and sister Donny and Marie Osmond.

How could you go wrong with Donny and Marie? I met them during my early cue card days on *The Andy Williams Show* and had worked with them as a producer and director over the years. They always delivered with their warm personalities and singing and acting talent. They were a perfect fit.

Recently, I had a chance to look at both shows they hosted in 1999 and 2000. They were really good shows. Just a quick side story about the importance of establishing friendships. I met Donny Osmond when I was working on *The Andy Williams Show*. Shortly thereafter, he introduced me to his little sister, Marie. One day, I ran into Donny in the hall at CBS and he said to me, "Hey, Jeff, where have you been? What's going on?" I told him, "I'm the AD on the new *Sonny and Cher Comedy Hour* now." He gave me a broad smile, a big hug, and said, "All right, Margolis!" He was thrilled for me. Some years later, Marie was given her own series on NBC by Fred Silverman and Saul Ilson (my friend who was now an executive at NBC), and she asked me to direct the show, which was being produced by two men who she didn't really know—Neal Israel and Pat Proft. I was a familiar face, and my presence gave her the confidence she needed to carry her own show. Fast forward to today. The telephone rang in my office, and it was Donny Osmond. He was looking for a piece of tape from the Miss America pageant because he was putting together a show in Las Vegas and needed to use a clip. I keep impeccable files and copies of all the shows that I have directed, and I was able to get my hands on just what Donny needed. We had the chance to catch up. It was a wonderful conversation—that's one of the many side benefits of being in this business—although Donny and I hadn't spoken in a while, it was just like "old home week," and I was happy to do him a favor.

I finally gave up Miss America in 2000. Leonard Horn had retired a few years earlier, and a new CEO came in, and I worked with him for a year. Then he was fired, and another CEO came in. I worked with him for a year. It was like a revolving door. I wasn't happy so I decided to move on to a new project, and the new CEO really wanted to bring in his own people anyway.

After the first year that we did the show in 1993, a tradition was born. Beginning in 1994, CEO Leonard Horn would always come to Los Angeles to meet with me, my producers, and the writer, sometime in October, about a month after the pageant had aired. He wanted to know what I was going to do with the show next year, so I never had a minute to catch my breath. He would always start the meeting by saying to me, "Just remember, Jeff, don't throw the baby out with the bath water." He had to go back to his board and the state pageant directors to tell them what my plan was every year. The pressure to keep it fresh and relevant was relentless. "Make everything new and different but keep it the same so we can hold on to our fan base but attract new viewers at the same time."

"Okay, what?"

In 2000, I did the show with yet another CEO. A month after the show aired, he came out to Los Angeles from New York. He was all over me and my staff with compliments. "God, the show was great," and "I've never seen or done a show like this!"

This was a guy who had never been in show business; that was why he had never done a show like this before! All of a sudden, he was getting executive producer credit on a television show. He was a corporate attorney, and now he knew how to produce? I had to pitch my ideas to him. Okay, whatever.

We met at a hotel on the beach in Santa Monica because he wanted to stay at the beach. Of course, when you visit Los Angeles from the East Coast you want to be near Rodeo Drive in Beverly Hills or stay at the beach in Santa Monica or Malibu. I took my producers,

Mick McCullough, Gloria Fujita O'Brien, and Benn Fleishman, and the writer for the show, Stephen Pouliot, to the luncheon meeting. We sat down on a patio overlooking the Pacific Ocean, with the waves lapping against the shore and a warm breeze blowing. It was a gorgeous setting and a gorgeous day, but what happened next did not quite match up to the setting.

The new CEO wanted to know about the show. He had one of his guys with him, the gentleman who ran the pageant in Atlantic City, and I told them everything I wanted them to know, and how it was going to be great again! In reality, we were still creating next year's show. They were smiling and asking all kinds of questions.

We finished doing the pitch, telling them how were going to lay out the show with as many new ideas as we had at the time. The CEO said, "Boy, that sounds fantastic. Listen, I wanted you to come to our hotel here, and I wanted to have this lovely lunch on the beach because I wanted to let you know that I'm not going to bring you and your team back next year." There was dead silence.

And then I said, "Pardon me?"

"I want to put my own stamp on next year's pageant, so I want to bring in my own producing team."

"But I just outlined a three-hour television show for next year."

"Yeah, thanks for all the great ideas. I'll be sure to use some of them."

Then they got up from the table and said, "Sorry it had to end this way. Buh-bye." Of course, they left the check for me to pick up. I felt like saying to him, "You can't let me go; I'm leaving anyway" (and besides that, you can go fuck yourself), but I didn't. That was the end of my eight-year run as the producer/director of the Miss America pageant.

It had been a really great eight years, but it was time to move on. Leave it to someone else to make it new and old again. Let someone else deal with the contradictions and a CEO who had visions of grandeur without the experience to back it up. Thank you. Next!

Miss America and Nancy O'Dell make me an honorary Miss America.

Marie Osmond and I always have a good time working together.

CHAPTER 19

BILL CLINTON: MR. PRESIDENT (1993-2000)

WHEN *ABC PRESENTS: A ROYAL GALA* WAS CANCELED IN 1991 AFTER PRINCE Charles and Princess Diana separated, I was so unhappy. It was such a great experience—going to London, working with royalty, my afternoons spent with David Frost, lining up all that great British and American talent, and producing the show at the famous London Palladium. The show had garnered all kinds of awards, including one for Robin Williams's performance in 1988.

I was saddened by its cancelation, and then I had an idea. "Wait a minute. Why don't we do a gala with Bill and Hillary?" A special with presidents had been going on for years at ABC, and I thought we should revive it. Past productions had been directed by Joe Cates, Gil Cates' brother. (You'll hear more about Gil Cates later. He helmed the Oscars.) I pitched the idea to John Hamlin at ABC.

John said, "I think it's a great idea. Let's do it. I'll get it approved by the network, and then you can pitch it to the President and Hillary." Clinton was riding high after his victory over George H. W. Bush and Ross Perot. He was extremely photogenic and personable, with that down-home folksy Arkansas twang. Hillary had warmed up on the campaign trail and was seen by many voters as a role model with brains, beauty, and guts. And like Prince Charles and Princess Diana, they had youth on their side and they loved the entertainment industry, so a television special with them would do well across a wide demographic.

A Gala for the President at Ford's Theater became part of my schedule for eight years, from 1993 to 2000, throughout Clinton's presidency. You can only imagine how excited I was to be orchestrating this special, but there were so many moving parts, including the all-important coordination with the President's busy schedule and the security team that surrounded him and the First Lady.

I made it a point to work closely with Hillary's social secretary and Bill's social secretary in order to make the evening run smoothly. Both assistants were probably in their late twenties and so efficient and so on top of everything, it was one-two-three and done. I met them over the phone. There was no Zoom or FaceTime then.

Eventually we met in person and had more great, productive conversations. I told them what information I would need from Bill and Hillary. I wanted to know who they would like to host the show and who they would like to see on the show. I did that every year. They requested Whoopi Goldberg, who hosted numerous times, Paula Poundstone, Jay Leno, and Natalie Cole, and I delivered in every case. After all who could say no to the honor of hosting a special for the President of the United States and the First Lady?

By the time I was ready to put the show together, get the hotel accommodations for the staff and the crew and get the airline deal done, I was already working closely with Bill and Hillary's two social secretaries on all aspects of the production. We were trying to figure out a way to get all my production staff through security before we got to Washington, DC. Could we get the FBI checks done while we were still in Los Angeles, before any of us left, so we didn't have to waste precious production time while we were in Washington? *No!* That was not going to happen. When we got to DC, we did it the way the Secret Service and the FBI wanted us to do it. Okay then, that was that. I had to keep reminding myself that this wasn't a normal TV special; we were actually working for the President of the United States of America.... Yikes! (But how fortunate were we to have this experience?)

We did two survey trips to Washington, DC. On one I took a small production crew: the writer Stephen Pouliot; my producers

Mick McCullough, Gloria Fujita O'Brien, and Benn Fleishman; the production designer Ray Klausen; the lighting designer Jeff Engle; and a production assistant.

The survey included scoping out Ford's Theater. We had to figure out where I could put cameras, the lights, where everyone would be seated—celebrities and politicians alike—and where the Secret Service had to be seated in relationship to Bill Clinton. Every year Bill and Hillary sat in the two center seats in the front row of the theater, and sometimes the vice president and his wife (Al and Tipper Gore) would sit next to them. Bob Iger was president of ABC at the time, and so he was either sitting on the other side of Bill and Hillary or behind Bill and Hillary. There was always somebody important next to them and behind them.

That first year, after I had my FBI and my Secret Service check and I passed, I then asked the President's and First Lady's assistants to introduce me to Bill's "lead," the Secret Service agent who is assigned to protect the President of the United States of America. I wanted to meet him so I could talk to him and tell him what I planned to do and make sure that it worked for the Secret Service. His name was Brian, and he looked like the kind of guy who would take a bullet for the President—he was straight out of central casting—a short, combed-back haircut, broad shoulders, and reflective sunglasses.

I became friendly with Brian because I was constantly checking in with him right up until the big day. The first year our performers included Michael Bolton, Boyz II Men, Brett Butler, Natalie Cole, William Hurt, and Rosie O'Donnell. Great headliners and all hand-picked by the Clintons. The gala aired on ABC and garnered good ratings. Everyone was happy, and so it was a slam dunk to do a second gala the next year.

The second year I produced and directed the show, I went back to Washington for the first survey meeting and met with Brian again in between meetings to prep for the Oscars and the Miss America pageant. (My schedule was chock-a-block full, but that's the way I liked it, and I could do it all because I had such a great production team surrounding me, and an understanding family.)

"I didn't get a chance to really *meet* the President last year," I said. "I was in a receiving line at the end of the show, and I got to shake his hand. He really didn't know who I was. I want to meet him one-on-one."

"Are you out of your mind? Bill Clinton is the President of the United States of America!" said Brian.

"I know that and I respect that, but I don't want to meet him in a receiving line with a hundred other people. I just want a few minutes alone with him."

Time passed, and one day Brian surprised me with a phone call.

He said, "I need to talk to you. I'm coming to pick you up."

"Oh shit, I must be in trouble. What's the problem?" He arrived at the production office with a police escort, and he was in one of those giant SUVs. He opened the door for me and said, "Get in. I'm taking you to the White House for a meeting."

I thought, "Okay, I better just get in the SUV." I could not figure out what was going on. I couldn't imagine that I was actually going to meet Bill Clinton, even though I had bugged Brian a number of times.

We went to the White House, drove past all the security check-points (what do you expect with a Secret Service police escort), and arrived at some private back entrance. Brian escorted me to an elevator which I knew was the only elevator in the White House that went up to the President's residence on the third floor. Nobody goes up to the third floor unless you're the family or Secret Service, or you're invited by the Clintons. We got on that elevator, and I thought, "Oh, *fuck*, I must be in some kind of trouble. (Or this could be great.) Going up to the third floor, really?!"

I didn't know what to think. But my heart was racing, and I kept repeating, "Brian, tell me what's going on here. What do I have to be prepared for?"

"Don't worry. You'll be fine."

We got off the elevator and walked toward a big wood-paneled door. Brian knocked on the door, and a voice from the other side said, "Who is it?"

"Mister President, it's Brian, and I have Mister Margolis with me." The door opened, and it was the President of the United States. He had obviously just come back from a jog. He was in his running shoes and sweatpants. Very relaxed.

Brian said, "Mister President, this is Mister Margolis."

He stuck his hand out, and I said, "Mister President, it's a pleasure to meet you."

"Can I call you Jeff?"

"Yes, you can."

"Then you can call me Bill."

That was the way it started. Whenever we were with other people, I called him Mr. President, but when we were alone, I called him Bill. I went in with a big smile on my face, and Brian said something like, "Well, you asked to meet the President. Ask and you shall receive. I just needed to completely check you out first."

I didn't say anything to him. I just smiled and shook his hand, and he said, "You've got fifteen minutes."

I went in and sat down, and we started talking, and all I remember is Bill asked, "You want something to drink?"

"Water would be fine."

"Do you want a Perrier?"

"Sure."

He went to a little refrigerator in his office and got me a bottle of Perrier, and he said, "Do you want it in the bottle or a glass?"

"The bottle's fine."

I remember he sat in a chair, and next to him were newspapers from all over the world. He was—and still is—an avid reader. I remember thinking, "Oh my God, does he do this every day?"

I knew that he took a run every day, so this is probably what he did when he came back from his run. After fifteen minutes, there was a knock at the door, and the President said, "Come in."

Brian opened the door and said, "Mister President, I'm here for Mister Margolis."

"It's okay, Brian. I'll let you know when Jeff and I are done." I spent about forty-five minutes with him.

He asked me all kinds of questions about how I got started. He was fascinated with the Academy Awards, which I was directing at the time. (Even the President is curious about the Oscars. You'll get your chance to learn a little bit about the Oscars in later chapters.)

We talked about the Oscars, and I said to him, "Can I ask you the same question? You asked me how I ended up producing and directing the Oscars. How did you end up being President of the United States of America?"

"You know what. We'll talk about that some other time. What you do is really *fascinating*. I want to know as much about it as I can." Bill Clinton had close ties to a lot of people in the entertainment industry. I am sure his curiosity was genuine, although he has the kind of personality that makes you feel like you are the only person he's interested in even when he's got hundreds of people around him. (In this case, it *was* only me.)

The whole conversation was about how I got started and the things that I had done and what it was like doing the Oscars and what it was like working with all those megastars.

Then after about forty-five minutes together he said, "I've got a country to run, so I'm going back to work."

"That's okay. I've got a show to produce, so I have to go back to work, too."

Brian came and got me. The President said, "It was really great talking with you."

"It was great talking to you, too. Next time, it's your turn to tell me about how you got to be President."

"Okay, you got it."

My Parents at the White House

All the guests that I booked every year for the TV show wanted to meet the President, of course. I didn't want them to just shake hands with him backstage when the show was over in a formal receiving line. I wanted them to really get to meet him. So, with the help of the President's social secretary, I arranged for a cocktail party before the taping of the show where each star was invited to the White House with one guest for an informal gathering. This was a way for all the talent to have some alone time with the President and First Lady, enjoy a cocktail, chat, and of course, have a picture taken.

It was generally a casual, friendly affair, except for one thing. To help Bill and Hillary know who everybody was, there was a formally dressed military sergeant at the entrance door. A line formed outside the Red Room or the Blue Room, and when it was your turn, you would go up to this uniformed sergeant and tell him your name. Then he would announce in a loud voice, "Mister President and Mrs. Clinton, this is Jay Leno and his wife, Mavis," for example (although I'm sure that the President recognized Jay—maybe his wife's name was less familiar).

After a couple of years of doing the show, I decided that I wanted to give my parents a gift, a real treat. I bought them two first-class tickets from Los Angeles to Washington, DC. I put them up in a hotel suite, and they came to the show. They watched the taping, and they sat two rows behind Bill and Hillary and Henry Kissinger and whoever else was in the row in front of them.

But before the show, I took my parents to the private reception. We were second in line, and they had heard this Marine sergeant announce, "Jay Leno and his wife, Mavis." Jay was hosting the show that year. We were next in line. I turned around to my parents—I had a very good relationship with them, and we could say all kinds of slightly inappropriate things to one another—I said, "And you wanted me to be a fucking dentist. Now look where you are." We all had a good chuckle and a hug.

Then the sergeant announced, "Mister President and Mrs. Clinton, meet Jeff Margolis and his parents, Robert and Temmie Margolis." We walked into the room, and my parents were smiling from ear to ear. And Bill did something very unexpected; he grabbed my dad and hugged him. I thought my dad was going to fall over. And then he kissed my mom's hand. Hillary was very lovely to both of them with a warm handshake and a "Welcome."

In his ebullient voice with the Arkansas twang, he said to my folks, "Let's take a picture, c'mon!" He organized the four of them; then Bill took a picture alone with my dad first, then my mom, and then Hillary took a picture with each of them. My parents were over the moon.

Bill Clinton Turns 50! Let's Celebrate!

Who doesn't like a birthday party, especially if it's a surprise? In 1996, I produced Bill's fiftieth birthday celebration at Radio City Music Hall. The event was not broadcast live; it was meant to celebrate Bill's birthday and to raise money for the Democrats in support of a number of upcoming critical elections. It was such a huge event to produce in such a short amount of time—I think we had maybe a month—so I brought in a director friend of mine, Liz Plonka, to help. This birthday present was Hillary's idea. She thought Bill deserved something special (there's that word again) for his fiftieth, and that Whoopi Goldberg should host. Whoopi and Bill were friends. We tried to keep everything a secret from him, and we did a pretty good job. Finally, on the evening of the show, Whoopi walked out on that enormous stage at Radio City Music Hall in front of six thousand people, and he had a smile on his face from ear to ear.

Whoopi could have called him Bill. She didn't have to call him Mr. President, although most of the time she did, out of respect. Halfway through her opening monologue one of the stage managers brought her a box of Kleenex. She took the box of Kleenex and walked off the stage, down to where Bill, Hillary, and Chelsea were sitting, and she handed it to Bill. "You're going to need this tonight."

Whoopi recounted a personal story about Bill that we had learned from his social secretary. He was a straight-A student (what else would you expect from Bill Clinton?), but somewhere along the way, a teacher gave him a C on his report card.

He couldn't understand how he could have gotten a C, so he asked his teacher. She said something like, "I felt that if I gave you an A, you wouldn't work as hard next year. So, I gave you a C." The *Los Angeles*

Times reported, "Sister Mary McKee, gave him a C in comportment for raising his hand too many times in class."

This special teacher who was committed to motivating her star pupil kept in touch with the President over the years, but what happened next at his birthday gala came as a complete surprise to him. Whoopi took the stage and said, "Mister President, we've got a special birthday present for you here." The curtains opened and there was his teacher, Sister Mary McKee, standing with the support of her walker, in a pool of light. When the President realized who it was, he lost it. The Kleenex came in handy! After finally composing himself, he couldn't run onto the stage quickly enough to give her a big hug and a kiss. (We had, of course, forewarned the Secret Service so that they weren't surprised! That would have ruined everything if they had run up on the stage, but I know they had all eyes on the President anyway.)

When the show wrapped, Bill and Hillary came backstage. They said to the Secret Service, "We want to go backstage and thank all the people who put this evening together for us." It was quite a crowd, of course, because everyone behind the scenes wanted to shake hands with the President and the First Lady. They worked the room and were so gracious, and it seemed like they were there for at least an hour.

A few days after this surprise birthday party, I received a letter from Bill—one of many I received over the years from him:

> *Dear Jeff,*
>
> *Thank you for everything you did for my 50th birthday party. It was perfect, and I can't imagine a better way to usher in the next half century of my life. You did a great job. Both Hillary and I are so grateful to you. Thanks.*
>
> *Bill Clinton*

After the typewritten portion, he added a handwritten note, "You were terrific!"

I'll tell you a little secret. When I worked on Bill's fiftieth birthday celebration, his personal staff shared with me home movies that we could use for the television special. They were of Bill from the time he was a little boy riding his tricycle being cheered on by his loving mother, all the way up to his inauguration. I transferred the material to DVD so that we could pull a few clips to use at his birthday party. (All of this exclusive material is in a vault, locked up somewhere, probably at the Clinton Library and Museum in Little Rock.) If I ever want to reminisce about my dear friend, Bill Clinton, I can look back at all the specials I did with him. I transferred every show to a digital stick which I can view anytime I want to remember some of the "good old days."

And of course, I gave Bill a copy of the shows for his archives. I wonder if he ever watches any of those shows and if they mean as much to him as they do to me.

The Christmas Tour of the White House

I also executive produced, with a gentleman named Bruce Nash, a one-hour special for Fox Television, *The First Family's Holiday Gift to America: A Personal Tour of the White House*. It was Bill and Hillary's last Christmas there in 2000, and Hillary always decorated the White House at Christmas time. How spectacular would it be for Bill and Hillary to give us a tour of the White House? As far as I knew, there hadn't been such a tour since Jackie Kennedy gave one in 1962.

Bill and Hillary were the hosts. It was a lovely special that celebrated Christmas and served as a retrospective of sorts of all the Christmases past during the Clintons' eight years in the White House. Hillary even pitched a book of recipes from the White House kitchen. The proceeds from the sale supported the White House Historical Society—the People's House. Talk about a promotional tie-in! Genius!

One More Surprise

Before Bill Clinton handed over the reins of the presidency to George W. Bush, members of his team thought it appropriate to throw a surprise goodbye party for him on the South Lawn of the White House, bringing together friends, family, loyal staffers, and members of his administration who had worked with the President for all or part of his eight years. Knowing how much he loved music, the party included a performance by Fleetwood Mac. Someone arranged for the driver of his campaign tour bus to pick him up outside the White House and drive him to the tent on the South Lawn where all the guests were assembled to wish him Godspeed and to thank him for his years of leadership. One guest showed up late. It was Al Gore, his vice president, who had to preside over the contested vote (remember the hanging chads) which put George W. in the White House. He made the party after fulfilling his duties to cast the deciding vote, and as we all know there was a smooth transition from one president to another. The democracy was saved, and the Clintons' sendoff was a success. What a privilege to be part of that final bash.

CHAPTER 20

MICHAEL JACKSON: ONE NIGHT ONLY (1995)

I MET MICHAEL JACKSON WHEN HE WAS SEVEN OR EIGHT YEARS OLD ON *THE Andy Williams Show*. He was fascinated when he saw me flipping cue cards. He came over to me after one of the rehearsals and said, "How do you do that? How do you know when to flip the card?" and "Can I hold them?" He was incredibly bright and inquisitive for a young kid, but I'd learn over the years that he wanted to know everything about what went on in the television studio.

When Andy Williams booked The Jackson 5 on his show again, Michael saw me and gave me a big hug. He remembered me as "the cue card guy." By this time the producers of *The Andy Williams Show*, Chris Bearde and Allan Blye, had moved on to produce *The Sonny and Cher Comedy Hour*. Art Fisher was the director, and I now was the assistant director. Moving on up!

Later on, The Jackson 5 were guests on *The Sonny and Cher Comedy Hour*. Michael saw me on stage. I wasn't holding cue cards; instead, I was carrying a script book. Michael and I hugged like old friends, and he asked, "Where are your cue cards?!"

I said, "I'm done with that. I'm now the associate director for Sonny and Cher." During a lunch break, I took him into the control room, pointed out all the monitors and what they did, the camera switcher, the audio and lighting consoles, where everyone sat, what their jobs were, and finally what I was doing to assist the director.

Then I looked at him and said, "Now you know where I am and what I do." He smiled at me, and I got another big hug and a "Good job, Jeff. Congratulations."

Over the years our friendship grew as we worked with one another. In 1989 he appeared on the *Sammy Davis, Jr. 60th Anniversary Celebration*, and his appearance was one of the highlights of the tribute. Then, at the height of Michael's career as a performer, composer, and the King of Pop, the unimaginable happened, dealing a bone-crushing blow to his image and his psyche. There were all kinds of terrible allegations made against him. The newspapers had a field day printing salacious stories. Some of his die-hard fans stuck by him, while others left in droves, believing every word they read or heard on the radio or on the evening entertainment news on TV. In addition to all of that, Michael, and his wife of one year, Lisa Marie Presley, whom he married in 1994, were going through a difficult time. He had leaned on her for emotional support when all these accusations broke, and now he thought he might be losing one of his lifelines. (They eventually divorced after trying on and off to reconcile.) It seemed as if Michael Jackson's whole world was falling apart. Those of us watching from the sidelines wondered how Michael would recover and whether he could withstand the bloodbath.

Michael had a tried-and-true manager, Sandy Gallin. I was very friendly with Sandy from the Sonny and Cher days, when he was their manager. Sandy and his partner, Jim Morey, had one of the biggest talent management firms on the planet. Not only did they manage Michael Jackson and Cher but Dolly Parton and many other stars. The list went on and on. Sandy and Jim were two of the most influential managers in Hollywood at the time. Sadly, Sandy is no longer with us, but I still get to deal with Jim, who is one of the nicest men in the business.

It's 1995, and a black cloud is hanging over Michael's head. Sandy Gallin and Jim Morey, together with Tommy Mottola, who was then the head of Sony Records, decided that Michael needed to do a television special—the most incredible special that Michael had ever done—as a way of rehabilitating his image and remind everyone that he was still the King of Pop. He needed to make a comeback. Michael had the same idea at the same time, but nobody knew that. So, he called me and asked me to help him design the special and produce and direct. I don't have to tell you how quickly I said *yes*! He could have had his pick of directors and producers who were on Team Michael, but he chose me. I think he sensed that I understood his complex personality and his genius. What I didn't say at the time was that I was worried about Michael, and whether he had the stamina to put himself through the rigors of an extravaganza. Hindsight is 20/20; and unfortunately, my premonition proved to be true. Besides, his track record wasn't unblemished. There had been several episodes where he had collapsed on stage from exhaustion. I hoped that we would not see a replay of this again—especially with so much riding on his taking to the stage.

I spoke to Sandy and Jim about Michael's special. Sandy kept saying, "What are we going to do to make Michael bigger than life?"

"I think that's the problem," I said. "You can't make him bigger than life. He's got to be relatable. He needs to be presented as a person, not an icon or an unapproachable idol. He's so big that he doesn't seem real anymore. Why don't we do something more intimate? That's what Michael wants to do anyway."

"Are you kidding?" Sandy said. "Tommy Mottola is never going to buy the idea of an intimate show, and neither is Michael when he really thinks about it—and neither am I. He's going to want a hundred thousand people to perform to, like he always does."

"Let's talk to him!" I said. "Then you can see for yourself."

"Forget about it. *Next*! What else do you want to talk about?" Sandy discounted the idea, but I persisted, because I knew I was right; I was following my instincts, which are often all that you have to go on—instincts and experience. As it turned out, Michael envisioned the same kind of event for himself. He had already been having conversations with some of his people (I have no idea who they were) before he went to Sandy and Jim about what kind of show he wanted.

I said, "Listen, Sandy, I want you to think about this. Let's do something in a famous venue. Let's find someplace small and intimate and special. There's a Fox Theatre that's special. I think it's in Atlanta. There's the Pantages Theatre in Los Angeles, which is well known, and there's the Beacon Theatre in New York. Or Carnegie Hall or Radio City Music Hall or something like that. Let's stay away from a large sports arena where Michael is mostly seen on huge television screens and the audience is kept at a distance."

"Well, Michael will never buy it," Sandy said.

But then Jim Morey said, "It's kind of interesting."

"Let me talk to Michael," I said.

"Not without me," Sandy said.

"Okay, you can come with me, but if you let me talk to him alone, I think I can make him see the value in doing it this way."

"I'm going with you to meet with him," Sandy insisted. He knew that Michael and I had already met, but he wanted to be there. It was fine with me; after all, Sandy was his manager, so he would have to give Michael his stamp of approval. I was hoping that Jim would come along too because he and I seemed to be on the same page, but he was busy putting out fires for other clients. At the meeting, I told Michael how we wanted to do the special and where we wanted to do it, and he looked at me and said, with his funny giggle, "What have you been smoking?" Basically, what he was saying was, "Are you out of your fucking mind?" Then he smiled again, giggled, and said, "Just kidding; of course, let's do it."

Michael decided he wanted to perform at the historic Beacon Theatre on Manhattan's Upper West Side on Broadway. Originally built for silent films and vaudeville in 1929, it was now home to many rock concerts and events. HBO, which was the network that bought the special, decided to call it *Michael Jackson: One Night Only*. It was going to be the biggest event in the history of television.

On July 25, 1995, the King of Pop announced he would be "participating in a television special broadcast" later that year. The production was scheduled to air exclusively on HBO at 8:00 p.m. on Sunday, December 10.

Now the media had something positive to focus on, and the excitement about the show was palpable. In an interview with one of the choreographers, Barry Lather expressed what everyone involved in the production was feeling: "We were all there for him, and to make history."

> *Jeff Margolis had worked hard preparing this show. It was going to be amazing. We all felt like this is a once-in-a-lifetime opportunity. We were all in it together for Michael. We all felt honored to be working on this show! That was definite. There was this buzz in the air that this was going to be another major highlight in Michael's career; a show talked about for years to come.*[7]

A month before announcing *One Night Only*, Michael released his next album, *HIStory: Past, Present and Future, Book I*, and promotion for the show and the album went into high gear. The record was his ninth album and his most personal, and some of the songs—if you listen carefully—seemed to reference the allegations against Michael and his tortured response. While DJs were spinning the album—which hit number one on the *Billboard* charts—we were busy preparing for the show at the Beacon Theatre.

HBO spent millions and millions of dollars in advertising alone. There were billboards all over New York—*Michael Jackson: One Night Only* and his logo—where you see him standing in the moonwalk pose and he's leaning forward with one hand on the brim of his hat.

For two months leading up to the show, there were sky-writing airplanes and banners and signs on the sides of buildings all over New York. In Los Angeles there were billboards down Sunset Boulevard and on the sides of city buses. Every other promo on HBO was for *Michael Jackson: One Night Only*.

Once everyone agreed on the venue, the date, and the promotional campaign, we gambled that by having the taping in Manhattan, we'd

---

7   Damien Shields, "Inside Michael Jackson's 1995 'One Night Only' Special That Never Was," *DamienShileds.com*, December 27. 2014. https://www.damienshields.com/michael-jackson-one-night-only/.

shield Michael from some of the paparazzi that followed him wherever he went. (That would turn out not to be the case, unfortunately.)

I visited Michael at his home in Los Olivos, California, just outside Santa Barbara. He had purchased a huge piece of property and turned it into Neverland Ranch (named after Peter Pan's "place where dreams come true and time is never planned"). We sketched out the concept for the show and identified some of the songs—all with an eye to keeping things intimate.

Michael sent a car to pick me up in West Los Angeles for the two-hour ride to Los Olivos. It was a schlepp to get there! It was always during rush hour which can be a nightmare on the Ventura Freeway.

Michael was a night owl, like I am. I didn't mind the commute, but after numerous trips, I said to him, "You know, Michael, for me to come out to Neverland and be with you for a couple of hours and then drive back home late at night, I spend more time in the car than I spend out here with you."

"So, stay here in my guest house," which I did. He had four or five guest houses at Neverland Ranch in addition to the main house, and they were fabulous, of course. So tasteful. Michael was such a class act.

He gave me a tour of Neverland, and I witnessed his amazing generosity. Once a week he would have a busload of school kids and their teachers visit him. He'd have a whole afternoon planned for them. It would start with a big lunch, and there would be some kind of fun entertainment, like a clown or somebody making balloon animals. He also brought kids out to Neverland who were sick and bedridden from special children's hospitals. He took care of all the logistics so they'd have a happy day. He'd usually show a Disney movie appropriate for their age group in a specially designed screening room. You don't hear that part about how kind, caring, and generous Michael Jackson was. Some of the kids who weren't bedridden were able to tour his zoo.

Michael asked me if I would temporarily stay in New York to be there with him while we were in production and early rehearsals, well before we moved into the Beacon Theatre. He wanted to be in

New York for four months to prepare for the HBO special, and I told him that I would not leave my family for that long but that I would come with him for two months. I said he had to let me fly home every other weekend, because I had a wife and two young kids at home that I would miss terribly. He agreed, but I think I only went home once during the entire rehearsal period. Every time I was ready to go, I would step in the limo to leave for Kennedy airport, and I would get a call from Michael and he would ask me to please stay and continue to work with him. He really needed a friend and lots of moral support. I stayed, and instead, I flew my wife and kids to New York so that we could still all be together. Otherwise, it would have been too difficult for me to be apart from them for such an extended period of time.

Michael was obsessed with getting everything right. He rehearsed and rehearsed and rehearsed. We had lots of great dancers to back him up, but we kept the scale of the production numbers small, at least by Michael Jackson standards. We talked about building a satellite stage right in the middle of the audience so that Michael could sit among his fans.

Michael planned on having only one guest on the show, and that guest was Marcel Marceau, the world-famous mime. (Marcel Marceau was a French Jew who during the Holocaust led many young children to safety by pantomiming to keep them calm and to remain silent so that they wouldn't be detected by the Nazis.) Michael idolized Marcel and called him personally to ask him to be on the special. Then Jim Morey took over and brilliantly made the deal. Marcel almost never appeared on television, but he had a passion for Michael and his music. It would be history-making for both of them. The whole idea had the genius of Michael Jackson written all over it and reflected Michael's creativity that went way beyond his music.

Michael sang a song that he wrote called "Have You Seen My Childhood?" while Marcel Marceau mimed the words. It was brilliant and incredibly moving. Unfortunately, nobody but the television staff and crew ever got to see it. You'll find out why in a minute.

You have to listen to the words carefully. If you know anything about Michael Jackson, you know he wrote his heart out in this song—the story about his troubled childhood and his tough father who drove him relentlessly to succeed. Anyone who has had a difficult childhood can relate to the words of this song—again, that is the genius of Michael Jackson! His ability to communicate raw emotions through music and lyrics.

I staged the song in such a way that the main stage was completely dark. Then, I brought a spotlight up center stage, and Michael stepped into that spotlight and started singing. Then I brought up a second spotlight just upstage left of Michael with Marcel Marceau standing and miming the words of the song.

A pitch-black stage with two pools of light shining straight down, Michael in one, Marcel in the other; it was incredibly dramatic and powerful. You should know that Michael studied Marcel's miming and incorporated some of his gestures into his own dances. And Marcel's face was so sad. It spoke directly to Michael's story, without words.

Anyway, every night when I used to go up to Michael's room at the Four Seasons where he was camped out, we would talk about the show and how we were going to make it the best show in television history. But, at some point, the conversation always turned into a discussion about his life and his problems. I was not only his good friend, producer, and director, but I became his therapist, a role I was not equipped to play, nor did I want to.

Finally, I said, "Michael, I'm only responding to your questions because we're friends. I'm like an older brother to you. And I'm only telling you what I know and how I feel. I'm not a doctor. You really need to speak to somebody about your issues."

He said, "My father always taught us that only sick people go to doctors."

I said to him, "Michael, let me tell you something with love." I wanted to say to him, "You're sick and you do need help," but I didn't. Instead, I told him, "It would be good for you to see a doctor, a really good therapist. You could use some help!" I felt comfortable enough with him to be totally honest and I wanted to be helpful. That's the kind of relationship we had.

One of his problems was that while we were working together in New York he was physically not well. He wasn't eating properly, and he was much too thin—obvious signs of stress. He was pushing himself to the brink of total exhaustion chasing perfection. He kept getting weaker and weaker, and he wasn't sleeping. I said to him, "Michael, you're not going to make it through this if you don't start taking better care of yourself." His "bodyguard" Wayne was trying to do everything he could to keep Michael healthy. But you can't force Michael to do anything he doesn't want to do.

As far as his performance and choreography on the show, I told him, with a huge smile on my face, "You've got to do something other than just the moonwalk and the crotch grab." He obviously always did an awful lot more than that. I was just trying to make a point, and he got the message.

I convinced him to let me hire a couple of different choreographers. Barry Lather, an incredible dancer and even better choreographer (he is Usher's choreographer today as well as Carrie Underwood's, and many others), and a young kid and a terrific dancer who was new to the game of choreography—Jamie King—and Michael's long-time in-house choreographers and favorite dancers, Lavelle Smith and Travis Payne. We also hired a new choreographer named Morleigh Steinberg who brought her own unique style to the special. My friend Kenny Ortega, director and choreographer extraordinaire, acted as the overall supervising choreographer along with the brilliant chore-ographer, director, producer, and my really good friend, Debbie Allen.

Kenny Ortega and Debbie Allen had worked with Michael many times, and Michael felt comfortable with them. Each choreographer was assigned two or three different numbers to design. There were dozens of dancers who rehearsed with the choreographers at the Sony rehearsal hall in Manhattan before they went into the Beacon Theatre, which was only available for a limited period. Once the cho-reographers felt sufficiently comfortable that their numbers were set, Michael would come in, watch, and then step into the act. Everyone rehearsed, rehearsed, and rehearsed. The schedule was brutal for everyone, especially Michael, who was in every number in the show.

Brad Buxer, Michael's musical director, came in from Los Angeles. He used to come into the dance rehearsals to make sure that all the rehearsal music tracks that he recorded off-site were correct and in sync with the dance numbers.

There was so much to coordinate but I had picked the best people for every job, and I knew they would deliver. I don't know what the budget for that show was for dancers and choreographers. And, of course, there were Los Angeles musicians that Michael insisted on using. I couldn't even fathom what HBO was spending, but I, along with everyone else, wanted to make sure that Michael was comfortable and that the show would be the best it could possibly be. Man, oh man, did we work hard; I mean, *everybody*! I don't know that I've ever worked harder, and I'm sure I'm not alone in feeling that way. And then of course the marketing was in full swing to ensure that all the money that was invested would pay off in viewership. The buzz about the show was off the charts.

The musical numbers that were slated for the show included "The Way You Make Me Feel," "Bad," "Earth Song," "You Are Not Alone," "Black or White," "Smooth Criminal," "Smile," "Man in the Mirror," and of course the Marcel Marceau-Michael Jackson duet, "Have You Seen My Childhood." The simplicity of that song provided a genius counterpoint to all the highly choreographed production numbers.

A few days before rehearsal and taping, the marquee at the Beacon Theatre read: "Michael Jackson: One Night Only," which attracted huge crowds outside the theater in the days leading up to Michael's performances. The audiences for the dress rehearsals and the taping were handpicked by Sandy Gallin and Jim Morey and a special staff of people at HBO chosen for this project only.

The set was gorgeous. It had a very different feel than what a fan might normally see at a big Michael Jackson concert. My production designer was my favorite, Joe Stewart. What a gifted designer, and you couldn't meet a nicer, kinder, more talented man. I so love working with him. The orchestra was wrapped around the stage, and there were two-story platforms built at the back for additional musicians on each level; and downstage right and left were Michael's regular band members led by Brad Buxer. The lighting was designed by Gregory Brunton in such a way that the band could appear and disappear, and whenever it disappeared there was a beautiful starry sky behind Michael. He looked as if he was floating in space.

As with every on-air HBO show, we scheduled two dress rehearsals and then two taped shows before a live audience that would be edited for the December 10 airing. HBO would run the taped dress rehearsal, simultaneously in sync—as close as they could get to the broadcast. If, God forbid, anything happened on the live show broadcast, they could switch over to the prior night's taped dress rehearsal, and hopefully the switchover would be close enough not to be noticed.

We started our run-through of the dress rehearsal, which we would tape later that night. That taping would become our "backup" show for HBO. Earlier in the day, Michael gave a brief interview with Marcel Marceau for the press and allowed the photographers to take pictures.[8]

We started the run-through right on schedule, and we were halfway through "Man in the Mirror." Michael was struggling, losing words, messing up the choreography, and then he suddenly collapsed. The music stopped, my stage manager, Dave Wader, ran out on stage to make sure that Michael was okay, and Jim Morey, who was sitting with me in the control room, jumped up, ran into the theater, down the aisle, and onto the stage. Michael's security team and his trusted bodyguard, Wayne, were right there making sure that he was protected and safe. Over the headset, the stage manager said to me, "Call 911," because I was closest to a phone in the truck. I couldn't dial fast enough. The NYC Police Department was amazing. The ambulance was there in less than three minutes. I later found out that Jim Morey had also called 911 on his way to the stage. I couldn't believe what was going on. Michael was on stage singing and dancing his ass off, I was calling camera shots and trying to make it look great (there's that word again), and then he fell forward right on top of the grat-

---

8   You can view the photo shoot, along with a few seconds of rehearsal footage with and without Michael, here: https://www.damienshields.com/michael-jackson-one-night-only/.

ing, which was built into the floor for special effects. It looked like he tripped and fell. He didn't even have time to put his hands out to break his fall. He was *out*.

Before the ambulance got there, the press was standing outside the theater doors. Are you kidding me? Really? I couldn't believe it! The press must have been listening in on the 911 emergency calls. Michael was rushed to Beth Israel Medical Center North. The *New York Times* reported the next morning, "Michael Jackson collapses at rehearsal." We continued rehearsals that evening with a stand-in while Michael was being attended to—some of us thought it might just be exhaustion and, knowing Michael's work ethic, we would see him tomorrow, but it didn't happen. Michael was in critical condition. His personal doctor, who was flown in from Los Angeles, told Sandy, Jim, me, and HBO that there was no way the show could go on. Holy shit! *What?* That couldn't be. Now what are we going to do? I had to deliver the devastating news to all the cast and crew who assembled in the audience at the Beacon Theatre that the show was canceled. I couldn't help myself. I started to cry.

All that work. All that time spent. Months of rehearsals. All of us involved in the show only wanted Michael to be okay. I think we were hoping for a miracle so that this incredible television special could still happen. Michael had his own small camera crew who taped everything he did as a performer. Somewhere, someone must have the tapes of all the rehearsals. I'm sure we could make an interesting documentary special about "The Making of the Special That Never Happened." Oh well, all of us who were there have incredible memories.

Everybody was concerned for Michael. It does me no good to say that I saw it coming, but practically from day one I could see that Michael was in a downward spiral. It was tragic! Devastating! I wish I could have done more to help him. I tried.

The doctors diagnosed Michael with low blood pressure, dehydration, and complete exhaustion. He recovered but not in time for us to tape the show, edit it, and air it on HBO. Afterward, he managed to weather the terrible allegations to the best of his ability despite its lingering shadow, even without *One Night Only*. He never lost his creativity and brilliant mind, but rumors swirled around for a while that Michael had faked his collapse because he wasn't sufficiently prepared.

After 9/11 he wanted to do something to honor the victims and their families and help heal the country. The special *United We Stand* was totally Michael's idea. I served as the executive producer and directed some of the segments along with my friend Alan Carter, whom I asked to come in and give me a hand. The show was too big and happened too quickly for me to try to do it all on my own. The show was pitched to John Hamlin at ABC. It was a no-brainer for him, and within days we were off and running. The concert was incredible. Let me share with you some of the artists who showed up to perform: Mariah Carey, James Brown, Al Green, Carole King, Rod Stewart, Bette Midler, America, Huey Lewis, Destiny's Child, P. Diddy, the Goo Goo Dolls, Train, Backstreet Boys, Usher, Pink, and NSYNC.

Michael appeared in the finale and brought everyone out on stage. While I was in the editing room after the taping of the event, I got a visit from John Hamlin, my friend at ABC, accompanied by a number of ABC lawyers. I thought, "Oh shit, now what?"

Unbeknownst to us, Michael had a contract with another network forbidding him from appearing on any other network special. Their lawyers told ABC, "You've got to take him out of the show. He can't appear on camera." We had no choice. As the producer/director I was so saddened by this turn of events and sort of pissed off at the amount of additional editing that this would entail. When I edited the show together, every time there was a shot of Michael, I had to cut to a wide shot or some other camera angle to make sure that he was never seen. For the finale of the show, all the people in the arena were holding their flashlights, waving them back and forth, which was certainly moving and emotional, and all the artists who appeared on the show were on stage, including Michael, but his face was never caught on camera.

When I spoke with Michael by phone after the taping, he told me he was so happy with the evening and that he was so glad that I was involved with the show, and then he thanked me for doing it for him. I didn't have the heart to tell him that he would never be seen on camera; besides, it wasn't right for me to be the one to break that news to him. His lawyer definitely needed to be the one to tell him.

I wished that Michael could have been front and center—after all, the show was his idea. If there was ever a show that would have enhanced his career and demonstrated what a giving, generous, kind person he was, this was the one! And only those of us who were there ever knew of his involvement.

What a sad story.

One of the good times working with Michael Jackson.

Michael Jackson and I were best buddies and made a really good team.

Dave Wader, my longtime stage manager with me and Michael Jackson.

CHAPTER 21

MY LIFE-LONG DREAM COMES TRUE (1989–1997)

WHEN I WAS SIXTEEN OR SO, I INSTINCTIVELY KNEW THAT I WOULD ONE DAY direct the Oscars.

The dream began in my family's living room. One night between commercials, while watching the Oscars, I heard a newscaster say that the Oscars telecast was the most popular television program in the world, challenged only by the Super Bowl.

I was intrigued. I filed this piece of information away in my head. I had some serious life decisions ahead of me. As I've already said, my parents expected me to become a doctor or lawyer, but that was not a commitment I felt ready to make, and that was not what I wanted to do. Of course, I wanted to please my parents, but I also wanted to figure out what my life's passion was and to follow it. How many people take a job just to put food on the table? Or follow in some-one's footsteps and do what is expected of them? I knew that wasn't going to be me. I was strong-willed and knew that I had to find my own way, and of course, I had Grandpa Sam Groper, giving me good advice and opening doors to my secret goal by introducing me to Uncle Monty Hall.

By 1989, I had spent twenty years building my career in Hollywood, directing TV series and specials, making valuable con-nections, and earning a good reputation. At the age of forty-three, I was one of the most experienced directors of live television in town.

It was so exciting to be working with talented people on a veteran team that functioned seamlessly with me at the helm. Jeff Margolis Productions was definitely one of the go-to companies that could be counted on to deliver first-class entertainment in many different genres of live television.

When the phone rang and the voice at the other end asked me if I wanted to direct the 61st Academy Awards show, I did what any ambitious director who dreamed of this his whole life might do. I passed out! I'm exaggerating here. I honestly can't remember if I was that carried away. It's not the image of me that I want to spread around. Let me just say that the phone call from my friend John Hamlin, who was then Vice President for Special Programs at ABC Entertainment, opened up a new world for me, and I couldn't wait to get started. When I hung up, I immediately called my wife, Leslie, who was beside herself with joy and pride, and then I called my parents. My dad cried. He said to me, "I might have to send you two corks for the Oscars."

The Academy of Motion Picture Arts and Sciences had a very interesting deal with the network. ABC aired the Oscars every year and was responsible for hiring and paying the director. I never understood the agreement between ABC and the Academy, and I really didn't need to know. All I knew was that I was going to direct the Academy Awards.

Apparently, there had been a falling out with the 1988 director, and word was going around that someone else would be taking over as the director. John Hamlin was a huge supporter and a huge fan of mine. (John is now in his nineties, and we still talk on the phone every few weeks.)

Anyway, John called me right away as soon as he knew the previous director was out. He said, "Jeff, ABC would like you to take over as director of the Academy Awards; are you ready to do the Oscars?"

I was speechless but John knew my momentary silence meant yes. I don't know how many other directors I was up against, but any one of them would have been thrilled to be chosen.

When I pulled myself together, I said, "What time do I have to be there, John?"

"I'm not sure but hold on."

John called Allan Carr, the movie mogul and Broadway producer, who that very day had been hired to produce the 61st Academy Awards. It would be his first time up to bat. (He was known as a talent manager, television, movie, and Broadway producer, and had a knack for thinking big, big, big.) I knew Allan Carr because I had worked on two Ann-Margret specials which he co-produced. The other producer was Ann-Margret's husband, Roger Smith. I was the associate director and Art Fisher was the director on those two specials. I was Art's right hand, so I was in the rehearsal hall when Art wasn't there.

John said to Allan, "Congratulations on producing the Oscars. Do you have any idea who you might want us to go after as a director?"

"Let me think about it. I need to think about the people I have worked with in television," answered Allan.

"Let me run a name by you. How about Jeff Margolis?"

"Done! Oh my God, Jeff Margolis, peeerfeeect!" (Only Allan could say perfect like that.)

Allan called me as soon as he hung up with John, and we chatted like two old friends who hadn't seen each other for years. He told me everything he wanted to do on the show. I knew that Allan wanted to break the mold—make the show different—and he was counting on me to realize his vision. I was up for the challenge. At the time, I did not know that producing the Oscars was Allan's lifelong dream. Hmmm? What a coincidence. As we started to put it together, I thought to myself: "Jeez, this is not like any Oscar broadcast in the history of the show! It's going to be very memorable." And it was! (And, unfortunately for Allan, not in a good way.)

Allan had produced the movies *Grease* and *Can't Stop the Music*, and *La Cage aux Folles*, a mega-hit on Broadway which ran away with all the Tony Awards imaginable. He had big ideas for the Oscars, which he shared with me on that telephone call and in the days and weeks to come. His assignment from the Academy and from ABC was

"Change the show. Make it young, but don't throw the baby out with the bath water. We're losing our young audience. It's become a show for the baby boomers, and we have to get the young kids back again." Talk about pressure, and pressure on Allan Carr, a guy who did not have a lot of years of television producing under his belt. He was in a sense a wild card to be the Oscars producer, but an interesting and smart choice. Before getting into films, he was known for staging big promotional events and had a gift for showmanship, and he was a talent manager guiding the careers of a lot of Hollywood and New York stars.

Producers expect me, as the director, to make their ideas work. They come up with the vision, and I make it happen. Sometimes, that vision feels like an insurmountable task. I get it done anyway. Other times, what they want, I know should not happen. Every fiber in my body tells me it should not happen. While I can express these concerns, in the end, I still have to realize what they want, and Allan Carr wanted something that I knew was wrong for the Oscars, wrong for television, and wrong for him, but I couldn't convince him. And thus began my adventure directing my first Academy Awards show in 1989, which became known thereafter as the "Rob Lowe sings to Snow White" debacle. This experience was not how I imagined my first foray into the world of the Academy Awards would be, but I was determined to make it successful so that I'd be invited back the next year, and the year after that. I wanted the Oscars to be on my calendar for at least sixteen years—for it to be the centerpiece of my schedule.

Allan relied on me to help him make decisions about how to do things because he had never produced a show like this before, and he knew I had years of television experience including directing live awards shows such as the AMAs. He kept saying, "I want a bigger audience in the theater, a lot more stars in those seats." I knew from all the years of the show being at the Dorothy Chandler Pavilion that seating was really tight.

I said to him, "Hey, I helped move the American Music Awards to the Shrine Auditorium so it could be bigger and better; lots more seats there to be filled by stars. Maybe we should move the Oscars back to the Shrine. There would be four seats for each of the nominees instead of the usual two." That was a big deal, and Allan loved it.

When I was hired, ABC had always wanted the show to be three hours.

But it never was. During the time I was directing the show, ABC decided to allocate three and a half hours of prime time. Before that happened though, the shortest show I ever did was twenty-four minutes too long. No matter what you try and do as the Oscars producer or director (and I had a few insurance policies up my sleeve to try to shorten the running time), the winners get to the podium and usually have a long list of people that they worked with to thank, and God forbid, they should forget their agent, their manager, their drama teacher from the twelfth grade, and oh yeah, their partner, their children, their parents, and so on, and so on. You can only hope they have a small family and they achieved their success without any help from their friends (too numerous to mention), but that's not going to happen. And also, God forbid, they should decide to turn their acceptance speech at the podium into a plea for some cause. *Boring!* Get the hook. (I have nothing against celebrities supporting important causes, but not on the Oscar clock when we need to drop the mic after three hours.)

It was Allan Carr's idea to have the presenters say, "And the Oscar goes to…" instead of "The winner is…." It seemed like a more genteel and inclusive way to present the award and make those nominees who didn't "win" feel less like losers. The concept of winners and losers has been late-night-talk-show fodder for some of the most outstanding, comedic host monologues in the history of the Academy Awards.

I created the "In Memoriam" package for the show in 1989. The Oscars used to do a memorial tribute to one movie star who died during the year. When I was creating the show with Allan, we were looking for moments. Allan really wanted to make the audience go through every emotion they could possibly go through on the show.

I said, "The memorial package that they always do is so heart-wrenching. It's always so meaningful and lovely. Let's not recognize just one person. Let's make it an 'in memoriam' package, and do a real tribute to those that make the movies we love. It could run as long as five minutes. In addition to actors, there are famous directors, famous writers, famous costume designers, and so on." It has remained part of the show today, and there are sometimes as many as thirty people acknowledged in the "In Memoriam" package. It's always one of the most touching and sincere moments in the show. Most of the other award shows on TV now have an "In Memoriam" package. Fortunately, Allan was receptive to this innovation, but it wasn't enough to keep the ship from sinking.

Sixteen Minutes of Hell with Snow White

Allan was hell-bent on a sixteen-minute production number to open the show with Rob Lowe and Snow White (actress Eileen Bowman) singing a duet. The number begins with Snow White talking to Army Archerd (the entertainment columnist for *Variety*) on the red carpet, then following dancers in star costumes down the aisle inside the Shrine Auditorium onto the stage, which was a recreation of the Coconut Grove, an old Hollywood nightclub.

(Oy, that's only the first minute and a half.) Then, Merv Griffin appears and calls out the names of some of the Hollywood old-timers like Cyd Charisse, Roy Rogers, and Dale Evans, who are sitting at tables in the club. Then he introduces Rob Lowe as Snow White's blind date. They sing a duet, "Proud Mary," and finally there is a kick line on stage, and the number ends with a few words from Lily Tomlin "trying to make sense of the whole thing" and reminding the audience that over a billion and a half people are watching.

I insisted that he cut the Snow White number down by six to eight minutes. That might have been acceptable (if it weren't so corny).

I said to Allan, "This is television! You can't do a sixteen-minute opening number. This isn't Broadway."

"Why not?"

"After about five minutes, viewers will start changing the channel. They'll find something else to watch. Television has to move fast. People don't have the attention span to watch a sixteen-minute song-and-dance number."

"You'll make it work! You'll make it live. You'll make it sing!" Oh God, how I tried.

All the planning in the world could not have avoided the Snow White debacle.

The biggest criticism of the 61st Academy Awards presentation was having Snow White on the red carpet. To make matters worse, she proceeded into the auditorium with cameras following her, and interrupted big stars who were nervous, waiting to see if they were going to win. She went up to them and in a high, squeaky voice said, "Oh, Clint Eastwood!" and made some kind of comment. Or she asked a star to do something ridiculous. Nobody in the audience liked that bit at all. Snow White wasn't a star. She was just an actor who was hired! If it had been some big personality, it might not have been as offensive, or they would have known how to handle the audience with more finesse. Imagine an unknown trying to kibbitz with Clint Eastwood, or Julia Roberts, or Denzel Washington, or Kirk Douglas, or Michelle Yeoh, or Brad Pitt, or Meryl Streep, or Viola Davis, or Leo DiCaprio, or Penelope Cruz, or Shirley MacLaine, or Morgan Freeman, or any other major star. Not a good idea. I don't really know what Allan was thinking at that point, but nobody could stop him, not even me.

Up until producing the Oscars, everything Allan did was magic. He was always on top somehow. But this time, for the first time, the press cut him off at the knees. And even with me having his back I couldn't help him. You never cut your teeth in television with the biggest show on the air—it's a recipe for disaster. You work your way up, just as I had.

And oh my God, I felt so sorry for him. I didn't know what to do. I couldn't make it better for him, as much as I tried. He was devastated! I think that could've been the beginning of the end for him. (Allan went into seclusion and died in 1999, ten years after his Oscar experience.) I don't think he ever really recovered from what turned out to be quite a traumatic experience for him. Even so, apart from the opening number, it was a great Oscars show.

And there was more trouble. The day after the Oscars, Disney went to the Academy and said to them, "Hey, nobody asked us for permission to use Snow White. You can't use Snow White without our permission. We're going to sue you."

The Academy said, "Wait a second. Let us talk to the producer."

Allan's response was, "Oh, I know the guys at Disney, and I knew they wouldn't mind, so I didn't bother, you know...."

Somehow, it got swept under the carpet. Disney never sued the Academy, and it went away. But I remember the following day, the Academy called a news conference, and Allan had to address the situation head-on.

Allan called me early in the morning—it was still dark outside—and he said, "You've got to come to the press conference with me. I just don't want to go alone."

We were in it together, and I said, "If you want me to be there, I'll be there."

I got all dressed and ready to go, and then his publicist called me and said, "Don't come. The Academy wants Allan to do this on his own. It's his problem, so let him handle it."

Oh my God...poor Allan. No use in kidding myself here. I knew there was no way he could talk his way out of this one. No one could with such a setup. Rob Lowe, bless his soul, even jokes about it to this day. Knowing what I knew, I had to put all my efforts into minimizing the loss. If I survived, maybe I'd get a chance to direct the Oscars the next year. But it was not guaranteed. I wondered if I'd end up being partially to blame, or if all the criticism would be aimed at Allan. (We all know what the outcome was.)

Choreographing the Oscars

The rest of the 1989 Oscars went without a hitch, and, thanks to Allan's brilliance and our collaboration, there were many memorable moments. Allan knew a choreographer that he liked very much who had a long-running live musical in San Francisco called *Beach Blanket Babylon.*

Allan loved that show. It was very, very San Francisco gay, with the costumes and the makeup and men playing women's parts. He wanted this choreographer for the Oscars. Of course, the choreographer had never done television before and didn't know anything about cameras and staging for television.

I said to Allan, "Okay, that's fine, but we need to bring in somebody who knows television or we'll never get through this." So, I brought in a couple of choreographers, and one of them was Kenny Ortega. (Remember, I brought Kenny in on the Michael Jackson HBO special?)

I don't think hiring the *Beach Blanket Babylon* choreographer was a huge mistake. I thought it was a good idea, but he needed guidance. The highest praise I can give to the first Oscars I directed with Allan was that we got through it. It was really a tough one, man.

He also made a brilliant choice of bringing Marvin Hamlisch on as musical director. He composed the music for the Broadway hit *A Chorus Line*, and Allan was also managing Marvin's career. He thought that the Oscars would be a great career move for Marvin, and it was. Over the course of his extraordinary career, Marvin Hamlisch earned an Emmy, an Oscar, a Tony, and a Grammy. What a joy to have worked with him!

~ ~

Hollywood always likes to guess who will host the Oscars. Allan couldn't make up his mind, so he asked me to make a list of people I thought could host the 1989 Oscars. I made a list, and he didn't like anybody on my list. He didn't like anybody on ABC's list. He didn't like anybody on the Academy's list.

The two of us were talking one night—just Allan and me. We were sitting in front of his fireplace, and he was drinking—a lot. He was in so much pain from something, God only knows what, and he always said, "Vodka makes my pain go away." We were chatting about hosts, and we both said, "What if we did a show without a host?" It was hard to have a conversation with Allan when he was drinking. He thought that alcohol made him smarter and more creative when he had a glass in his hand, and most of the time he was right, but sometimes it did negatively affect his judgment.

We came up with the no-host idea together. I wanted to include Allan in all the ideas that I had because even if an idea was mine, he was the producer and at the end of the day, they needed to be his ideas. It was so important to him. That was okay with me. It doesn't matter who gets credit for an idea as long as it's good and it works.

Finally, Allan decided that we would not have a host. Instead, he wanted presenters who were married or living together or had starred in a movie together or were just best friends. He called it "Compadres, Comrades, Companions, Co-Stars, and Couples"—a description that the Hollywood crowd loved.

If you look at the show, that's how he booked it. For example, it was Melanie Griffith and Don Johnson, or Burt Lancaster and Kirk Douglas, Demi Moore and Bruce Willis, Sammy Davis Jr. and Gregory Hines, and Sean Connery, Michael Caine, and Roger Moore, Edward James Olmos and Max von Sydow all together—all well-known and much-beloved stars. It was brilliantly booked and a great idea. Danette Herman was the talent producer and was Allan's biggest cheerleader and support system on this gigantic undertaking. Each presenter was the host of the award they were presenting.

Holding It All Together

Did I worry about anything? Of course, I did, but I didn't want to put a kibosh on it by thinking, "Ugh, this is going to happen, or that is not going to happen." I just approached it as if "everything's going to be great!" (There it is again.)

I keep everyone calm if I'm calm. It all comes from the top. I've seen directors completely destroy a show by getting the production staff and the crew so nervous and worked up by yelling and screaming, that of course they're going to make mistakes!

WE'RE LIVE IN 5

The number of people under my direct or indirect "command" is greater than anything I had done or will have done in my television career, and I would guess that anyone directing the Oscars would probably make the same claim.

Here's what I'm talking about. For example, on a special like *Amy Grant: A Christmas to Remember* we had two cameras. It was a location shoot done location style, like making a movie. Staff and crew totaled about fifty people. For the SAG Awards (which you will hear about later), on rehearsal day and show day, there were probably 350 staff and crew. In terms of the total people credentialed for the SAG Awards, there were probably over 2,000 people involved on the day before and on show day. That includes groups like security guards, catering, press, and publicists.

The number of people on Oscars rehearsal day and show day was probably roughly 4,500–5,000. A small town!

What happens if someone makes a mistake on a live show? There's nothing you can do. I always compare what I do to a pilot flying a jet. Once he pushes that throttle forward and that plane lifts off, he's committed. When he leaves the runway, he's got to get to 35,000 feet in the air. When I'm in the control room looking at the clock before a live show, my associate director counts down from 10; then I hear 5...4...3...2...1, and liftoff, we're LIVE on the air. There's no turning back. Whatever happens, happens. That's what I love about live television.

I have another analogy that describes my role as a director of specials and award shows. A lot of directors have a tough time holding it all together. And a lot of directors rely to a greater or lesser extent on their associate director and technical director to get them through a show. Those directors usually only want to look at one monitor—the program monitor—and they want to see what's being broadcast to the home audience. I can never do that. I'm like a conductor with a full orchestra in front of me. I need to stay a "bar" or two ahead of what the orchestra is playing. Just like the conductor, I have to be ahead of what's happening with all my cameras. When I'm cutting from one camera to the next, my associate director is readying the next shot while I'm looking at a preview monitor to make sure the next shot looks good before I snap my fingers and tell the technical director to take the shot. One of the key principles that I follow when picking a camera for a moment, is to imagine myself sitting in the fifth row center of the theater. As the director, I want to see the performers on stage exactly the way it would look like from that seat—not too close and not too far. It's the way I give the home audience a "fifth row center" seat to everything that's going on.

I'm usually watching at least twenty camera monitors, and about seventy other monitors with playbacks, graphics, live satellite feeds, and so much more—all at the same time—as well as the script, which is rolling at the same time that a presenter is reading it. It's crazy; it's nuts; it's insanity, but I love it. And I must say that not a lot of people have the visual bandwidth to cope with all of that. I'm glad I do.

It's never happened to me yet, but I've seen this on other live award shows. A performer will come out like Adele did on the Grammys a couple of years ago. She started a number with a live orchestra; about twelve bars into the song, she said, "Wait, stop, stop, everybody, stop!"

Everyone thought, "Oh my God, is she having a heart attack?" Elton John was getting a special award, and she was doing a tribute to him. She stopped and said, "I'm so, so sorry. Let me apologize to all of you who are watching. I'm paying tribute to Elton John. He's my friend. I messed up, and I have to start over. Forgive me." And then she said to the conductor, "Whenever you're ready."

And she started over. Oh man, the critics loved it. No one faulted her for being a perfectionist and really caring that her song be the best it could be for her friend Elton. And she did it with such confidence. As the director, you always have to be ready for the unexpected, and respond as seamlessly as possible.

One task I did not take on during my first Oscars gig with Allan Carr was picking the presenters. That was something Allan was so good at and really wanted to do mostly on his own. He would say to me, "What do you think about so-and-so?" Most of the time his ideas were really good. He worked with the talent producer Danette Herman, and they were the perfect team. She had done the Oscars for many years, and she was able to keep Allan focused. She also knew every talent agent, manager, and publicist in Hollywood.

To keep track of what we were doing, we used a board. We built the rundown of the show, and put it up on The Board. How do we want the show to open? What is the first award to be presented, and who should present it? What comes after award number one? When do you go to commercial? How many awards do you do in the next act? Do you do awards two, three, and four? You build a board that way until you have a complete show from beginning to end in however many acts it takes to make a rundown and put together a good show. Using the concept of acts is a great way to keep everything organized, and using a board helps you visualize the show.

Once you know what the award categories are and who the nominees are in each category, you can start to fill in the time slots. Are we going to do a production number to highlight the costume design of each nominee and show all the costumes that were in their movies? Maybe it doesn't work in Act 2 because it's going to be too long. It can't be in an act that's got two other awards in it. Maybe it's got to be in an act that only has one other award. It's a puzzle! Putting The Board together is so much fun but so much work to get it right. Ultimately, we come up with a rundown for the show which we feel will be the most entertaining evening for Hollywood's biggest night and will make the best television special with just the right pacing—at least on paper. This technique of using a board and slotting in numbers is still used today as a tried-and-true organizational tool. It gives you a visual layout of the entire event and helps highlight what might be a problem and where to move awards around to make the event a success!

Projecting the Right Image at the Oscars

When I started directing the Oscars in 1989, I wanted to present myself in the right way all the time, especially on show day. If somebody happened to notice me, I couldn't very well be wearing a Hawaiian shirt and tennis shoes. I felt that would be disrespectful to the Academy.

My solution was, on show night only, to wear a tuxedo. How could I go wrong in a tux? Let me count the ways. First of all, the tux I rented that first year was too tight across the shoulders. I looked like an aging bodyguard, even though I was only in my early forties. And by the way, how do you direct a three-hour live television special, and the biggest event on television, in a tuxedo? Especially if you're as active as I am while you're directing. I was miserable, and at the first commercial break, I had to take my jacket off. You'd think I would have learned after that first year, but no, the next year, there I was again in a tuxedo. However, I did remove my jacket before the show started. I wanted to look nice because when the show was over, I was invited to the Governor's Ball to speak to the guests along with Gil Cates, who was the new producer. After that year, I never wore a tux again during the show; I wanted to be comfortable. I now knew to only get changed into my tux when the show wrapped and I thanked everyone for a great job.

When the third year rolled around, I was ready. I decided I would wear jeans and a T-shirt in the control room, and as usual, I would rent a tux and change after the show. (Why own a tuxedo when you only wear it once a year?) That way I could dress comfortably for work, and after I thanked everyone personally for all they had done to make the show a success, then I would change. Thank yous to everyone were really more important to me than going to the Governor's Ball, so that always came first.

That was the true me—hugging, kissing, shaking hands, and being as personable as possible despite the stress of keeping the show on time and budget. It was one of my rituals—to make sure that I acknowledged everyone who had worked so hard to make me look good on the Oscars, or any show that I do, and to come off as seamlessly as possible. Don't forget, the Oscars were live, and anything that could go wrong might go wrong if everyone wasn't on their A game, myself included.

I eventually sprang for a tuxedo, by the way—I was in it for the long haul—and I wore it on the occasions when I was nominated for an award and had an event to attend. I have pictures of me accepting Emmys and DGA Awards in my own tux and looking every bit the part of how the public thinks a Hollywood producer/director should look. Quite honestly, though, I would always rather be in jeans, some sort of T-shirt, and my Converse sneakers.

Before the show started, I always walked out to the red carpet to make sure that my crew had no problems. Along with my brother, Peter, I had an associate director named Debbie Palacio, and she was so good, totally under control handling the red-carpet arrivals. I would go out there just to wish everyone well and to make sure that everything was set up properly for the big parade of stars, many of whom hoped to walk away that night with an Oscar.

Nervous? Who, Me?

I never get nervous when I have to speak in front of a group of people. I never have and I probably never will. Here's a good example. In 1989, ABC put together my very first production meeting for the Academy Awards. Everybody who had the slightest connection to the Oscars was there—from ABC and Academy staff members to publicists and managers, Los Angeles City Police and Fire Department heads, security, catering, Governors Ball planners, and anyway, I think you get the picture. There were probably 250 to 275 people at this meeting.

I didn't realize that so many people were going to be attending, but it was my meeting and I did what I had to do. I talked through the show and discussed every single element of the rundown. I was as thorough as I could be with each segment.

Then I asked for questions from the attendees and answered all the ones that I could. Those I couldn't answer I directed to someone in the department that was responsible. Then I ended the big meeting and asked everybody to break out into smaller groups, all those who needed to talk about their particular area of responsibility. I thanked everyone, wished them good luck, and told them that it was "going to be great."

This intense planning was essential, and it made people realize the importance of this event—the biggest television show on the air.

So, as you may already have gathered, I made it through the 1989 Oscars unscathed, and the prospect of doing many more became a reality. I just needed to pass muster with whoever was ordained as the producer for 1990.

Hanging out with the Oscars statues.

Clint Eastwood backstage at the Oscars rehearsal.

Samuel L. Jackson and John Travolta join me at the Oscars rehearsals.

CHAPTER 22

CHANGING OF THE GUARD AT THE OSCARS

KARL MALDEN, THE PRESIDENT OF THE ACADEMY OF MOTION PICTURE ARTS and Sciences, hired Gil Cates to produce the Oscars in 1990. Gil was on the Academy's Board of Governors and had a long career in film, television, and on Broadway. ABC was responsible for supplying the director, but the director had to be approved by the Academy and the producer of the show. The Academy said, "Well, we've hired a new producer, Gil Cates, and we'll have Gil and Jeff meet. We're fine with Jeff, and if Gil's fine with him, then we're all good."

I met with Gil, and we hit it off right away and tried to figure out what took us so long to get together.

We met for lunch, and we had a great time. Gil told the Academy and ABC that he wanted to work with me and that he loved what I did on Allan Carr's show, as much as it was criticized for the Snow White debacle. From a technical standpoint he thought the show was flawless.

With Gil producing the Oscars instead of Allan Carr, the environment was much calmer. Gil included me in everything. I would plan out all the acts of the show with him. We would sit and play with The Board every day. "Let's move this to Act Three." We would look at it, and I would say, "Well I have a great idea for Act Four. I have an idea of how we can hold the audience and make sure they don't change the channel during the commercial." Gil and I would agree or not, and if not, we'd change it. Lots of hours, lots of hard work, but I loved it.

Once we were happy with each act and what award was going to be delivered in each act, then we would start the who-is-going-to-present-the-award game: "Gee, Sandra Bullock would be great for that award, and she was in such-and-such a movie this year. Quincy Jones would be great to do the award for such-and-such." There were certain award presenters that were a matter of tradition. For example, whoever won Best Actor in a prior year would present the Best Actress the following year, and the Best Supporting Actor winner would present the Best Supporting Actress winner the following year.

We would play that game, and it was lots of work, and never a slam dunk. Booking presenters on an awards show is one of the most difficult aspects of the show, believe it or not. Ask Danette Herman, who has booked over twenty-five Oscar shows. There are so many performers who are afraid of live television. They're used to being able to do as many takes within reason as they want when they're making a movie. There are no second takes on a live television show. Some stars are scared to death to go out on a live show even with the script rolling right in front of them on a big screen prompter. We get a lot of turndowns. And there are always practical considerations such as scheduling; for example, the "perfect" presenter for a specific award might be on a film shoot overseas and unavailable.

So, we depended a lot on Danette Herman, the talent producer on the show. She was always in the presenter meetings. She was a great booker with excellent ideas. She'd say, "Oh, gee, we've gone after him four times before, and he always says no."

Gil would say, "Well, hopefully he won't say no for a fifth time. Give him a call."

Danette would instigate the calls by contacting a publicist or an agent. There were some calls that Gil wanted to make on his own. I never made a call for a presenter. That was for Gil and Danette to do.

Debbie Allen as the choreographer was fantastic. Gil loved her, and she loved doing the show. Debbie and I were best friends forever, so that was all good. Gil brought on Bill Conti, who was known for writing the theme song for *Rocky*, and he was also the musical director for the movie. It was Bill's first time as musical director for the

Oscars. He was masterful, and the musicians loved working with him. He was suave and sophisticated and had the chops. Bill reprised his role as musical director up until the 1996 Oscars when Quincy Jones took over as producer and hired a new musical director.

During Gil's time in charge, he wanted to put his stamp on the show, so he brought in a lot of new people and new ideas. They pretty much stayed through all the Gil Cates years. Gil takes credit for bringing Billy Crystal on as the host, and we both take the credit for Whoopi Goldberg.

We came up with a format for the Oscars which seemed to work very well. We gave the show a theme every year. One year it was "Women in Film," and one year it was "Films around the World." That seemed to work for us. We just lucked out the year that we did "Women in Film" as four of the five nominees for Best Costume were women in 1993. We were able to make a big deal out of that. I wanted to contribute to the "Women in Film" idea, but I couldn't come up with anything. Not at first, anyway.

Well, I was in the habit of listening to my favorite FM radio station, 94.7, the Wave, every morning on my way to work. And my favorite DJ was a woman with the greatest voice, and the smoothest style of delivery, and she made the music so much more enjoyable; I fell in love with her. Her name is Randy Thomas. So, I'm driving into the Oscar office one morning, listening to Randy on the radio, and it hits me...OMG, Oscars theme, "Women in Film," why not have a woman announcer on the live telecast for the very first time in Oscars history? Wait a minute, for the very first time in *live television broadcast history*! Epic! I couldn't get to the office fast enough to share my idea with Gil.

"Gilbert, I have an incredible idea, women in film, a female announcer for the very first time in television history, on the Oscars...."

"Jeffrey, let me think about that for a minute, my boy...."

Wait, what? Think about it? I wanted Gil to be jumping up and down with joy, but then I remembered that he wasn't quite as spontaneous as I was when I thought that an idea was brilliant.

He finally said, "I like your idea, but I'm not familiar with Randy's voice. We need to get her voice on tape."

I didn't know Randy, but I called the radio station, and as soon as I mentioned that I was calling from the Oscars, the next thing I knew was that the voice on the other end said, "Hi, Jeff, this is Randy…." And the rest shall we say is history. Randy did the Oscars, she hit a home run out of the park, and before she knew what hit her, she was doing the Emmy Awards, the Tony Awards, and more. She opened the door for women announcers on television. It makes me feel proud that I had a little something to do with her success and for giving other women a shot at a role that had typically gone to men.

After working with Gil for six years, Quincy Jones was hired to produce the 1996 Oscars. Quincy had never produced an awards show. That year Gil had too much on his plate, and he couldn't do the Oscars. As the dean of the film and television school at UCLA, he had taken on responsibility for the Geffen Playhouse, which was named after media mogul David Geffen, who had donated $5 million, the largest gift toward buying and renovating the historic building (formerly known as the Westwood Playhouse). It was located just off UCLA's Westwood campus and had strong support from the local community. It was up to Gil to make sure it continued to be successful but make it even more relevant in the theatrical community.

Gil said to the Academy that he needed to take a year off, and the Academy agreed to his request. (What else could they say?) Then, they went to Quincy Jones and said, "It's only going to be a one-year deal to produce the show."

Quincy said, "That's fine with me. I don't want to do it more than one year. From what I understand, it's way too much work to do for more than a year."

Quincy and I had worked together before, and he knew I had seven Oscars award shows under my belt: one with Allan Carr and six with Gil. Quincy called me and said, "Before anybody else calls you, I just want to make sure it's okay with you if I tell ABC and the Academy that I want you as the director."

I said, "I'm there, but I feel like I need to touch base with Gil and make sure he's comfortable with all of this."

Quincy said, "Of course, Jeff, you're such a mensch."

Gil had no problem. He said, "My son, go with my blessing. Make us proud."

I enjoyed working with Quincy, who wanted the show to be musical from fade-in to fade-out. He wanted there to be music everywhere under everything. We pretty much did that, except when the recipients were doing their thank yous and giving their nods to the other nominees.

One of Quincy's major contributions was nailing down presenters. He was unbelievable. He had a personal phone book like nobody else. He wanted to make a lot of the calls himself. I remember in a meeting, Quincy said, "Let them say no to me, or better yet, let them try to say no to me." That was the power of Q. And with the help of Danette Herman, I think Quincy got commitments from everyone he asked.

It was such a joy to work with Quincy. Remember, I was his "brother from another mother." We couldn't have been closer and more in sync with our creative ideas. When Gil picked up the producing reins again after Quincy's term, I expected to stay on board. But as you will find out later, something happened that was so unimaginable that I could not have made it up had I tried.

Me and my buddy Oscar.

Directing the Oscars, my happy place.

Peter, my brother, is my associate director.

Producer Gil Cates and me going over the Oscar show rundown.

Debbie Allen's brilliant choreography helped me win the Director's Guild
Of America Award for directing the 65th Annual Academy Awards.

CHAPTER 23

OSCARS PRESENTERS AND HONOREES

As the director of eight Academy Awards, there were so many memorable moments during each show (some in front of the camera and some behind the scenes). Every award is important to the person who receives it, but the six awards that everyone in the home audience waits for are Best Actor, Best Actress, Best Supporting Actor and Actress, Best Director, and Best Picture. No one in Nebraska pays that much attention to the award for costume design, for example, but costume designers do and so do the producers, directors, and stars who work with them. The same is true for set designers and cinematographers as well as all the other awards. Winning an Oscar can be a career changer and move a name from a "maybe" to the top of everyone's list in the blink of an eye. The same is true for the person who directs the Oscars; having that credit—whether for one year or eighteen—puts you into an elite club that forever changes your career trajectory.

I have so many *personal* stories about the Academy Awards, and I've worked with literally thousands of people who stood on the stage to take home the Oscar statue, but here are some of my favorite tales of presenters and honorees.

Steven Spielberg and His Mother

Clint Eastwood presented Steven Spielberg the Oscar for Best Director for *Schindler's List* in 1994, when I was directing the show. (It was up against another favorite, Jane Campion and *The Piano*. In an ironic twist of fate, both directors were up for the award again in 2022, but this time it was Jane Campion who won for *The Power of the Dog*.)

Steven brought his mother with him to the 1994 awards. When I cut to an audience reaction of him sometime early in the evening, I saw that sitting on one side of him was his wife, Kate Capshaw, and on the other side was his mother, whom I recognized from a magazine article I had read about her. She owned a kosher delicatessen called the Milky Way on Pico Boulevard in the Fairfax district of Los Angeles. She was a petite woman with short gray hair, a quick smile, and an unmistakable presence. I thought, "Oh, how sweet. If he wins an Oscar, it'll be a great moment. I can cut to his wife and then his mom." During the commercial break before the award, I told one of my camera operators who was covering the side of the audience where Spielberg sat, "You've got the shot of Spielberg. If he wins, you'll follow him out of his seat. Then I'll pick him up with another camera to cover his walk up on stage. You put your camera back on his mother, and if she has a reaction as I think she will, I'll cut to her." And sure enough, she was touching her heart and weeping and kvelling, and I cut to her as her son accepted his Oscar. Of course, Spielberg referred to his mother in his acceptance speech. After thanking his wife, Kate, "who got me through ninety-two difficult days in Krakow, Poland," he said of his mother, "She is my lucky charm, and I love her very much." His mom was so emotionally wrapped up in her son winning; she looked up at him like a proud Jewish mama who is watching her son receiving his first Cub Scout badge in grammar school, or like a thirteen-year-old delivering his Torah portion at his Bar Mitzvah, not as if she were watching her big-deal son, the producer/director who had made *Jaws* and was now accepting the film industry's highest honor. Knowing how my mom would have reacted, I understood completely. The very next award, for Best Picture, went to *Schindler's List*—the win was announced by Harrison Ford. In some ways the film was a long shot; in other ways it was a sentimental favorite and a recognition of Spielberg's body of work. Spielberg went back up on stage to receive Best Picture honors together with his two coproducers, Gerald R. Molen and Branko Lustig. The entire audience stood after their emotional acceptance speeches.

Two days later, I was in the production office. We were wrapping up, and somebody came in and said, "Steven Spielberg sent you a gift, but they can't bring it into your office. It's too big."

"Okay, what is it?"

I walked out, and he had sent this big box full of all kinds of gorgeous succulent plants. I'd never seen anything like it.

I thought, "What a mensch this guy is." He also sent a card. I don't remember the exact wording, but he thanked me and said he was so grateful that I had the courage to stay on a shot of his mother and see her emotion and her expression. That almost meant as much to him as holding the Oscar. It was a big-deal moment for Spielberg. He had been nominated numerous times, but winning the Oscar for a black and white film based on the life of Oskar Schindler, a Christian industrialist who saved the lives of many Jews during the Holocaust, was poignant. You can only imagine what that meant to his mother and to him.

Hey, Barbra! That's My Dressing Room!

Working with major stars can sometimes be challenging. I found Barbra Streisand to be very difficult because she's a perfectionist. She knows what works for her, and she wants everything done her way. I admire that, but when you're doing a show that's not the Barbra Streisand Special, it makes it very difficult. A show like the Oscars, where it's a three-hour-plus live special and has fifty other personalities that also need attention to one degree or another, it's not easy to cater to one person's needs at the expense of another's.

Barbra and I worked together on the 1991 and 1993 Oscars. She came on as a presenter, and I gave her most of what she wanted. And when I knew I couldn't, I suggested what I thought would satisfy her.

Every year that we presented the Academy Awards at the Shrine Auditorium in downtown Los Angeles, we erected a whole village of trailers in the parking lot. The trailers for me as the director and

Gil Cates or Quincy Jones as producer were luxurious. They were around five hundred square feet with a master bedroom, a bathroom, and a full kitchen plus a living area. I used to do a lot of work there and held many production meetings as well. I never spent a night in the trailer because I always wanted to be home with my family, but I needed to use it from the minute I got there in the morning until I left late at night.

The Academy Awards aired on ABC on Monday night, and because of that, I knew I couldn't go home on Sunday night, so I stayed in a hotel near the Shrine Auditorium. Monday morning on the 10 freeway from Beverly Hills where I lived to the Shrine in downtown Los Angeles was impossible due to early Monday morning commuter traffic. I'd stay late in my trailer, check into a hotel, take a nap and a shower, and then come back early on Monday morning to have a meeting with my associate directors and my stage managers in my trailer before the show.

When I got to my trailer this particular Monday morning, my name had been taken off the door with my gold star, and in its place, it said "Barbra Streisand." I thought, "Well, that's interesting."

I put my key in, and I opened the door and walked in. Her assistant looked up at me and said, "Can I help you?"

I said, "I'm Jeff Margolis. This is my trailer."

She said, "Um, I don't think so, not anymore."

"Pardon me?"

"Ms. Streisand is going to be here all day. Between her dress rehearsal and the time she's on the show, she doesn't want to drive all the way home to Malibu and then try to get back here in time. We assumed that since you would be in the remote truck directing all day, you wouldn't need your trailer."

"Really? Who gave you access to the trailer? It's my office! It's my home!"

"I don't know who gave us your trailer, and I'm really sorry about this, but it's not yours anymore. It's Ms. Streisand's."

"That's not going to work for me. I have a meeting. Look, every-body's starting to gather outside, and the Shrine Auditorium won't be open for several hours. I need my trailer for a meeting."

"I'm sorry. I don't know what to tell you." (I soon learned how this all came about.)

Fortunately, the remote truck was open because all the technicians were getting ready for the full, long Oscar day. So, I held my meeting in the truck although it was very distracting with all the preparations for the show going on around us. We could hardly hear one another over the commotion. I thought, "Thanks a lot, Ms. Streisand."

Before the dress rehearsal, Barbra asked to speak to me. She sent one of her assistants to the remote truck to get me. She seemed very concerned about the trailer situation.

When I got there, after that beautiful Streisand smile and a hello, she said, "Well, I'm so sorry to inconvenience you, Jeff. We figured you'd be busy all day and you'd be in the remote truck. You wouldn't be in this trailer, so we thought, why should it sit here empty? I needed a place to spend the day when I wasn't needed on camera, and I was so happy not to have to drive home or check into a hotel. I apologize that you were unaware of this situation."

I said, "Okay. No problem." (What else was I going to say?) "I'll see you on camera shortly. The dress rehearsal is going to start in an hour. If I don't see you again before the show, good luck." I found out that Barbra's team had cleared all of this with Danette Herman and the talent department, but somehow in all the confusion of the day, the message had not reached me. In the end, no harm, no foul. What was most important was that Barbra was comfortable so that she'd bring her A game to her appearance. That would be all that anyone would remember (except me).

As the day proceeded, and we continued rehearsing, she was very gracious to me. But she continued to be in her Barbra Streisand mode for everybody and everything else. "Don't roll the prompter so fast. I can't read that quickly." "Does that light have to be there?" "Can you move that light?" It never stopped. But that's Barbra, that's why she is so good.

When you are the director of a huge operation and you need the stars to do what they do best, it's wise to pick your battles. This was not a battle worth fighting over. Neither was the next one—which was a twofer—not one but two stars to deal with at the same time. But this was a fun one.

Jack Nicholson and Warren Beatty Crash My Dressing Room

When the Oscars were still at the Dorothy Chandler Pavilion, I had an office dressing room backstage that was normally used by the conductor of the Los Angeles Philharmonic Orchestra. It was very comfortable, and everyone knew that was where I hung out.

It was show day, right after the dress rehearsal. There was a two-hour break before the show went live. I put all my notes together in the remote truck and wrapped up everything I needed to do before the show. Then I wanted to go to my dressing room and relax, take a shower, unwind, and maybe even have some time to chat with friends.

This time I walked back to my dressing room, and there was a young kid named Scott, whom the Music Center hired to be the dressing-room coordinator. It was his job to make sure my dressing room was ready for me when I needed it.

When I got there, Scott stood in front of my door; he was white as a ghost, and he had that look on his face that catastrophe was about to ensue.

"Hey Scott, is everything okay?"

In an exaggerated whisper, he said, "Jack Nicholson and Warren Beatty are in your dressing room."

"Oh, really?"

"Yeah. They wanted someplace to go between the dress rehearsal and the live show. Jack pointed to the door and said, 'What's in that room?' I told him it was the director's room, and he said, 'Well, I'm sure he's busy, so let's go in there.'"

I walked into the dressing room, and there they were—Jack and Warren—just sitting there schmoozing. Jack said to me, "You must be

Jeff Margolis; your name is on the door. You don't mind if we stay in here 'til the show starts, do ya, pal?"

What was I going to say? "No, I don't mind. Let me just grab my stuff, and I'll get out of your way."

"How about if we take a picture with you?" they said. "That'll be our thank you for letting us stay in your dressing room."

I took my stuff and found somewhere else to shower and change before the show. But I do have a great picture with Jack and Warren!

The King of Cool: Paul Newman

Paul Newman was no stranger to the Oscars. He had been nominated ten times and won Best Actor in 1986 for *The Color of Money*. He was a presenter on several Oscars I directed. It was a thrill.

Paul fuckin' Newman—you know what I'm saying?

Every time I spoke to him, he was wearing glasses—either sunglasses or reading glasses—and he had a habit of pushing them up to his eyebrows or resting them over his forehead. I don't know if he did it with everybody, but with me when I used to talk to him, he'd put his elbow on my shoulder.

I always asked him if he was happy with his dialogue, and he would say, "I'm fine with it." I would tell him it would be on the prompter, and then I would show him how he was making his entrance, which podium he was going to, when the envelope would be handed to him, and when the trophy ladies were going to come out.

He would say, "I got it. I got it. I got it." And then I said, "After you open the envelope, when the winners come up, you can shake hands or hug or do whatever you want. Then the trophy ladies will show you where to stand while the winner or winners make their acceptance speech. When they're done, you'll all walk off together. The trophy ladies will escort you in the right direction."

"I got it. Let's go. Don't you have to be in a control room directing the show?"

"I'm on my way."

We would hug, I would thank him, and I was gone.

Paul Newman was low-key and so easy to work with. He demanded very little of me and listened attentively when I ran through the segment that he was part of. Film stars are much more likely to listen to the director than the producer—in television it's the producer who has the ultimate say, but in films the directors usually have the last word, so when I worked with film stars—even someone as monumental as Paul Newman—they paid attention to what I had to say, and they knew that I was there to make everything go smoothly for them.

One time, I was talking to Paul on stage, and he saw a photographer out of the corner of his eye. He called the photographer over and said, "Please take a picture of us and let me know how to get a copy." Then he said to me, "I hope you don't mind, but I want a picture of us for my collection." Not only did he get his photo, but so did I. What a great memory for me to have. That was only one of my interactions with Paul Newman, but it was a memorable one.

My only regret about the Oscars is that I often have just a fleeting moment with some of the greatest celebrities of the film industry—people who are my heroes who I might see from one year to the next—but only for an instant. They do their thing—introduce a category, present an award—and then they are gone. It's a very different experience than directing and producing a show like the American Music Awards, for example, where I might work with an artist on stage rehearsing numerous times.

Three Unforgettable Appearances

Spartacus

Do you remember when Kirk Douglas had his stroke? His very first appearance two months later was on the 1996 Academy Awards, the year that *Braveheart* won Best Picture. Kirk was there to accept the Honorary Life Achievement Award which was presented to him by Steven Spielberg. He wanted to walk out on stage despite the aftereffects of his stroke. It was so brave of him. When he stood at the microphone and gave his speech, it was difficult to understand him.

The audience hung on his every word, and they were clearly moved by the effort it took to deliver a speech. Here was the man who played Spartacus—he showed a different kind of courage to do what he did that evening.

I remember talking to him backstage at the dress rehearsal, and he didn't really say much. But just to be standing there with him, oh my God. I wasn't really directing him. I was just telling him what he needed to do. When we were live on the air, he walked out on stage and got a full-on one-minute standing ovation. His wife, Anne Douglas, and his son, actor Michael Douglas, and his other sons were in the audience. I cut to a shot of them after Kirk started to speak, and again when he received his second standing ovation. His family was weeping, and I lost it. That was one of those moments when I couldn't give out directions; I just pointed to the camera monitor and I had to rely on my associate director and technical director to call the shots. I couldn't speak; I too was weeping!

Kirk thanked his sons and his wife, Anne, and said, "I am proud to be part of Hollywood for fifty years." I certainly know what he means. As hard as it is to fathom, I've been working in this business for fifty years behind the camera. It has all gone by so fast. But when you are doing what you love and interacting with extraordinary celebrities like Kirk Douglas it's fleeting.

Superman

I met Christopher Reeve at the 1996 Oscars. He was a surprise guest. He came to rehearsal in his wheelchair, paralyzed from his neck down as a result of a horseback riding accident. It was so heartbreaking to see him like that. I had to turn and walk away for a moment because I couldn't take it. He was wheeled out of the back of a van on a ramp, hooked up to a breathing device, and he had two doctors and a nurse with him at all times. I spoke to him at rehearsal and told him what we were going to do. He had a smile on his face and said, "Just have my people roll me out there, and when the curtain opens, I'll speak."

Whoopi Goldberg was the host. She introduced the surprise guest but didn't say who it was. The curtain opened, and there was Christopher Reeve, sitting by himself, in his special wheelchair, all alone in the middle of the stage. There was no set, no nothing.

He got a standing ovation that lasted well over a minute. Every time I cut to somebody in the audience, they had tears in their eyes.

In his speech, Chris asked Hollywood to produce more movies about social issues. He then introduced a montage of movies that he said "courageously put social issues ahead of box-office success. They've enlightened us, they've challenged us, and they've given us the opportunity to learn." Whether his message made a lasting impact on the choices that Hollywood makes about the movies that it greenlights is not for me to judge, but I can say unequivocally that the messenger was unforgettable. I will never forget that moment when the curtain opened and there he was.

Another Survivor

The honoree for the best documentary short in 1995 was Kary Antholis, who produced and directed *One Survivor Remembers*. The documentary was based on the life of Holocaust survivor Gerda Klein's memoir, *All But My Life*. When Kary went up to the podium to accept his award, he brought Gerda Klein with him. Looking over the audience, she listened intently while Kary delivered his acceptance speech. Gil Cates asked me to start the music because his speech was running long. Instead of saying thank you and goodbye, he introduced the woman standing next to him. When Gerda Klein started to speak, I stopped the music. By the time she was done thanking everyone, there wasn't a dry eye in the house or in the control booth, including mine. I couldn't call the shots. Here is what she said:

> *I have been in a place for six incredible years where winning meant a crust of bread and to live another day. Since the blessed day of my liberation, I have asked the question, why am I here? I am no better. In my mind's eye I see*

those years and days and those who never lived to see the magic of a boring evening at home. On their behalf I wish to thank you for honoring their memory, and you cannot do it in any better way than when you return to your homes tonight to realize that each of you who know the joy of freedom are winners[9]

Her remarks embodied the true meaning of gratitude, and I shall remember what she said for the rest of my life.

Spielberg and Lucas, what more can I say?

---

9   Michael Berenbaum, "Remembering Holocaust survivor, author and Oscar winner Gerda Weissmann Klein, a 'testament to tenacity,'" *Forward*, April 6, 2022. https://forward.com/news/485087/remembering-holocaust-survivor-author-and-oscar-winner-gerda-weissmann/.

Are you kidding me...Sophia Loren?!

Warren and Jack taking over my dressing room.

Paul Newman, a real movie star.

The extraordinary Halle Berry and I share a moment backstage at the Oscars.

Rehearsing with Liza on the Oscars.

I loved directing the Oscars.

CHAPTER 24

OSCARS HOSTS

I'VE ALLUDED TO THE FACT THAT THE OSCARS HOST IS A BIG DECISION. THE host sets the tone for the evening and keeps things moving and is available to the director for a Plan B rescue, should something go wrong. In the recent past, the Oscars have mixed it up by having not one but two hosts (Anne Hathaway and James Franco). In 2022, they thought that three was the charm with comedians Amy Schumer, Wanda Sykes, and Regina Hall. It was a bit of a stretch giving each woman equal airtime. Maybe next year, they'll try the no-host model again. Who knows?

During the eight years I directed the Oscars, I worked with three great hosts: Billy Crystal, David Letterman, and Whoopi Goldberg. Each one brought their particular brand of humor to the task and created some memorable moments that were chatter at the water cooler the next day.

The Blah Blahs

Producer Gil Cates and the Academy selected Billy Crystal to host the Oscars, and I was thrilled. I had worked with Billy years before on the TV show *Presenting Susan Anton* and many times after that on one television special or another. So when he signed on to the Oscars, it was like old home week. I was happy that he was hosting, and he was glad to be there. We decided that for his opening monologue—because I had worked with him so many times and knew his style—the only thing he would tell me was how he was going to come out on stage. He always did something hilarious. He would always show me the way that he was going to make his entrance so that I would be able to cover it properly. Remember the year he rolled out on the big Oscar statue? And one year he came out on a horse. They were all very well thought out and very funny entrances.

He also gave me fair warning if he planned to directly engage some star in the audience. One year he walked out into the audience and sat on Clint Eastwood's lap and talked to him. I knew it was coming so I had all the right camera coverage. But as far as what his monologue was going to be, absolutely not. He told me nothing. That was going to be his surprise to me and the audience, both in the theater and at home. Some other directors might not have been happy with this plan, but I trusted Billy and he trusted me. I knew that I would cover it properly, and I knew that it would be great!

I did say to him, "Billy, there are a billion and a half people around the world watching this."

"I'll tell you what. Whenever I'm going to go to the audience to talk to someone like Jack (he loved to talk to Jack Nicholson, who was always in the first row), I'll tell you who I'm going to talk to. That way you can get a camera there to get a reaction from them." Which he did. But he never told me what the bits were. I just shot them for the first time live on the air. It was so exciting! I loved it! When I am directing, I always put myself in the fifth-row center of the audience, and I try and shoot whatever is happening on stage the way I would see it if I were actually sitting there. That way the audience at home can feel like they're part of the audience in the theater.

Billy worked closely with the writers on the show. I wasn't involved with that. He would come to dress rehearsal, and he would do his monologue in what we call "blah blahs." Occasionally he would tell a joke just to see if the crew laughed but most of his dialogue was, "Okay, Jeff, then I'll walk over here and blah blah, and then I'll move over here and blah blah."

Billy brought in a creative team with him, but most of the ideas were his. He would throw out something to the writing staff, and then they would come up with something comedic to embellish his concept. But Billy knows what Billy does, what works for him, and how to make Billy funny. He's just naturally funny anyway. He does great impersonations. He does the best Sammy Davis Jr. I've ever seen. He's famous for that!

Usually, his jokes are PC. But sometimes he can't help himself, and the censors let him get away with it. (Besides, they are lightweight compared to some of Richard Pryor and Ricky Gervais's ad-libs.) Here are just two:

> *When talking about* The Crying Game *in his open-ing monologue, Crystal said, "That big scene proved one thing—white men can jump. Talk about a stocking stuffer, I'll tell you that right now."*
>
> *He later joked, "But it has been a great year for all kinds of movies, like big Hollywood extravaganzas like* A Few Good Men, *the J. Edgar Hoover story. Talk about a best-kept secret. Hoover was the master of disguise, really for seven years he was on the* Andy Griffith Show *as Aunt Bee. Gotta admire him, not only did he catch Dillinger, he was the lady in red."* [10]

Billy is a great song-and-dance man as well as a great comedian and actor. He can mix it up. That's what makes him such a great host. He comes on stage like a man shot out of a cannon and his energy doesn't drop until the final moment of the show. That's a rare gift that comes from years of experience as a standup, an actor, and a director. His singing medley of Oscar-nominated Best Pictures was always one of the highlights of his opening monologue. No one could do it better. "*The Silence of the Lambs*, a bouillabaisse of cheeks and arms." What? Who else could deliver that mouthful? Billy hosted the Oscars four times under my direction, and it was a treat every time.

Billy is still working hard. He wrote, produced, directed, and starred in a movie with Tiffany Haddish called *Here Today*, released in May 2021. And in 2022, Billy put together the Broadway show *Mr. Saturday Night*, which will also be filmed. If you can't see it live, you'll

---

10   "Politically Incorrect Oscar Jokes Through the Years," *The Hollywood Reporter*, February 26, 2016. https://www.hollywoodreporter.com/lists/politically-incorrect-oscar-jokes-years-869987/.

be able to catch it wherever you view your movies. He performed an excerpt of one of his show monologues on the 2022 Tony Awards telecast, which was one of its highlights. He hasn't lost his timing and his incredible ability to engage the audience.

I had a great time the four years that Billy hosted the Oscars. I have had the opportunity to work with him so many times. He couldn't be more professional, and you couldn't work with a nicer man. He always looks like he's having a good time and doesn't mind poking fun at himself. At the 1992 Oscars he said, "I know what you are thinking…I thought Billy was taller." He's like a vaudevillian in an Armani suit. And if he doesn't get a laugh, he pauses for a moment and with an impish grin says, "That was a good joke." Love his humor.

Billy and I don't go out to dinner together, or even hang out, but the last time I flew to New York, many years ago, I ran into him at an airport. It was hugs and kisses and "How've you been?" and "Where've you been?" and "How come you never call me?" I said back to him, "How come you never call *me*?" We just smiled at each other and hugged again.

It's All About the Dog

Dave Letterman really wanted to host the 1995 Oscars. Then when he realized that he was actually doing it, I'm not so sure he wanted to anymore. I think he was glad to be there, but when he saw the size of the Shrine Auditorium and realized the magnitude of the event, he might have had second thoughts. The job of hosting the Oscars can be intimidating.

David Letterman was very intense and wanted to know exactly what he had to do and how much time he had to do everything. Could he ad-lib at a certain point? Or if it was information, did it have to be presented exactly as written? These were all questions that he needed to discuss with Gil Cates, who was producing that year.

He was never uncomfortable or nervous because that's not Dave. He had years of experience hosting his own shows, but the first time he walked out on the stage with me, he said, "Holy shit! Look at this place!" The Shrine Auditorium holds 6,300 people, and the Ed Sullivan Theater in New York where he held court every night holds only a couple hundred. (Remember when I had to fill all those seats for Dick Clark's AMAs?) He surprised all of us in his opening monologue. On his late-night show he'd bring a dog out, and he'd have a piece of carpet on the floor, and the dog would perform all kinds of tricks on the carpet. It was one of his regular shticks. We had no idea he was going to do that in his opening monologue at the Oscars. Surprise!

I remember one of my stage managers, Dency Nelson, was with Dave, and he opened up his headset and said to me, "Jeffrey, put your seatbelt on!"

"What does that mean?" I was sitting in the truck watching all the monitors.

"You'll see—he's just about to—" and *boom*! There it was. The guy came out with the carpet, and I didn't know what was going on; I just had to wing it! The carpet guy left, and then Dave said something and called the dog out. Dave talked to the dog, and the dog spun around and rolled over and did God only knows what else. And then the dog left, and the carpet guy came back on stage to get his carpet. The audience (as well as all of us) had no idea what was going on, but it was funny. Dave has a way of making anything he wants to be funny just that—funny.

Dave is really quick, and he's really smart, and as I just said, he's really funny. He looked out into the audience, and there were Oprah Winfrey and Uma Thurman sitting next to each other. It just hit him that there were two ladies with the names Oprah and Uma. He ad-libbed a whole thing about Oprah Uma, Uma Oprah. The audience laughed, but Oprah and Uma didn't. They didn't get it. (I think it's actually a bit that might have been inspired by a "tongue-twisting television sketch" written for Mel Brooks's wife, Anne Bancroft.[11]) I

---

11   In the sketch, written by Tom Meehan, Anne tells her psychiatrist about a dream in which she throws a party for Yma Sumac. One of the lines she delivers in introducing the party's guests is: "Oona, Yma. Oona, Ava, Oona, Abba." And it gets crazier from there as more guests arrive. From: Mel Brooks, *All About Me* (New York: Ballentine, 2021), pp.332–334.

had, of course, spoken to Dave before the show and during rehearsals. I told him that "the stage managers will always be there to tell you everything you need to know in enough time before you have to do something so that you don't feel rushed or uncomfortable." Dency Nelson was the stage manager alongside Dave, and they had worked together numerous times in other situations, so Dave felt comfortable.

Because Dave did a live show every night, he was comfortable with live television. There were no nerves involved at all. He did everything he was supposed to do. When I would say to him, "You're going to do this" or "You're going to do that," he would look at me with his eyes rolled up and that "Dave look," which said, you're really starting to piss me off.

During rehearsals, he also did the same blah blahs as Billy Crystal. (Was this catching?) He came out and said, "Welcome, everybody, to the Sixty-Seventh Annual Academy Awards. Glad you're all here tonight." He continued, "Then I'm going to go to Jack Nicholson, and then I'm going to come over here to Meryl Streep (by this time the important seats in the theater had large cards on them with the names of the stars who would be sitting in them), and then I'm going to blah blah blah blah blah, and then I'm going to walk over here and do blah blah blah blah blah." That's the way he talked me through his opening monologue. I would have preferred to hear his opening monologue for real, but that's not the way David Letterman rolls. But about that dog.

I would sit in the truck during dress rehearsals, listening to the blah-blahs, doing some camera cutting. I'd tell the cameramen, "Roll with me here," and we would do what I liked to call "zone defense." That means that I'd always have a closeup shot on one camera, a head-to-toe shot on another, a reverse shot over his shoulder to the audience, and so forth, so I'd have choices when the show went live, and I could pick and choose the best shot for a particular moment in Dave's monologue. He had his blah blahs, and I had my zone defense, and between the two of us and my camera team we made it all work. And don't forget, I'm looking at God only knows how many monitors all at the same time, making instantaneous decisions about which camera would be best to make the joke work. And there was no going back for a retake because we were live on air—it's one and done.

I'd tell the camera operators, "Okay, ladies and gentlemen, it's zone defense time," which meant give me cover—give me all the shots. It was the Margolis way of shooting an unknown situation. Many directors of live television use the zone defense technique, but I'm pretty sure we all have different names for this style of coverage, but it became standard operating procedure for me. (Take it and use it!) The trick is to be able to look at multiple monitors simultaneously, and instantaneously pick the best camera shot. And as I said, there are no do-overs!

Who Is that Oscar?

The year Gil Cates took a hiatus from producing the Oscars in order to focus on the future of the Geffen Playhouse and his obligations at UCLA, the Academy chose Quincy Jones to step in as the producer. He was the ideal choice as far as I was concerned. He had produced television shows, and films, as well as orchestrating film scores for numerous movies, and produced pop music albums for so many major recording artists. He is a man of many talents, and it was exciting for me as the director to have him as the producer and a partner for the 68th Annual Academy Awards.

I sat with Quincy, and we talked about hosts. I said, "There are a lot of good people out there, but when Whoopi hosted the first time, she was incredible. She falls into the Bob Hope, Johnny Carson, Billy Crystal group. I love working with her. What do you think about Whoopi?"

Quincy smiled. "I love her. She's a good friend of mine. That's a great idea."

(I think he already had the same idea.)

"So can you call her?"

Quincy picked up the phone and of course, she said yes. She was ready to go. When you are as important as Quincy Jones, and he calls you personally, that's how it works. He wasn't asking Whoopi to appear in a car commercial; he was asking her to host the Oscars. How could she say no? (Although I'm not knocking car commercials—that from someone who appeared in a Continental Airlines plug with Dick Clark on the AMAs!)

Whoopi knows what she wants to do, and she knows what works for her and what doesn't. That's part of what makes a celebrity a great talent. They know what's right for their personality and their style—whether it's a joke or a piece of dialogue, the way their face is lit; what camera angle serves them best, and so forth. It's like a singer who knows what key works best for their voice.

Whoopi didn't want any surprises for her or for me, unlike Billy Crystal and David Letterman who were big with the blah blahs. She wanted to run through her monologue with me word for word, and she was very definite about how it would come off and whom she would engage with in the audience.

Quincy and I tried to come up with ways to showcase her unique personality and her comedic style and make her appearance as the host something to celebrate, which it was. I remember the opening of the show. I started outside the theater, when we were still at the Dorothy Chandler Pavilion in downtown Los Angeles. We had rows of Oscars sitting on the ledge of an outdoor fountain. I zoomed into a full shot of one of the Oscar statues and did a match dissolve (put one picture on top of the other and blended them together to reveal a new picture) to Whoopi inside the theater, and she was wearing a giant Oscar costume. So, it looked like the Oscar outside near the fountain became the real-life Whoopi Goldberg dressed as an Oscar inside the theater. Sounds more confusing than it really is. Then I did a special effect that peeled away the Oscar costume that she was wearing, and viola, there was Whoopi. (It was a novel effect back then and quite difficult to pull off, but today it would be so much easier, more real, and much more effective, but hey, it was 1996, and it was really creative back then.) Today, almost anything is possible in the area of special effects. So many "toys" to play with as a director.

Whoopi totally delivered, and Quincy and I could not have been happier. I worked with her several times after the Oscars, including

on the *Ebony* magazine special, and, of course, on Bill Clinton's fiftieth birthday celebration, which she hosted at Radio City Music Hall.
(We've remained good friends, and I suppose if I picked up the phone
and called her today, she'd take my call with a huge smile on her face,
happy to hear my voice.)

Billy Crystal was brilliant at hosting the Academy Awards.

Whoopi, what a gem, and so much fun to work with.

Quincy Jones, my brother from another mother.

CHAPTER 25

ALMOST DISASTERS AT THE OSCARS

WHEN YOU ARE DIRECTING LIVE TELEVISION, YOU NEVER KNOW WHAT'S GOING to happen, and when you are directing the Oscars with all the awards to present, stars to get on and off the stage, and time pressure from the network to bring the show in at three hours, the possibility of a disaster increases exponentially. That's what makes it so exciting and a challenge for a rare number of directors who have the experience and the temperament to deal with it. Managed chaos to the nth degree.

Let me tell you about three Almost Disasters at the Oscars.

I'm Losing You

One year the theme for the Oscars was "Movies around the World." We sent some major stars to different countries, and we were doing live satellite feeds from those locations. Jack Lemmon was in Russia, and this is where the almost-disaster occurred.

I had a whole day scheduled where I connected with each location we had selected. The idea was that at each location one of the actors or actresses would present an award on the show, which would be: Actor, Actress, Supporting Actor, Supporting Actress, Director, and Picture. So, on that day, the plan was to check in at all six locations and rehearse to make sure that there were no technical issues. The audio delays were not too bad, and the pictures looked good a million miles away.

Some of the locations were Tokyo, Buenos Aires, London, Sydney, and Moscow. Jack Lemmon was in Moscow. On this rehearsal day, he was being very patient because the Russians couldn't get a video feed to me. I couldn't see Jack. I was communicating with him through a stage manager in Russia who fortunately spoke fluent English. I could hear all of the technicians talking over their headsets, but I couldn't hear Jack's microphone. We worked for about an hour to try and get something going, and nothing happened. I never saw Jack and I never heard Jack, but we ran out of time. Uh oh, now what?

On my next day of rehearsals, I had scheduled another hour to go to Moscow and make sure that everything functioned flawlessly. This day I could finally see Jack, but I still couldn't hear him. I ran out of time again. Oh shit, we're screwed! The following day was the show. There was the dress rehearsal, and then the show aired live. I always conducted the dress rehearsal as if it was the actual show, live on the air, so we'd all be fully prepared to deliver the best show we could, and fix any last-minute glitches. No such luck, not in Russia anyhow, but I still had hope. I knew it was "going to be great (maybe)."

So, it's Jack Lemmon's turn during the final rehearsal. We cut to Moscow, and we couldn't hear a word. The picture was pixelated, and I thought, "God, we are screwed." Everything was perfect on our end; all our technicians were in communication with the Russian technicians trying to talk them through the process to make it all happen. Of course, our technicians had been doing that for two days prior. We were about to go on the air, live. I thought, "Well, just in case, I need to have a Plan B."

So I went to our host, Billy Crystal, and said, "Look, if we don't get to see or hear Jack Lemmon in Russia, and he can't read off the names of the nominees, then I'm going to have to get you out on stage, and you're going to have to say, 'We're having technical difficulties.' Then, you're going to have to present the award."

Okay, now it's show time; we're live on the air. By the way, the audience loves when crap like this happens at the Oscars, when technical things go wrong. It always seems to be the headline in the news the next day. So now it's time. Billy Crystal says, "And now we go live to Russia, to Moscow, where Jack Lemmon will be announcing an award." I cut to Jack. Everything is perfect. I can hear him. I can see him. The picture is beautiful. The sound is good. The Oscar gods and goddesses were shining down on us. And if they hadn't been, I always had Billy Crystal to save the day. He is the consummate pro and would have kept everything moving.

Get the Mic

Another almost-disaster was Madonna's Oscars appearance in 1990. She was performing one of the five nominated songs for Best Score. We rehearsed her number endlessly in the rehearsal hall for weeks, then on stage at the Shrine Auditorium for way more time than any other performer was allotted. We had two elevators installed into the stage floor, one for Madonna to come up on and the other for her microphone. The microphone would come up after Madonna arrived on stage so that the camera could get a head-to-toe shot and a clear view of her spectacular gown. And then she would walk down to the microphone which was supposed to come up on the other elevator just in time for her to sing. Unfortunately, it turned out to be a recipe for disaster.

During rehearsals, her elevator came up to the stage, she walked down to her mark and the microphone wasn't there. Twice, no less. Not good. The elevator for the microphone was not working. I had audio assistants standing by on either side of the stage just in case the same thing happened when we were live on the air, so they could run out, hand her a microphone, and look like they were choreographed dancers wearing tuxedos.

Madonna was royally pissed off that it wasn't working, and she was yelling and screaming at anybody who would listen. The audio technicians and the stage crew were trying to figure out what the problem was. They thought they had it solved by the next rehearsal, but they didn't, and Madonna threatened to walk out.

She was singing a Stephen Sondheim song, "Sooner or Later (I Always Get My Man)" from *Dick Tracy*, which had been nominated for song of the year. It was at the time she was dating Warren Beatty, and she wanted it to be perfect because it was Warren's movie. I thought, "Oh my God. If we're on the air and this microphone doesn't come up, I hope that she doesn't turn around and walk off the stage."

Anyway, once we were live on the air, the microphone started to shake and jiggle its way up on to the stage. We thought it wouldn't get there in time, so the audio assistants started to drift out on stage like choreographed dancers. The microphone came up just in time for her to sing without missing a beat, and everyone had a chance to look at her stunning ensemble which included a white fox stole and a clinging dress made of sequins, crystal, and silk that made her look like an old-time Hollywood starlet. She worked it for all it was worth, and it was worth a lot. When she sings the lyric, "I'm getting my man," you believe her.

My approach always on a live show is that it's live! There's nothing you can do if something happens. There's nothing you can do to fix it, and you have the rest of the show to get on the air! Just keep moving forward, let it go, stay focused, and hope that your Plan B saves the day if Plan A fails. As a director it's a good idea to think about the worst-case scenario while simultaneously thinking, "It's gonna be great." The ability to hold two opposing thoughts is a gift for a director, just as is watching seventy-plus screens, a script crawl, and communicating with 150-plus people over a headset all at once. Try it! You might love it.

Whole Lot of Shakin' Going On

On a scale of one to ten, earthquakes elicit an eleven in my gut. I have always been afraid of earthquakes going back to my childhood when we were hit by a huge one. My sister and I huddled together while my father tried to comfort my mom, who was having a full-blown panic attack as our house shook, rattled, and rolled. I have never gotten over that experience, and each earthquake since that time has only added to my own panic attacks. You don't want to be with me when the Big One hits, which seismologists have promised us Los Angelenos. And what you may not know is that there are usually a series of after-shocks once the initial earthquake has had its way with us. Some of them feel just as severe as the initiating tumbler.

On January 17, 1994, Los Angeles was hit with a 6.7 which may actually have been worse since it was a confluence of two fault lines. It was referred to as the Northridge Earthquake. The Santa Monica freeway buckled, some older buildings that were not properly ret-rofitted collapsed, and a highway bridge gobbled up a motorcyclist. It was terrifying, and we experienced numerous aftershocks. It was two months before the 66th Academy Awards were to air on ABC on Sunday night, March 21. My nerves were still jangled, but the show must go on.

I was running the dress rehearsal that Sunday afternoon. Whoopi Goldberg was the host, and she had just introduced the presenter for Best Visual Effects. Each nominee was to demonstrate the visual effect that earned them their nomination. One of the nominees was for the movie *Jurassic Park*. (I think you might know where this is going.) Just as the presenter announced Special Effects Director Phil Tippett and *Jurassic Park* an enormous dinosaur poked his head out from behind the curtain and growled. At that very moment, there was a huge aftershock, and the entire Music Center shook, and made hor-rible groaning sounds adding to the dinosaur's. I was in the control truck and for a moment, I wasn't sure if all of that was part of the special effects or my number eleven fear factor. It took a second or two for everyone to register what was going on and to go into "fight-or-flight mode." It was up to me to calm everyone down since I was the only person who could communicate with the six hundred people on my headset. I pushed the button on the PA system so I could also address the audience. It was my finest performance. I was able to get everyone back on track and the rest of the rehearsal went without a hitch. But don't ask me to do it when the Big One hits! By the way, congratulations to the ground-breaking work of Phil Tippett, who won that evening.

Insurance Policies

On every awards show, I always had insurance policies where you needed to have insurance policies. In any situation where there was a stand mic on stage or some kind of special mic, I always had an audio person on either side of the stage, ready to walk out with a hand mic if there was a problem, so that the performer on stage could always speak, or sing, and be heard. That's a good example of an insurance policy.

When shows are running extra long, you have to try and pick up as much time as you can. To try and pick up a few seconds or minutes along the way is not an easy task. Here are a couple of my insurance policies:

One: When a presenter is introduced, you cut their walk from off-stage to the podium. You just have the presenter at the podium when they are introduced, and you save ten to twelve seconds. And ten or twelve seconds, when you're running long and the network wants you to get off the air on time, is significant and adds up to help you keep the show ending close to three hours.

Two: Coming out of a commercial break, usually the theme music of the show is played, the title card is on the screen, and the announcer welcomes you back to the show. That normally takes about five to seven seconds. To save that time, just come back to the host and move on.

Three: Going into a commercial break is the same thing. You play the show's theme music, the title of the show is on the screen and the announcer teases the upcoming act. That's usually five to ten seconds.

So, as you can see, a couple of seconds here and a couple of seconds there, they start to add up. Every little bit helps when you're trying to get off the air on time.

In retrospect, every Oscars show I directed had its memorable moments. I expected that I'd have the opportunity to remain its director for the same number of years as one of my idols, Marty Pasetta, who directed sixteen telecasts for most of the 1970s and '80s, but it was not to be. I recently watched an interview that Marty gave to the Academy, long after he left, and I am reminded of what a gentle, thoughtful guy he was. He referenced me in his interview when talking about working with the same people over and over again through the years. "Oh yes, Jeff Margolis was my cue card boy on the *Smothers Brothers*, and now he's directing the Oscars."

Scouting a Russian location for Jack Lemmon's live shot on the Oscars.

With Madonna at the Oscars rehearsal.

Sidney Poitier, what an honor.

Keanu Reeves arrives at the Oscars rehearsal.

CHAPTER 26

BOOKENDING THE OSCARS

Karl Malden and the Oscars Retrospective

If you happen to be one of the billion people from over ninety countries who watch every minute of the Oscars, you may know about the special I was asked to produce and direct, *Oscar's Greatest Moments: 1971–1991: Unforgettable Highlights from the Academy Awards*, a twenty-year retrospective. It runs for one hour and forty-nine minutes to be exact. Or you may have missed it because it has only been available on VHS (remember those cassettes?) and DVD for home viewing until now. I'm certain these days you can find it on YouTube.

The Academy of Motion Picture Arts and Sciences never, and I mean *never*, makes clips available from this most-heralded yearly event. If you love the Oscars and the sometimes-outrageous behavior that occurs on stage when several thousand actors and their friends and family get together to celebrate, you will want to track down a copy of this unique special, which was released in 1992 and is now available from Sony's film library.

It took me a year to complete this retrospective and a few more to relax enough to watch it at my leisure. But I promise you it's worth it. Where else will you see and hear 1985 Best Actress Oscar winner (*Places in the Heart*) Sally Field say to those watching, "You like me! You really like me!" Or you might want to check out a young Sylvester Stallone and an equally young Muhammad Ali wrestling with each other on stage.

For a great host moment, watch Johnny Carson from the 1978 Oscars—suave, mischievous, and funny—tell the audience, "Welcome to two hours of sparkling entertainment spread out over a four-hour show," followed by a sarcastic and hilarious rib as he looks out over the audience, "I see a lot of new faces, especially of formerly old faces."

Or you can study *Crocodile Dundee* actor Paul Hogan's advice in 1986 to nominees when they hear someone else's name called as the winner in their coveted category: "Here's the 'I'm so glad she won smile,'" Hogan says, showing off his pearly white teeth. "Then you storm out of the building. Or you could try old-fashioned boo-hooing." He continued giving advice from the podium, "If they read someone else's name other than mine because I've been nominated, it's not going to be pretty. Everyone is here to sweat. This program is live. Millions of people are watching you. And if you win, remember the three Gs: Be gracious. Be grateful. Get off."

Despite Johnny Carson's joke, everybody looks youthful in this 1992 retrospective, starting with footage of Liza Minnelli, who bounds up on stage to welcome the audience singing "Everybody Loves Oscar!" The show never pauses for a breath. It's exhausting, invigorating, and surprising, especially if you love movies.

Karl Malden, who was then the twenty-seventh president of the Academy, appropriately provides the on-camera narration and could not have been a better choice to host this "main event." I suggested shooting him on camera at his home, but Karl is a very private person and did not like the idea of millions of people peering into his living room.

So, I came up with the idea of renting the presidential suite at the Beverly Wilshire Hotel for the day and shooting the wraparound material there. I set up dolly tracks in the suite so that the camera could move smoothly and create an artistic effect.

We lit the suite beautifully, and I positioned Karl in various locations for variety.

Karl was delighted with this idea. We have shots of him sitting by the fire casually dressed, a counterpoint to the formality of the Oscars presentation where all the men are in tuxedos and the women bejew-eled and bedecked in gowns.

Oscar's Greatest Moments was mainly an editing assignment with hours and hours spent in an editing room picking out the "special moments" and putting them into an entertaining order. I want to give credit to my producing partner, Maria Schlatter, the daughter of producer George Schlatter, who did a monumental job splicing and dicing. She worked daily with the editor. I worked very closely with Maria. Without her this project would not have happened. She did a brilliant job. Watching twenty years' worth of Oscars telecasts to put together roughly three hours' worth of material by picking out the choice moments was quite a chore, but I think you'll agree that it was worth the effort. Thank you, Maria.

How did I get the job? I was hired because of my relationship with the Academy. By the time the documentary was slated for production, I had already directed the Oscars for three consecutive years. Many times, I would have to get approval from the Academy to use certain material in the context that I felt was appropriate for its position-ing in the documentary. The segments included Oscars Hosts; Best Actress; Best Actor; Best Picture; Best Song; Bloopers; and Special Moments. There were lots of funny clips, usually in the monologues delivered by the hosts or in unrehearsed acceptance speeches.

There are some "over the top" moments in this special. One in particular stands out. Charlton Heston didn't arrive on time for his presentation, so Clint Eastwood came out on stage to read from the teleprompter. Clint said, "It's very funny that the guy who has the least bit of dialogue in movies is asked to stand in for Charlton Heston." The audience exploded in laughter and just at that moment, Charlton strode across the stage and took over, reading from the teleprompter the material that he had rehearsed the day before. Clint stood there and listened to Mr. Heston with a giant smile on his face. A segment of the documentary included short clips from Charlie Chaplin's mov-ies followed by the appearance of the Little Tramp himself at the 1971 Oscars. It was his first return to Hollywood in twenty years of self-imposed exile in Europe. In his acceptance speech for a special presentation to him, Charlie Chaplin said, "Thank you for the honor of inviting me, all of you wonderful, sweet people." For anyone who loves the movies, this is a documentary that brings together some of the extraordinary talent that the Academy has seen fit to acknowledge.

No Good Deed Goes Unpunished

No matter how carefully you plan your next career move, some decisions are simply out of your control. In this case the hiccup came in 1996. I had directed eight consecutive Academy Awards shows. Allan Carr had produced the first one with me as director in 1989, and I had survived that tumultuous-yet-exciting experience. Unfortunately, Allan did not. The Snow White blunder was his downfall. There was no saving him, hard as I tried. He was not invited back by the Academy. Too much damage had been done to his reputation by the press and the powers that were.

Then I directed seven more Oscars nights. Six of them were with producer Gil Cates, and the seventh was with Quincy Jones: his first foray as producer of the Oscars. I knew Quincy wasn't returning as a producer the following year because he had made it very clear to the Academy that he only wanted to produce the show for one year. He had too many other projects on his plate—composing music, producing movies, and putting together television specials. The Academy Awards would be put back in Gil Cates's capable hands. And I expected to be working right alongside Gil once again. (Remember, I intended to direct at least sixteen Oscars, following in the footsteps of Marty Pasetta, who had hit the Big Sixteen. There was no reason why I couldn't match his record, or even exceed it if I was lucky.)

Here's what happened the year that Quincy and I did the show in 1996, which had received phenomenal ratings. Gil called me afterward. I knew for sure he was coming back to the Oscars, and I thought, "Oh, good. I get to work with Gil again." It was a great experience with Quincy, but I was looking forward to working with Gil once again. Gil loved producing the Oscars. He was quoted by a reporter, "I've always been a fan of the circus, and this is the greatest circus." That's one way of putting it.

The call finally came, but it wasn't what I expected. Gil said, "Jeff, you know how much I love you. You know how much I care about you. You know I think you're the best director in variety television. However, I'm not inviting you back to direct this year."

I said, "Pardon me?"

He said, "I've decided to go another way."

"Gilbert! Really?"

"Yes."

"What happened?"

"You're a smart guy. You'll figure it out."

"Really?"

"Yep. We'll talk soon. I love you. Bye-bye." Click. I sat with the telephone in my hand for about fifteen minutes before I could breathe again or even move. I was in shock. Then I called my wife to commiserate with her and tell her that I felt completely blindsided. There was no warning for what had happened, and ostensibly I had done nothing wrong. I had done everything right!

This was the biggest disappointment of my entire career. I had worked steadily with Gil on six of the eight Oscars shows I directed, and when he came back to produce the 1997 Oscars, he decided not to bring me back. What the *fuck*? I wasn't let go. I just wasn't invited back. It's splitting hairs, but that was how it was communicated to me.

I couldn't understand why Gil did not invite me back. I was absolutely crushed. First of all, Gil and I were really, really good friends, and I didn't know how you could do that to a friend. I had done such a good job working with him. I just couldn't figure it out, and there was no discussion. But this is Hollywood, and sometimes shit happens. Up to this point in my career I had always been rewarded for a job well done, and I expected that trend would continue. And why not? But there is life after the Oscars...even for the little boy who stood in front of the television set wondering how all those people fit behind that piece of glass and made me laugh and cry, and whose dream to one day direct the Oscars did come true. At least for eight marvelous years working with literally thousands of talented people, some of whom were the sweetest individuals in the world (to take a note from Charlie Chaplin).

Lucky for me, when one door closes another one opens.

Like I just said, another door opens!

Here with SAG Awards statuettes.

CHAPTER 27

ACTORS CONGRATULATE THEMSELVES: THE SAG AWARDS (1999–2014)

I WON'T LIE. I WAS STUNNED, HURT, AND ANGRY OVER WHAT HAPPENED WITH Gil Cates and the Oscars. I had directed the show for eight years and counted on directing them for another eight, at least. I licked my wounds, spoke with friends, my wife, and my parents, and had a general pity party for a few days. I was so upset that I fantasized that maybe the phone would never ring again, which is very unlike me, and my days of getting a cork from my dad were over. Catastrophic thinking! For a few days my glass was definitely half empty (really, *me?*), and telling myself, "It's going to be great" was just not cutting it. But, at the same time, I just kept telling myself that something good would happen, and that my calendar was already full of specials that had been booked as well as series episodes. For most directors/producers that would have been plenty, but for me it didn't take away the pain of what had happened.

Word quickly got out that I might be available to direct/produce another awards show during awards-show season. Soon after I got a call from the Screen Actors Guild asking me to come in for a meet and greet. After the meeting, they asked me if I would consider executive producing their awards show.

The Screen Actors Guild Awards is right up there with the Oscars; it is a very important show in the industry because it is all about actors honoring actors for doing outstanding work. It was an honor for me to be asked to be the executive producer of this important event. So, the SAG award for executive producing the awards show goes to... Jeff Margolis, and I had a sixteen-year run, no less. (Coincidentally, the same length of time I had dreamed about directing the Oscars.)

The SAG Awards and the Golden Globe Awards are both run-ups to the Oscars. The Golden Globes are usually held in December, the SAG Awards the following January or February, and the Oscars at the end of March (except for 2021 when the Oscars were held mid-April due to COVID) to wrap up awards season.

Both the SAG Awards and the Globes are different because, unlike the Oscars, they hand out awards for productions in both film *and* television—and not only to one-off productions but series as well. Oscars only recognize individual films. SAG is the award for the members of the Screen Actors Guild, for acting only, whereas the Golden Globes are handed out by the Hollywood Foreign Press Association in numerous categories for both film and television. The Screen Actors Guild Awards wanted to be as big as the Oscars. I was hired in 1999 to help them achieve their dream. (Lots of dreams going on here, right?)

By the time I arrived, the SAG Awards had been on NBC for four years, and they were floundering. NBC didn't pick them up again, and the board was looking for a place to go. They ended up at TNT where the SAG Board deemed that they would have more freedom to do what they wanted by being on a cable network. The executives at SAG shared with me their aspiration to become as big as the Oscars, and it was my job to make that happen. Since I had directed the Oscars for eight years, they believed I had the secret sauce to make their dreams come true. It was a tall order, but I promised to do my best to make it happen.

Once settled in at their new home at TNT, the Screen Actors Guild formed a committee, which consisted of actors assigned to oversee the production of the awards show. SAG wanted to make sure that nothing could happen to embarrass the Screen Actors Guild or their actors, and that nothing would tarnish the reputation of their union. The committee was made up of actors who weren't producers.

It was an interesting way of working. I'm trying to be as diplomatic as possible here. I had never been involved in producing a television show by committee. What's that joke about a camel: it's a horse that is designed by a committee. You get the picture.

There was an actual committee called—wait for it—The Committee. We met each year, and I had to go through the rundown of the show, tell them what I wanted to do and the order that I wanted to do the awards. That was the first meeting. They had the right to ask for changes, and they had the right to approve the final rundown. Once they approved it, I could move forward. Mind you, I was the executive producer, but I still had to deal with this.

It wasn't easy. It wasn't easy for anybody. In a subsequent meeting, I would sit with the talent producer, Maggie Barrett-Caulfield, and my other producers, Gloria Fujita O'Brien, Mick McCullough, and Benn Fleishman, and we would decide who should present each award before we presented our ideas to the committee.

But there was a catch. We couldn't go after people until the nominations were announced because The Committee asked me to use as many of the nominees as possible to serve as presenters. The thinking was that these actors were already in the audience, so why not use them to present? (Remember when I presented the same idea to Dick Clark for the American Music Awards in the early eighties?)

Maggie Barrett and I would decide who we wanted to present each award. Then we would put those names up on the board with the approved rundown. The Committee would come in, and I would go through the rundown again and wait for their approval.

Beyond painful! I can't tell you how time-consuming this process was. After the first couple of years, The Committee now felt that they were more knowledgeable about how to produce a television show. (Of course, each year, we were teaching them Television Producing 101.) Okay, here it comes. By year three, The Committee wanted the production designer, Joe Stewart, to submit three different ideas of what the set might look like. I had to have him sketch me out three set looks for them to choose from. I had Joe design three sets that I knew I would be happy with. I could make any of the three work, so it really didn't matter to me which one The Committee chose. But the exercise of having to go through the Committee approval process was challenging. Everyone had an opinion, and many times, they disagreed with one another. And, by the way, did I mention how beyond painful this process was?

Over the years some of The Committee members stayed on while others left. One actor moved to the East Coast because she had a gig there so she couldn't be in LA for all the meetings. Somebody else got a role in a movie and left. But there were a couple of people who were permanent fixtures. During the time I was there, two of them died.

Finally, a couple of years after I started, and for several years, Scott Bakula was part of The Committee, and it was such a relief and such a pleasure to have him be part of the process because he was a working actor, and he knew the business. And he was one of the nicest men you'd ever want to meet! His opinion mattered. Shelley Fabares was another gem. I remember being infatuated with her as a teenager when she was on *The Donna Reed Show*. And later she had a running part on *Coach*. What a thrill for me. Others on The Committee, not so much. But somehow, I made it all work. There were days when I felt like I needed the patience of a saint not to say something I might later regret.

Over time, the SAG Awards improved, and the viewership went up. The actors that won usually were contenders to win an Oscar. On many occasions the SAG Awards were a preview of what was to come at the Oscars. That was not as true of the Golden Globes. They often picked a wild card as a winner, being mindful of the international audience. The Golden Globe committee was made up of members of the Hollywood Foreign Press Association and came from all around the world. In 2020 the Golden Globes were criticized for the lack of diversity on their committee, and, in front of millions of viewers, they vowed to do better. It was a cringe-worthy moment. The Awards were canceled but were renewed in 2023 with a glamorous show, but the jury is still out on whether they will be booked in the future.

I insisted that everyone presenting a SAG award be at rehearsals the day before the show. If they couldn't come to rehearsal, I replaced them. That was a policy that I instituted which was really important because I wanted to be sure that everyone was ready for the live show. I didn't want any surprises! At least ones that were within my control to avoid. On the day the presenters came in for rehearsals, I set up a comfortable "producers' lounge" backstage.

The stage managers would meet the actors as they got out of their cars or limos and bring them back to the producers' lounge. I'd sit and schmooze with them for a while and then go over their copy to make sure that they were comfortable with their dialogue.

Did you know that we never had a host at the SAG Awards? I had to sell that idea to The Committee in the beginning. I thought that a no-host show would be a good idea because the SAG Awards was the shortest awards show on television. It was only two hours, and all the other award shows were three to three-and-a-half hours, especially the Oscars. I suggested to The Committee, "Why don't we do a show without a host? When you have a host on an awards show, most often that host is a comic. You've got to give them an opening monologue, and then ample dialogue during the show, and it eats up a lot of time. Let's make every presenter for each award be the host for that segment." (I was taking a page out of the Allan Carr playbook—one of his better ideas!) The voice-over announcer really could be considered the host of the show because he or she would say, "Ladies and gentlemen, please welcome," and then introduce the presenter. I used a few different voice-over announcers over my sixteen years on the show. Les Marshak, my favorite male voice; Ellen K, whose voice I loved and Randy Thomas, my favorite female voice of all time. I shared the story with you earlier about how I met Randy on the Oscars telecast with Gil Cates where we honored women in film. She's still my favorite female VO announcer and a really good friend.

The Screen Actors Guild Awards show was held in the Expo Hall of the Shrine Auditorium. It looked like the Beverly Hilton Hotel's Ballroom, which is where the Globes are presented, only ours was much nicer and twice the size. There were tables, and meals were served. It was a very casual, comfortable evening, although I'm sure the nominees might not agree. They'd always be on pins and needles wondering if they'd hear their name called as the winner.

Taking a screenshot of my sixteen years executive producing/directing the SAG Awards, one of the shots that stands out for me is my interaction with Clint Eastwood. I had, of course, met him during my Oscars tenure and knew him to be a gentleman to the *n*th degree, but he demonstrated just how much of a class act he was the year that he presented a SAG award for Ensemble Cast in a Motion Picture. During rehearsals, he was so accommodating and loved what the writers gave him to say. Two days after the show I was sitting in my office, and one of the production assistants brought in a gift. I opened the card, and it was from Clint Eastwood thanking me. Then I opened the gift (I was taught by my mother to always read the card first. It's the right thing to do even when no one is around!), which was a beautiful brown leather toiletry travel bag with my initials monogrammed in gold letters. What a class act!

The last year I executive produced and directed the SAG Awards was 2014—I had a great run, but it was time to move on.

At the SAG Awards rehearsal with Anthony Hopkins.

Brooke Shields at the SAG rehearsals.

James Earl Jones, a legend.

Rehearsal time with Leo DiCaprio.

Backstage at the SAG Awards with Kate Hudson.

Sharing a hug with John Krasinski and Amy Poehler.

With Forest Whitaker at the SAG rehearsals.

Tom Selleck and me backstage at the SAGs.

Rehearsal with the classy Sandra Oh.

With the incomparable Willem Dafoe.

A Few Words About Other Awards Shows I Directed and/or Produced

I do not want to be too repetitive here about award shows, so I will keep this section rather brief.

Primetime Emmy Awards

I love directing any live award show. The Emmys are special because they are all about the business that I am in and it's always a thrill for me to see my colleagues get nominated and win. I enjoyed making our evenings of recognition as special as I could make them.

Daytime Emmy Awards

To talk about this show, I would just be repeating what I told you about the Primetime Emmy Awards.

TV Land Awards

This show was all about nostalgia, honoring the shows and stars on TV Land. Most of the shows were reruns of past network sitcoms, dramas, game shows, and variety shows. A fun look back at television's history. The stars being honored were genuinely appreciative of the recognition of their good work over the years. Knowing that this award was not going to get them more work, they just enjoyed the evening. The acceptance speeches were short and heartfelt.

~ ~

Here are the numbers for all the awards shows I directed/executive produced:

> Sixteen SAG Awards
> Twenty-two American Music Awards
> Eight Academy Awards
> Three Primetime Emmy Awards
> Two Daytime Emmy Awards
> Three TV Land Awards
> Two Academy of Country Music Awards

Fifty-six shows in all. I never got bored or complacent because everything was *live*. I had to stay alert because anything could happen, at any minute, that could derail a show if I didn't have my insurance policies, an experienced team, and the adrenaline to carry me to "drop the mic."

The Academy Awards was one of my most favorite shows to direct.

Once again, with Whitney, at The American Music Awards.

Bruce Willis and Cybill Shepherd preparing for the Emmy.

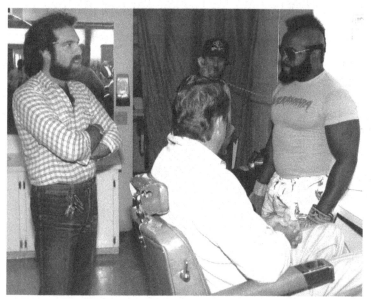

Mr. T and me at the TV Land Awards.

With Trisha Yearwood at rehearsals for the Academy Of Country Music Awards.

Checking on music cues with Jon Bon Jovi at the American Music Awards.

CHAPTER 28

TAKEAWAYS AND MOVING FORWARD

OVER THE COURSE OF MY CAREER IN TELEVISION, WORKING WITH HUNDREDS OF actors; thousands of creatives in lighting, set design, costume design, and every other creative field; executive producers, network executives; agents, managers, and publicists; and talented and hardworking crew, I have created my own playbook of sorts—a list of eleven rules that I live by, and that hopefully you will see fit to adopt in your own life. These rules can be applied in any field of endeavor—not just to the entertainment industry—but this is the field that I know best.

Number 1: Be kind.

Number 2: You must do your homework. Know what you're doing in all areas of production.

Number 3: There's no reason to ever raise your voice and yell or scream. You get so much more from people when you are kind—but know what you want and how to get it.

Number 4: Know the artists that you're working with. Know all the aspects of those artists.

Number 5: Be kind.

Number 6: Stay on schedule and on budget.

Number 7: Create a family around you. You need to work as a team. You have to realize that what you do, you cannot do alone.

Number 8: You must be a leader. That's what you're hired to do; that's what you need to do.

Number 9: You must gain the respect of everybody in your cast, on your crew, and on your staff.

Number 10: Don't forget to thank all the people who helped to make it possible.

Number 11: Be kind.

LONGER VERSION

If I was asked to give advice to someone coming up in the ranks (and my short list wasn't enough) here's what I would say (in no particular order but more in-depth):

1: Be kind.

2: I guest-lecture to film and television producing and directing classes at colleges, and the first thing I say is, "Always remember to be kind. You're behind the camera. They're in front of the camera. Be kind, be accommodating, be firm. Know what you need and what you have to deliver to the network or the studio or the executive producers. You'll always have somebody to answer to. Know what you're talking about. Do your homework."

3: Don't raise your voice. I have never, ever, ever raised my voice ever at talent, staff, or crew. Ever. Never. When you work with somebody difficult, you need to be firm. You try to give them what they want, but if they ask for something that you can't accommodate, you have to be able to be firm enough in a nice way to tell them no. But then you need to give them an alternative.

4: Be sympathetic when you're dealing with somebody who is so uncomfortable or so insecure or someone who just needs to be angry. Most of the time the reason that an artist gets angry and goes off at you is because they're not happy with what they're doing. They're angry at themselves for not making themselves happy or satisfied with their performance. Just understand that. They're blowing off steam at you. I'm the first guy they see. It's me and/or the stage manager. Sometimes, if I'm not producing, I have said to an artist who goes off, "Look, you need to speak to the producer." When somebody goes off, there's nothing you can say or do to appease them. The best thing to do is just listen and then walk away or say, "Okay, fine. Give me a minute, and I'll try to make it work for you."

5: Be kind.

6: I've never had alcohol at a wrap party. Because you never know who you are going to run into. And first impressions are really important. Network and studio executives are very important people. If they meet you at a wrap party and the alcohol has affected you in any way, you make the wrong impression and you don't know how it's going to affect you.

7: Work hard, but have a good time. It's important to do a good job, but nobody wants to work in an oppressive atmosphere, so make it fun when you can. If you are upbeat, chances are that the crew members will make the effort as well. If you're not having a good time, try to figure out why. Maybe suggest that the cast and crew take a ten-minute break while you get it together.

8: Hopefully you got some sleep and had a good meal before work because, God knows, you need the energy to make it through the day....

9: Think positively and tell yourself, "It's gonna be great!" I say that on every show I work on. First at the production meeting, then during production over the headset, I always say, "It's gonna be great." You have to have a positive outlook. You have to know that you're gonna work hard and that "it's gonna be great."

10: Don't forget to thank the people who made it all possible with you. Thank you doesn't cost you anything and can mean everything to someone who is not often recognized. From the biggest star to the assistants in wardrobe and makeup to the cue card holder (remember I was one of those!). They are all important. Producing and directing is a team sport, and you want to show your love all around. Always say "thank you."

11: And above all else, be kind!

What's Next

Thank you, Dad, for bringing that little black box home that you plugged into an outlet when I was five years old. Thank you, Mom and Dad, for letting me watch television all the time, and thank you for letting me follow my dream. I love what I do, producing and directing television shows and working with talented and creative people. I have been blessed with the incredible opportunities that I have been given in this business. And when you are given an opportunity, you better have the talent to make it work.

I don't ever want to stop working.

God only knows what the next chapter has to offer.

We shall see.

Onward and upward.

We're live in 5...

ACKNOWLEDGMENTS

THIS BOOK WOULD NOT HAVE COME INTO BEING WITHOUT THE ADVICE AND prompting of my father, an engineer by training, and a man of many talents blessed with a great sense of humor and a way with words. Had I known how long it takes to write a memoir I might not have embarked on this journey, but it's been worth the many drafts. When I typed "The End," like my good buddy Quincy Jones says, "It's not the end; it's really just the first fifty years of my career, and I'm looking forward to the next chapter."

Had my publicist and friend Steve Rohr not put us together, I don't think I would have seriously put my butt in the seat and done the work. So a special and heartfelt thank you to Loren Stephens, my collaborator. Two of her many fine qualities are her patience and perseverance. Throughout the time that we worked together, she consistently repeated, "It's gonna be great," when I found myself doubting whether this book would see the light of day and find an appreciative audience. I had nothing to worry about. But when it's your life you're talking about...hey! Also a shoutout to Loren's colleague at Write Wisdom, Nancy Mills, who helped us get organized and contributed to the first draft, turning her journalistic skills on this guy.

A number of readers gave me comments during various draft stages including Leslie Margolis, Adam Margolis, Peter Margolis, Jan Esterkin, Stephen Pouliot, and Marc Freeman. Thank you for your honest and valuable comments. As this is my memoir, when we remembered something differently I deferred to myself—after all, I take full responsibility for what's on the page.

To Jim Berg for the first editorial review of the manuscript, and to Clayton Farrell of Post Hill for fine-tuning. And that was no easy task as you'll see in the long list of thank yous at the end of this acknowledgments section.

A special thank you to the Post Hill publishing team for giving *We're Live in 5* a welcoming home, and once again, a special shout out to Loren Stephens, Steve Rohr, and Nancy Mills for their valuable and endless input.

Lots of appreciation to my friends who wrote such nice endorsements: Quincy Jones, Bruce Vilanch, Whoopi Goldberg, and Donny Osmond. I know that readers will be drawn to this book not just because it has my name on the cover or they like the title.

And much appreciation to Billy Crystal for the over-the-top foreword. You have been on your own journey to write a memoir, so you know what it takes, and I will be forever grateful to you for writing such flattering words. It means the world to me and is a reflection of our many years working together at the Oscars and elsewhere.

To Ron Wolfson, whose many photographs complement the text. You captured some great moments. I appreciate your keen eye that caught some priceless moments with so many people.

And a heartfelt thank you to my immediate family, especially to my daughter Sam, who has been there for me to teach me and save my butt every time I complained that my computer was not doing what I wanted it to do.

And now, just in case you don't think you matter to me, I want to say thank you, and list from A to Z all the people who have contributed one way or another to giving me an opportunity as a kid, opening doors for me as I honed my craft, and sharing credit with me on this great ride. I really tried to remember everybody to the best of my ability.... If your name is not on the list, I'm sorry; fifty years is a long time, and a lot to remember, but I thank you just the same.

Paula Abdul	Patrick Baltzell
Susan Abramson	Bob Banner
Wendy Charles Acey	Sarah Barry
Doug Adams	Chris Bearde
Evan Adelman	Richard J. Beck
Debbie Allen	Diane Biederbeck
Dan Andresen	Allan Blye
Jon Aroesty	Tom Boles
Ted Ashton	Dave Boone

Christine Bradley

John Bradley

Robert Bradley

Kristen Hansen Brakeman

Fred Bronson

Ron Brooks

Paul Brownstein

Greg Brunton

Curt Burich

Bruce Burmester

Hugh Camargo Jr.

Chris Carr

Alan Carter

Dave Casella

Joe Cashman

Gil Cates

Maggie Barrett-Caulfield

Brian Chambers

Ernie Chambers

Jerri Churchill

Dick Clark

Kari Clark

Rac Clark

Adam Cohen

Bill Conti

Joe Coppola

Michelle Cornelius (a.k.a. Speedy)

Linda Cowan

Sarah Cowperthwaite

John Cox

Rocky Danielson

Tina Cannizzaro DeBone

Robert Dickinson

Heather Douglas

Bobby Douglass

Bob Dussault

Dave Eastwood

Rick Edwards

Jeff Engel

Jeff Fecteau

Tisha Fein

Charlie Fernandez

John B. Field

Valdez Flagg

Benn Fleishman

Damita Jo Freeman

Bron Galleran

Tyrone George

September George Hill

Tom "Scoop" Geren

Pat Gleason

Tara Grace

Ed Greene

Paige Hadley

Keith Hall

John Hamlin

Marvin Hamlisch

Don Harary

Bill Hargate

Kevin Hayes

Larry Heider

Corinna Heuer

Dave Hilmer

Joan Huang

Garrett Hurt

Saul Ilson

Carrie Ann Inaba

Vanessa Ioppolo

Dave Irete

Quincy Jones

Spike Jones Jr.
Ellen K
Allan Kartun
Art Fisher
Jamie King
Cynthia Kistler
Bill Klages
Ray Klausen
Booey Kober
Rachel Korman
Dennis Langston
Barry Lather
Keith Lawrence
Norm Levin
Alissa Levisohn
Dave Levisohn
Gloria Levisohn
Diane Louie
Rick Ludwin
Jon Macks
Jenn Main
Howard Malley
Kristin Malley
Anita Mann
Dee Dee Marcelli
Adam Margolis
Erin Margolis
Leslie Margolis
Peter Margolis
Matthew Margolis
Rachel Margolis
Samantha Margolis
Les Marshak
Dennis McCarthy
Crisa McClees

Mick McCullough
Pete Menefee
Simon Miles
Julie Miller
Rickey Minor
Don Mischer
Lisa Moceri
Ron de Moraes
Shawnee Myers
Gary Natoli
Hank Neimark
Dency Nelson
Gloria Fujita O'Brien
Kenny Ortega
Debbie Palacio
Shawn Parr
Ken Patterson
Ron Paul
Travis Payne
Joe Petrovich
Bill Philbin
Dave Plakos
Stephen Pouliot
Vince Poxon
Sandy Prudden
Fred Quillen
Hector Ramirez
Eric Ross
Michael Ross
Gail Rowell-Ryan
Paul Sandweiss
Kevin Sanford
Chantel Sausedo
Phil Savenick
Todd Schulze

Tom Scott
Murray Seigel
Rob Sellers
Cheri J. Seltzer
John Shaffner
Ken Shapiro
LaVelle Smith Jr.
Laura Staat
Lenny Stack
Kenny Stein
Douglass M. Stewart
Joe Stewart
Mikael Stewart
Patti Stone
Edgar Struble
Sid Tessler
Todd Tessler
Jenn Thomas
Randy Thomas
Jeremy Tominberg

Ret Turner
Bruce Vilanch
David Wader
Josh Wader
Keaton Walker
Tom Ward
Melissa Watkins Trueblood
Dan Webb
Allan Wells
David West
Debbie Williams
Kris Wilson
Keith Winikoff
Jenny Wise
Dee Dee Wood
Don Worsham
Easter Xua
Olin Younger
Lisa Zugschwerdt

JEFF MARGOLIS CREDITS (*PRODUCING*) FROM IMDB

1. 2014 20th Annual Screen Actors Guild Awards (TV Special) (executive producer)
2. 2013 19th Annual Screen Actors Guild Awards (TV Special) (executive producer)
3. 2012 A Hollywood Christmas Celebration at the Grove (TV Special) (executive producer)
4. 2012 18th Annual Screen Actors Guild Awards (TV Special) (executive producer)
5. 2011 A Hollywood Christmas Celebration at the Grove (TV Special) (executive producer)
6. 2011 Pipe Dream (TV Series) (executive producer - 8 episodes)
7. 2011 17th Annual Screen Actors Guild Awards (TV Special) (executive producer)
8. 2010 Oscars Red Carpet 2010 (TV Special) (executive producer)
9. 2010 16th Annual Screen Actors Guild Awards (TV Special) (executive producer)
10. 2009 15th Annual Screen Actors Guild Awards (TV Special) (executive producer)
11. 2008 14th Annual Screen Actors Guild Awards (TV Special) (executive producer)
12. 2007 13th Annual Screen Actors Guild Awards (TV Special) (executive producer)
13. 2007 E! Live from the Red Carpet (TV Series) (executive producer - 1 episode)
14. 2006 L.A. Holiday Celebration (TV Special) (executive producer)
15. 2006 12th Annual Screen Actors Guild Awards (TV Special) (executive producer)
16. 2005 46th Annual Los Angeles County Holiday Celebration (TV Special) (executive producer)

17. 2005 11th Annual Screen Actors Guild Awards (TV Special) (executive producer)
18. 2004 In Search of the Partridge Family (TV Series) (executive producer)
19. 2004 Motown 45 (TV Special) (executive producer)
20. 2004 10th Annual Screen Actors Guild Awards (TV Special) (executive producer)
21. 2003 Fame (TV Series) (executive producer)
22. 2003 9th Annual Screen Actors Guild Awards (TV Special) (executive producer)
23. 2003 The Disco Ball (TV Special) (executive producer)
24. 2002 The Honeymooners 50th Anniversary Celebration (TV Movie) (executive producer) / (producer)
25. 2002 CBS: 50 Years from Television City (TV Special) (executive producer)
26. 2002 8th Annual Screen Actors Guild Awards (TV Special) (executive producer)
27. 2001 United We Stand (TV Special) (executive producer)
28. 2001 7th Annual Screen Actors Guild Awards (TV Special) (executive producer)
29. 2000 The First Family's Holiday Gift to America: A Tour of the White House (TV Special) (executive producer)
30. 2000 Powers of the Paranormal: Live on Stage! (TV Special) (executive producer)
31. 2000 6th Annual Screen Actors Guild Awards (TV Special) (executive producer)
32. 1999 79th Miss America Pageant (TV Special) (producer)
33. 1999 Up Close and Personal: The Search for Miss America (TV Special) (executive producer)
34. 1999 5th Annual Screen Actors Guild Awards (TV Special) (executive producer)
35. 1998 The 78th Annual Miss America Pageant (TV Special) (producer)
36. 1998 Quincy Jones... The First 50 Years (TV Special) (producer)
37. 1997 77th Miss America Pageant (TV Special) (producer)

38. 1996 Celebrate the Dream: 50 Years of Ebony Magazine (TV Special) (executive producer)
39. 1996 Miss America Pageant (TV Special) (producer)
40. 1996 All-Star Countryfest '96 (TV Special) (producer)
41. 1995 Michael Jackson: One Night Only (TV Special) (producer)
42. 1994 A Gala for the President at Ford's Theatre (TV Special) (producer)
43. 1993 A Gala for the President at Ford's Theatre (TV Special) (executive producer)
44. 1992 Roseanne Arnold (TV Special) (producer)
45. 1992 Oscar's Greatest Moments (Video documentary) (producer)
46. 1992 The Jaleel White Special (TV Special) (executive producer)
47. 1990 An Evening with Friends of the Environment (TV Special) (executive producer)
48. 1990 Night of 100 Stars III (TV Special) (producer)
49. 1989 Sammy Davis, Jr. 60th Anniversary Celebration (TV Special) (co-producer)
50. 1988 ABC Presents: A Royal Gala (TV Special) (producer)
51. 1987 Happy 100th Birthday, Hollywood (TV Special) (producer)
52. 1986 America Votes the #1 Song (TV Special) (producer)
53. 1984 Be Somebody... or Be Somebody's Fool! (Video) (producer)
54. 1984 Perry Como's Christmas in England (TV Special) (producer)
55. 1983 Perry Como's Christmas in New York (TV Special) (producer)
56. 1983 NBC Saturday Morning Preview: The Yummy Awards (TV Special) (producer)

JEFF MARGOLIS CREDITS (*DIRECTING*) FROM IMDB

1. 2014 20th Annual Screen Actors Guild Awards (TV Special)
2. 2013 19th Annual Screen Actors Guild Awards (TV Special)
3. 2013 2013 Golden Globe Awards Red Carpet Special (TV Special)
4. 2012 A Hollywood Christmas Celebration at the Grove (TV Special)
5. 2012 Golden Globe Awards Red Carpet Special (TV Special)
6. 2012 The Screen Actors Guild Awards (TV Special)
7. 2011 A Hollywood Christmas Celebration at the Grove (TV Special)
8. 2011 17th Annual Screen Actors Guild Awards (TV Special)
9. 2011 Golden Globe Awards Red Carpet Special (TV Special)
10. 2010 79th Annual Hollywood Christmas Parade (TV Special)
11. 2010 The Spirit of Mississippi (TV Special)
12. 2010 The Gulf Is Back (TV Special)
13. 2010 The 37th Annual Daytime Emmy Awards (TV Special)
14. 2010 The 8th Annual TV Land Awards (TV Special)
15. 2010 16th Annual Screen Actors Guild Awards (TV Special)
16. 2009 The 36th Annual Daytime Emmy Awards (TV Special)
17. 2009 The 7th Annual TV Land Awards (TV Special)
18. 2009 15th Annual Screen Actors Guild Awards (TV Special)
19. 2008 The 6th Annual TV Land Awards (TV Special)
20. 2008 Teleflora Presents America's Favorite Mom (TV Special)
21. 2008 14th Annual Screen Actors Guild Awards (TV Special)
22. 2007 Do You Trust Me? (TV Series) (pilot)
23. 2007 13th Annual Screen Actors Guild Awards (TV Special)
24. 2006 Christmas Celebration at the Grove (TV Special)
25. 2005 American Music Awards (TV Special)
26. 2005 The 40th Annual Academy of Country Music Awards (TV Special)

27. 2004 The 32nd Annual American Music Awards (TV Special)
28. 2004 The 39th Annual Academy of Country
    Music Awards (TV Special)
29. 2004 Motown 45 (TV Special)
30. 2003 Fame (TV Series)
31. 2003 The Disco Ball (TV Special)
32. 2002 The Honeymooners 50th Anniversary
    Celebration (TV Special)
33. 2001 United We Stand (TV Special)
34. 2000 The First Family's Holiday Gift to America:
    A Tour of the White House (TV Special)
35. 1999 79th Miss America Pageant (TV Special)
36. 1999 Amy Grant: A Christmas to Remember (TV Special)
37. 1998 The 78th Annual Miss America Pageant (TV Special)
38. 1998 To Life! America Celebrates Israel's 50th (TV Special)
39. 1998 Quincy Jones... The First 50 Years (TV Special)
40. 1998 The 25th Annual American Music Awards (TV Special)
41. 1997 77th Miss America Pageant (TV Special)
42. 1997 Happy Birthday Elizabeth: A
    Celebration of Life (TV Special)
43. 1996 Celebrate the Dream: 50 Years of
    Ebony Magazine (TV Special)
44. 1996 Miss America Pageant (TV Special)
45. 1996 All-Star Countryfest '96 (TV Special)
46. 1996 The 68th Annual Academy Awards (TV Special)
47. 1995 Michael Jackson: One Night Only (TV Special)
48. 1995 Rudy Coby: The Coolest Magician on Earth (TV Special)
49. 1995 The 67th Annual Academy Awards (TV Special)
50. 1994 A Gala for the President at Ford's Theatre (TV Special)
51. 1994 Dennis Miller Live (TV Series) (6 episodes)
52. 1994 The 66th Annual Academy Awards (TV Special)
53. 1994 The 21st Annual American Music Awards (TV Special)
54. 1993 A Musical Christmas at Walt Disney World (TV Special)
55. 1993 The American Music Awards 20th
    Anniversary Special (TV Special)

56. 1993 A Gala for the President at Ford's Theatre (TV Special)
57. 1993 Battle of the Bands (TV Special)
58. 1993 Roseanne (TV Series) (1 episode)
59. 1993 The 65th Annual Academy Awards (TV Special)
60. 1993 Billy Ray Cyrus: Dreams Come True (TV Special)
61. 1993 The 20th Annual American Music Awards (TV Special)
62. 1992 Holiday Greetings from 'The Ed
    Sullivan Show' (TV Special)
63. 1992 The 64th Annual Academy Awards (TV Special)
64. 1992 The Jaleel White Special (TV Movie)
65. 1992 The 19th Annual American Music Awards (TV Special)
66. 1991 The 63rd Annual Academy Awards (TV Special)
67. 1991 The 18th Annual American Music Awards (TV Special)
68. 1990 An Evening with Friends of the Environment (TV Special)
69. 1990 Sinatra 75: The Best Is Yet to Come (TV Special)
70. 1990 Jerry Lewis MDA Labor Day Telethon (TV Series)
71. 1990 Night of 100 Stars III (TV Special)
72. 1990 The 62nd Annual Academy Awards (TV Special)
73. 1990 The 17th Annual American Music Awards (TV Special)
74. 1989 Sammy Davis, Jr. 60th Anniversary
    Celebration (TV Special)
75. 1989 The Magical World of Disney (TV Special)
76. 1989 The 61st Annual Academy Awards (TV Special)
77. 1989 The 16th Annual American Music Awards (TV Special)
78. 1988 The Gong Show (TV Series)
79. 1988 Whitney Houston: Love Will Save the Day (Video)
80. 1988 ABC Presents: A Royal Gala (TV Special)
81. 1987 Motown Merry Christmas (TV Special)
82. 1987 Dolly (TV Series) (3 episodes)
83. 1987 Happy 100th Birthday, Hollywood (TV Special)
84. 1987 Superstars and Their Moms (TV Special)
85. 1987 The 14th Annual American Music Awards (TV Special)
86. 1986 The 38th Annual Primetime Emmy Awards (TV Special)
87. 1986 America Votes the #1 Song (TV Special)
88. 1986 The 13th Annual American Music Awards (TV Special)

89. 1985 Miss Hollywood Talent Search (TV Special)
90. 1985 The 37th Annual Primetime Emmy Awards (TV Special)
91. 1985 The ABC All-Star Spectacular (TV Special)
92. 1984 Be Somebody... or Be Somebody's Fool! (Video)
93. 1984 Perry Como's Christmas in England (TV Special)
94. 1984 Puttin' on the Hits (TV Series)
95. 1984 The Magic of David Copperfield VI: Floating Over the Grand Canyon (TV Special)
96. 1984 The 11th Annual American Music Awards (TV Special)
97. 1983 The Righteous Brothers: Live on the Sunset Strip (TV Special)
98. 1983 Perry Como's Christmas in New York (TV Special)
99. 1983 Kenny Rogers Live in Concert (TV Special)
100. 1983 NBC Saturday Morning Preview: The Yummy Awards (TV Special)
101. 1983 Battle of the Beat (TV Special)
102. 1983 The 10th Annual American Music Awards (TV Special)
103. 1982 The American Music Awards (TV Special)
104. 1981 Perry Como's French-Canadian Christmas (TV Special)
105. 1981 A Gift of Music (TV Special)
106. 1981 Sixty Years of Seduction (TV Movie documentary)
107. 1980 Dinah and Her New Best Friends (TV Series)
108. 1980 Marie (TV Series)
109. 1980 Olivia Newton-John: Hollywood Nights (TV Special)
110. 1980 The Beatrice Arthur Special (TV Special)
111. 1980 Sensational Shocking Wonderful Wacky 70's (TV Special)
112. 1979 Presenting Susan Anton (TV Series)
113. 1979 The Captain & Tennille Songbook (TV Special)
114. 1978 Ringo (TV Movie)
115. 1978 Julie Andrews: One Step Into Spring (TV Special)
116. 1977 Good Old Days (TV Special)
117. 1976 The Peter Marshall Variety Show (TV Series)
118. 1976 Cos (TV Series)
119. 1974 Tony Orlando and Dawn (TV Series)

Special Credits:

Film

1979 Richard Pryor: Live in Concert (directed by)

Home Video

1992 Oscar's Greatest Moments (Video documentary) (directed by)

Special Events

1996 President Clinton's 50th Birthday Celebration (Live Event, Radio City Music Hall) (produced by)

2001–2006 The 13th–18th Annual Spotlight Awards

ABOUT THE AUTHORS

JEFF MARGOLIS

Emmy Award winner Jeff Margolis is one of the most successful live TV event and variety special directors of all-time. As a kid, he was introduced to showbusiness by his uncle, gameshow legend Monty Hall. What followed is a career spanning five decades including directing mammoth hits of the 1970s like The *Sonny & Cher Show*, and *Tony Orlando and Dawn* and continuing with mega specials like *Michael Jackson: One Night Only, Sinatra 75: The Best Is Yet to Come, Whitney Houston: Love Will Save the Day, Kenny Rogers Live in Concert, Quincy Jones... The First 50 Years*, and *Happy Birthday Elizabeth [Taylor]: A Celebration of Life*. Jeff also achieved live television's biggest and most coveted directorial prize–directing the Academy Awards, which he's directed eight times along with multiple director and producing duties at the Emmy Awards, Screen Actors Guild Awards, American Music Awards, and Miss America Pageant.

LOREN STEPHENS

Pushcart Prize and Emmy Award nominee Loren Stephens is a novelist, biographer, and widely published essayist. Her critically acclaimed novel "All Sorrows Can Be Borne," is inspired by her husband's epic story of being raised in Montana after being adopted from his native Japan. As founder and president of Write Wisdom and Bright Star Memoirs, Stephens has co-written dozens of books with notables from fashion and entertainment world. Collaborations include "Paris Nights: My Year at the Moulin Rouge," by Cliff Simon and "Fighting for the Truth" by actor and singer Aki Aleong. As an essayist, her work has appeared in the *Los Angeles Times*, *Chicago Tribune*, *MacGuffin*, *Jewish Women's Literary Annual*, and the *Montreal Review*. She lives in Los Angeles. Prior to her career in writing, Loren was a documentary filmmaker. Notably, she was Emmy nominated for her PBS film "Legacy of the Hollywood Blacklist narrated by Burt Lancaster. Additional credits include "Sojourner Truth: Ain't I A Woman" which won a Golden Apple Award from the National Education Association (NEA); and "Los Pastores: The Shepherd's Play" for PBS.